D0077166

HANDBOOK OF EDUCATIONAL DRAMA AND THEATRE

HANDBOOK OF EDUCATIONAL DRAMA AND THEATRE

Robert J. Landy

Foreword by RICHARD COURTNEY

GREENWOOD PRESS
WESTPORT, CONNECTICUT • LONDON, ENGLAND

OLD WESTBURY LIBRARY
PN3171
.L28
copy 1

Library of Congress Cataloging in Publication Data

Landy, Robert J.
  Handbook of educational drama and theatre.

  Bibliography: p.
  Includes index.
  1. Drama in education—Handbooks, manuals, etc.
I. Title.
PN3171.L28   371.3'32   82-6111
ISBN 0-313-22947-3 (lib. bdg.)   AACR2

Copyright © 1982 by Robert J. Landy

All rights reserved. No portion of this book may be
reproduced, by any process or technique, without the
express written consent of the publisher.

Library of Congress Catalog Card Number: 82-6111
ISBN: 0-313-22947-3

First published in 1982

Greenwood Press
A division of Congressional Information Service, Inc.
88 Post Road West, Westport, Connecticut 06881

Printed in the United States of America

10 9 8 7 6 5 4 3 2 1

CONTENTS

ILLUSTRATIONS

FOREWORD:
ROBES, ROLES, AND REALITIES

> Sure, this robe of mine
> Does change my disposition.
> Shakespeare, *The Winter's Tale*, IV, 4: 134-35.

Shakespeare understood the significance of dramatic action. For him, it was not simply that "All the world's a stage" but that playing a part changes us in some way. When we "get into the skin" of another human being (in life or in theatre), we learn something both about the other person and about ourselves. In *The Winter's Tale* when Perdita puts on a costume of someone else, it alters her personality; once she has identified with and impersonated the other person, she can never be the same again. Once dramatic action has taken place, reality shifts.

Humanity has acknowledged this quality of drama from the beginning. Tribal people all over the world use dramatic dance to promote the mental health of the community, and the ancient Athenians used it for both education and therapy. Rhetoric was at the heart of medieval learning. In the Renaissance the speaking of Latin dialogue and the staging of plays were components of the school curriculum. Mme. de Maintenon, wife of Louis XIV, established the convent of Saint-Cyr where the girls improvised dialogue and conversation; they also performed plays by Racine and Corneille. By the nineteenth century, however, drama in schools had dwindled to the production of the occasional school play.

A remarkable revival was born in the first decades of the twentieth century in Great Britain and the United States. The first steps were taken by major pioneers: in Britain by Caldwell Cook through classroom work; and in the United States by Alice Minnie Herts through theatre. In the 1920s and 1930s Robert G. Newton developed improvisation amongst unemployed miners in the Depression, and, also in Britain, "the primary school method" incorporated the learning of all school subjects around activity, specifically dramatic activity. In the United States at the same time, John

Dewey's educational philosophy (filtered through the work of Hughes Mearns) brought a parallel growth: Winifred Ward developed creative dramatics for young children, and Charlotte Chorpenning created children's theatre specifically designed for the attention span of youngsters.

By 1945 drama and theatre had established a bridgehead in educational systems. On both sides of the Atlantic programs of teacher education developed a strong cadre of good drama instructors who infiltrated the schools and colleges; theatre performances for children so increased their quality that experiments with the form began, particularly by Peter Slade and Brian Way with participation (a link with spontaneous drama in the classroom). Excellent "how-to" books for teachers appeared in considerable numbers: by Isabel Burger, Geraldine Brain Siks, and Nellie McCaslin in the United States; and by Slade, Way, and E. J. Burton in Great Britain. Meanwhile, Canada and Australia produced their own pioneers who began to adapt the British and American work to their own situations.

By 1968 there had been sixty years of steady improvement in educational drama and theatre; increasing numbers of high-calibre people were involved; and there were isolated examples of excellence. But drama and theatre were still not essential components of all education, nor was the field well justified in ways that senior educators could understand. New needs were being asserted, and they had to be satisfied. In Britain several young drama educators from Trent Park College began to experiment with form: Gordon Vallins established Theatre in Education (TIE) at Coventry, and Mark Long and Sid Palmer began the unique People Show at the extreme of London's "fringe" theatre. Dorothy Heathcote and Gavin Bolton developed spontaneous drama as a "lived-through" experience in schools and for the handicapped. In the United States Viola Spolin's work, which involved improvisation per se, opened up new avenues of exploration for both school and theatre. From Maine to California experiments of all types abounded; old techniques were turned inside out, and new techniques flickered and then either died or flowered. In Australia the state of Victoria established its remarkable Drama Resource Centre under Graham Scott with every type of drama assistance available to unite education with drama and theatre. In Canada undergraduate and graduate programs in both English and French were widened beyond their traditional boundaries.

It is for this expanding field of educational drama and theatre that Robert J. Landy has written this book. It is different in style from other books in this field written only a few years ago in three main ways. First, it reflects the remarkable diffusion of dramatic activity into a wide range of situations and environments. Spontaneous drama and theatre are now not merely components of school life but take place in galleries and museums, churches, and all types of community settings. School learners, the deaf, the disabled, prisoners, the elderly, multiethnic groups, the disturbed—for all types of persons in a community, drama and theatre are used. Theatrical experiments are taking place with ancient forms (like puppetry) and new ones (like participation). This book reflects the amazing range of drama and theatre activities happening today.

Second, the book reflects a serious intellectual approach to understanding the place of drama and theatre in the lives of human beings. Dr. Landy's work is not, like so many publications a few years ago, based on a romantic appeal that drama and theatre "are good for us." His arguments are carefully reasoned, and most of his postulates are based on the findings of existing research. Thankfully, sound research has begun in this field, and if the necessary rigor is maintained, it should prove fruitful for future generations.

Third, the book reflects many diverse views. By basing it on a series of television interviews, Dr. Landy has allowed many leaders in the field to express their points of view. These views are not always in agreement with one another—a most healthy situation! A critical appraisal of both theory and practice is an essential element in a viable educational field. (As Brian Way is so apt to thunder at teachers: "There is no *one* way!") Dr. Landy has fully accepted that there are both complementary and differing views about the nature of educational drama and theatre, and this provides the book with a salutory quality.

Whether in the classroom or on a stage, dramatic action is never static. The dramatic world, as Shakespeare has shown us, is a world of change—of reality and illusion, of time and space, of shifting perspectives, and of the dynamic learning for those who are in it. It provides what Michael Polanyi called "personal knowledge"—knowledge that is deeply embedded in the individual person and unique to him or her. In contrast, when we discuss it or write about it, we are concerned with "discursive" knowledge. Thus when we are engaged in creative drama, improvisation, or theatre, we are learning *directly* and creating "personal" knowledge. But when we stand outside the dramatic experience and examine it critically, we are engaged in an activity that is qualitatively different from the "doing" of drama and theatre. Because Dr. Landy's book so expertly covers the many different aspects of educational drama and theatre with a solid intellectual basis and incorporates so many diverse views, this should not blind us to the fact that it remains at the level of "discursive" knowledge. Its success will be judged if it will allow us to be better prepared to face the essence of drama and theatre: the dramatic act of the human being performing in both life and art.

RICHARD COURTNEY
Toronto, Ontario; and
Elephant Butte, New Mexico

ACKNOWLEDGMENTS

This book developed from two basic sources. The more immediate one is the *Sunrise Semester* series "Drama in Education," produced by WCBS-TV and New York University in 1979-1980. The more primary one is my own dramatic education.

From the *Sunrise Semester* project, I owe immense gratitude to the more than ninety students and colleagues from the United States, England, and Canada who appeared on the program. I especially want to thank my colleagues Lowell Swortzell and Nellie McCaslin for their continuous support and guidance throughout the processes of planning and executing the television series and writing and editing this book. The *Sunrise Semester* series would not have been possible without the collaboration and expertise of my colleague Nancy Swortzell, who coordinated so many aspects of the experience. It was Nancy who phoned me one week after I was hired at New York University (NYU) to say that we were going to put together forty-eight half-hour programs in six weeks.

I would like to acknowledge the contributions of my assistants Fran Van Horn, who also read the manuscript, and Mimi Flaherty, who worked throughout with patience and intelligence.

I would like to thank CBS, Inc., and WCBS-TV for allowing me to publish portions of transcripts from the *Sunrise Semester* "Drama in Education" series. Mike Price, the NYU producer, was invaluable in getting us through this challenging endeavor, as was Shirley Fischer, the production assistant at WCBS-TV. I owe much gratitude to Roy Allen, producer-director of *Sunrise Semester* for his support and continuing help in securing materials for the book.

I am grateful also for permission on reprint from: Miles, D. *A Play of Our Own*. One act play. (With the Hartford Thespians, 1937). Unpublished, c. 1973.

Also, I am grateful to Helen Kelly of New York University for her support and advice during the production of "Drama in Education."

I would like to recognize those individuals who have contributed substantially to my understanding of educational drama and theatre: Gavin Bolton, James Moffett, Sheridan Blau, Dorothy Heathcote, Brian Way, and especially Richard Courtney, who is a perpetual source of inspiration. I must also acknowledge my debt to my students at the Adams School in New York City, at California State University, Northridge, and at New York University who have indelibly shaped my thinking and acting.

HANDBOOK OF EDUCATIONAL DRAMA AND THEATRE

INTRODUCTION
AND OVERVIEW

This book represents an attempt to specify many and various applications of drama and theatre to the education of all human beings. Outstanding uses of educational drama and theatre are surveyed as they occur in schools, communities, and theatres for young audiences. Underlining all that follows is the search to clarify educational drama and theatre as a field of inquiry that is inclusive and interdisciplinary, incorporating not only aesthetic but also pedagogical and therapeutic aims and techniques.

The field is vast, with many problems of definition and unresolved issues. But educational drama and theatre is indeed a growing discipline throughout the United States, Australia, Great Britain, and Canada. In the following pages we take a look at the work of some of the outstanding experts in the field, many of whom appeared on the televised WCBS-TV series "Drama in Education," broadcast on the program *Sunrise Semester* from September 1979 through January 1980. Throughout this book we cite workshop experiences and interviews from the *Sunrise Semester* program as well as other sources.

The literature of educational drama and theatre has developed substantially since the early chronicle of teaching academic subjects through drama, Caldwell Cook's *The Play Way*, first published in 1917. Cook called his book "An Essay in Educational Method," characterizing the method as follows:

> The natural means of study in youth is play, as anyone may see for himself by watching any child or young animal when it is left alone. A natural education is by practice, by doing things, and not by instruction, by hearing how, as you may see in the flight of a young bird.... It would not be wise to send a child innocent into the big world; and talking is of

poor avail. But it is possible to hold rehearsals, to try our strength in a make-believe big world. And that is Play.[1]

In speaking about the dramatic education of children, *play* and *drama* have become almost synonymous terms. The British educational drama expert Peter Slade has said: "Whenever there is play, there is drama."[2] Even when we speak of more formal theatre production, we use the language of play: we *play* roles; we act in a *play*.

Today, there are publications, tapes, films, and other educational materials available on all aspects of educational drama and theatre. These resources are specified within each chapter of this book.

In recent years the educational application of drama and theatre has expanded beyond the classroom and beyond the age range of the child or youth, which roughly corresponds to the school years kindergarten through high school. Today, we see a growth of significant educational drama work in museums, hospitals, churches, and playgrounds. We see drama applied to the education and recreation of the elderly, the handicapped child, and the incarcerated adult. The possibilities seem endless, especially in light of research in the social sciences supporting the notion that human learning is intimately related to play, role-taking, imitation, and identification, all elements inherent in the experience of drama and theatre.[3]

DEFINITIONS

Historically, drama is one of the oldest known activities. It occurred when a community would gather for a ceremonial purpose: to assure a good hunt, an ample rainfall, or a long life to a new leader. The dramatic elements included chanting, dancing, storytelling, and dressing up in the costumes and masks of gods, animals, or elements. As in most rituals, the learning that occurred was social and cultural: an affirmation of community, common values, needs, and hopes.

In anthropological films such as *Dead Birds*, documenting the lives of a primitive culture, the Baliem Valley people of New Guinea, we still can clearly see the significance of drama in everyday life as, for example, children battling each other with sticks, rehearsing for future adult roles as warriors.

This kind of dramatic war-play is, of course, prevalent in most all cultures. Most of us have, no doubt, been playful victim to a child with a toy gun or cocked thumb, who in his own way is making a statement about his society and his role identifications.

We adults, too, have developed very sophisticated kinds of dramas. Our war-play is more prevalent in our minds, though, as we symbolically execute our enemies and reward our allies in fantasy and dream. These internal dramas occur spontaneously and frequently. Before confronting a new experience, a job interview, for example, we pre-view in our minds what the interviewer will be like, what he or she will ask us, and we rehearse how we will sit, speak, shake hands, and so on. Having completed the interview, we re-view the experience and perhaps play it out again in fantasy: "If only I had answered differently; if only I could have been the boss and he, the hopeful applicant." These reflections occur so frequently that we ordinarily would not give them a second thought. But they are internal dramas, and like dreams, they allow us to gain a new perspective on reality.

In the developmental history of a human being, drama also becomes a natural means of learning. Its elements—imitation, imagination, role-playing, and interpretation—account for much of a child's learning of language, movement, and social behavior. By acting out the roles of father or mother, for example, the child learns what a parent is and what is expected of the child in relationship to the parent.

Generally, then, drama is an active, everyday process of human enactment. It occurs regardless of age and culture and can be acted out behaviorally or "acted in" in thought. Like play, it is spontaneous and natural. Like ritual, it is social and ceremonial. Like thought, it concerns rehearsing, previewing, and reviewing experience, and often touches upon fantasy, wishes, and dreams.

Furthermore, drama is not necessarily performed to an audience. The term *performance* is used throughout this book to signify dramatic enactment to an audience.

In form, drama can be highly idiosyncratic, from the formal ritual dance of hunters to the informal play of children. Unlike narrative, it demonstrates rather than tells about. It means, literally, a thing done.

It is primarily in this century that educators have consciously applied drama to the learning of individuals in schools and other educational settings. One term used by American educators to describe the process of learning through drama is *creative drama*, a term attributed to Winifred Ward, one of the outstanding pioneers of educational drama in America.

A recent committee of the Children's Theatre Association of America, reexamining the terminology of educational drama, stated the following definition:

> Creative Drama is an improvisational, non-exhibitional, process-centered form of drama in which participants are guided by a leader to imagine, enact and reflect upon human experiences. Built on the human impulse and ability to act out perceptions of the world in order to understand it, creative drama requires both logical and intuitive thinking, personalizes knowledge, and yields aesthetic pleasure.[4]

The term *improvisation* is also essential to our understanding of educational drama. Improvisation is an unscripted, unrehearsed, spontaneous set of actions in response to minimal directions from a leader, usually including statements of whom one is, where one is, and what one is doing there.

Other terms used to describe the process of educational drama include *drama in education, dramatic education, developmental drama, child drama,* and *informal drama.* The term *creative drama* is used less often in England where the term *drama in education* seems most popular.

Several educators, such as Richard Courtney, have commented upon the differences not only in terminology but also in educational philosophy. Much of the difference between American and British educational drama practice seems to lie in the American preoccupation with behavioral objectives, as opposed to the British reliance upon empiricism and concrete logic.[5] But whatever terminology or philosophical perspective is subscribed to, most all educational drama leaders begin with the child's natural predisposition to play, identify with characters, enact roles, and enter into the inner experience of imagination and fantasy. Although their techniques and philosophical perspectives may be different, their commitment to using the art of drama for human learning and development is constant.

Theatre, unlike creative drama, implies the development of a product, a script that is rehearsed and performed to an audience. The essential ingredients of theatre are actors, script, and audience.

Many theatre artists are uncomfortable with the notion of theatre as educational. With so much attention to economics and entertainment in the professional, commercial theatre, for example, it is difficult and undesirable to attend to its educational values. Furthermore, although the practice of training actors, directors, and writers for the professional theatre is certainly a form of theatre education, it is not strictly educational theatre, where the emphasis must be not only upon the individual's growth as a theatre artist, but more significantly upon his or her development as a human being. We, therefore, do not discuss the commercial professional theatre, but rather the kind of theatre most notable for its concern and attention to therapeutic and educational values, which, for our purposes, is theatre applied to specialized community environments—such as the church, hospital, inner city—and theatre for young audiences.

The Children's Theatre Association of America defines *theatre for young audiences* as "the performance of a largely predetermined theatrical art work by living actors in the presence of young people, either children (young persons typically of elementary school age, five through twelve) or youth (young persons typically of junior high school age, thirteen through fifteen)."[6] The educational values in theatre for young audiences concern the experiences of writing, directing, acting, and viewing a play, all of which are examined in chapter 10.

Under the umbrella term *theatre for young audiences,* the Children's Theatre Association includes the terms *theatre for children,* indicating an audience of ages five through twelve, and *theatre for youth,* indicating a junior high school audience. Furthermore, the association describes two other forms of theatre for young audiences: *participation theatre*, where audience members both observe and participate in the action; and *theatre by children and youth*, where the roles are played by young people rather than adults. Generally, though, adults are most often the primary actors in theatre for young audiences.

There is another term we refer to that represents an attempt to bridge the gap between drama and theatre: *theatre-in-education*, or *TIE*. TIE refers to the presentation of plays in schools or theatres by a trained team of actor-teachers who prepare ways to relate the experience of theatre to the regular classroom curriculum and to the lives of the students.

ISSUES IN EDUCATIONAL DRAMA AND THEATRE

One of the central issues in the field of educational drama and theatre involves the relationship between the nonperformance, informal process of drama and the more performance-oriented product of formal theatre. Most schools tend to stress one over the other. In American dramatic education, kindergarten through grade twelve, for example, we find a plethora of school plays performed during holidays, despite the influence of Winifred Ward and others in creative drama. On the other hand, we find a greater emphasis on the process of creative drama and play in British primary education.

The reasons for these differences are varied, including diverse educational philosophies, teacher-training procedures, and administrative policies. In moving toward a reconciliation of process and product, though, we might look again at the Children's Theatre Association, which represents drama and theatre not as polarities but as a continuum that begins with the natural drama of everyday life and then moves toward creative drama, participation theatre, and, finally, toward the art form of formal theatre.[7] But this should not imply that all drama necessarily leads to theatre, since a child at play will not necessarily become a performer on stage. The relationship between drama and theatre is not linear. Within any informal dramatic process there exist elements of more formal theatre, as, for example, when children at play create a spontaneous script, a content that they perform to a projected audience of parents, peers, or imaginary others. So, too, do we find elements of play, spontaneity, and informal drama in theatre when the actor on stage is taught to "live the moment," as if it were happening for the first time. It is now commonplace in rehearsing theatre for directors to use many of the process-oriented techniques of improvisation.

It might be most accurate, then, to view drama and theatre as interrelated, where all aspects of the drama/theatre experience are relative to the performer, whether old or young, whether at work or play; the performance, whether in a theatre or classroom or street; the script, whether written down or improvised; and the audience, whether real or imagined. For educational drama and theatre leaders, this interrelationship implies a full knowledge of the process and product aspects of both drama and theatre as they relate to human learning. In meeting the demands of an administrator who feels a drama program only exists for plays to be produced during holidays, the teacher still has recourse to using creative drama methods and techniques during rehearsal. Likewise, playground leaders sensitive to the needs of their children to bring their dramatic play to a more artful, polished form also have recourse to help them fashion a play to be performed to an audience.

This raises another important issue concerning children as performers and more generally, the overemphasis upon performance at the expense of reflection and understanding. In the 1950s the British educational drama specialist Peter Slade made a case against formal performance before the age of twelve.[8] Fearing that it would promote showing-off behavior, he noted that young children need unrestricted space in which to play. He observed that children between ages five and seven naturally focus their actions all around themselves as new ideas occur. If they were limited to performing to an audience directly in front of them, they would be violating their natural inclinations to move about freely.

In our contemporary society children experience many pressures to perform. Their parents might demand that they recite the alphabet or read from a book to demonstrate their literacy long before they set foot in a classroom. Because of early childhood education and television programs such as "Sesame Street," more and more children are able to perform these tasks. But at what price? If children are learning to perform to please their proud parents, a dramatic principle has been violated. The principle is that drama is a developmental process of learning and should reflect a child's readiness and natural inclination to play and to dramatize.

For Peter Slade, that principle relates to an understanding of human development in terms of spacial, physical, and emotional readiness. For the psychologist Jean Piaget, readiness to perform is based upon cognitive development.[9] If we can understand the importance of an integrated cognitive, physical, and emotional development, we will have an accurate picture of when a child is ready to perform.

Another educational drama issue concerns the content of dramas and plays to be performed. When the British drama educator Gavin Bolton was asked in a recent interview what an observer would see during one of his sessions, he replied, "Not much, really."[10] Upon further questioning, he clarified the point that one would not see much action but rather a process of exploring issues, thinking, and reflecting upon experience. But what issues and what experiences should be explored?

Millions of children around the world now routinely watch television representations of adult issues and concerns—sexuality, birth, death, violence, and so on. Should they deal with these issues in creative drama work and view plays concerning adult subjects?

Generally, educational drama and theatre leaders have played it safe. Noncontroversial material is most often chosen to dramatize. The published plays for young audiences, at least in America, generally abound in adaptations of fairy tales, legends, popular novels, and historical incidents, carefully screened to avoid controversy.

Certainly, *Tom Sawyer* is fine material to dramatize, especially when it is fashioned imaginatively and skillfully. But what about the classical dramatic literature? What about contemporary plays dealing with the concerns of children? What about a child's feelings toward death and violence and sexuality? Should these feelings provide the basis for a creative drama workshop or new scripts for young audiences?

Issues of product and process, of the values inherent in performance, of developmental learning through drama and appropriate material to dramatize, are discussed in the context of the many and varied applications of drama and theatre to the education of individuals in several learning environments.

We examine some current uses of drama and theatre in schools at all levels and see how dramatic methods relate naturally to the regular school curriculum. We then move out of the classroom to explore how educational drama and theatre has become a vital force in community life. We look at institutions such as the museum, the church, and the nursing home to understand how drama and theatre are beginning to play a significant role in therapy and community education.

Then we take a look at the theatre as an educational environment for young audiences. Through examining recent plays and through looking at the role of the playwright, director, and actor, we attempt to understand the educational value of this very vital institution.

There is another area of growing importance to the field—puppetry in education. Like creative drama and educational theatre, puppetry is used as both a learning process and a performing art in schools, communities, and theatres. Puppetry has also become an important therapeutic tool in working with the disabled.

Following our overview of puppetry in education, we discuss ways of training for a career in educational drama and theatre and look at the kinds of vocational and avocational opportunities available.

Finally, having completed an overview of the present, we speculate about the future directions in educational drama and theatre.

NOTES

1. H. Caldwell Cook, *The Play Way* (New York: Stokes, 1919), p. 1.
2. Peter Slade, *Child Drama* (London: University of London Press, 1954), p. 23.
3. See, for example, Richard Courtney, *Play, Drama, and Thought*, 3d ed. (New

York: Drama Book Specialists, 1974); Jean Piaget, *Play, Dreams, and Imitation in Childhood* (New York: W. W. Norton, 1962); and Dennis Brisset and Charles Edgley, eds., *Life as Theatre* (Chicago: Aldine Publishing Company, 1975).

4. Jed H. Davis and Tom Behm, "Terminology of Drama/Theatre with and for Children: A Redefinition," *Children's Theatre Review* 27, no. 1 (1978): 10-11.

5. Richard Courtney, "In My Experience," in John Hodgson and Martin Banham, eds., *Drama in Education: The Annual Survey*, vol. 2 (London: Pitman, 1973), pp. 56-69.

6. Davis and Behm, "Terminology of Drama/Theatre."

7. The position of the Children's Theatre Association of America is consistent with that of the Society of Teachers of Speech and Drama in the United Kingdom, the Canadian Child and Youth Association, and the National Association for Drama in Education in Australia.

8. Slade, *Child Drama*.

9. See, for example, Jean Piaget, *Language and Thought of the Child* (New York: Harcourt, Brace, 1926).

10. WCBS-TV, *Sunrise Semester*, "Drama in Education: An Interview with Gavin Bolton" (October 15, 1979).

PART I

THE SCHOOL AS AN ENVIRONMENT FOR EDUCATIONAL DRAMA AND THEATRE

1

EDUCATIONAL DRAMA IN SCHOOLS

EDUCATIONAL DRAMA IN THE ELEMENTARY SCHOOL

In any given elementary school day, drama is occurring naturally and spontaneously in myriad ways. During nondirective recess and play periods, children, alone or in groups, will act out, in role, scores of imaginary scenes. They will be warriors, teachers, heroes. They will act out entire improvised, free-form dramas based upon a television program, fantasy, or recent incident from their everyday lives. During class, when they become disinterested or distracted, they will act out elaborate internal dramas, based often in fantasy material, much of which is not accessible to their consciousness.

There is available, then, a wealth of dramatic material for teachers to draw upon. Should teachers chose to ignore the natural dramatic play and rich inner lives of children, they are limiting their natural resources and potential to expand the educational experience.

Most skilled teachers use drama every day in their classrooms without even knowing it. In fact, whenever teachers move from a method of telling about to one of demonstrating, they are moving into the realm of dramatic education.

Not all demonstration is drama, though. A demonstration of how to change water into ice and steam through freezing and boiling is not a dramatic activity. It becomes drama, though, when teachers ask their students to think imaginatively, as if they were water, and then to enact the various states of water as it changes from liquid to solid to gas. The essence of dramatic experience lies in the inner process of imagination, of thinking as if one were someone or something else, and the concomitant external process of impersonation or enactment.

The old elementary school stand-by "show and tell" implicitly represents two basic means of education, demonstration and description. Competent teachers, whether or not trained in drama, will know that the quality education of young persons depends upon the development of their ability to describe and to enact. They will also know that a mechanical, unimaginative demonstration is as educationally unsound as a description that lacks detail, clarity of thought, and creativity.

With some training in drama, the teacher should be able to help sharpen a student's ability to demonstrate or act out. In beginning directed drama work in the elementary classroom, the teacher must always remember to draw upon the child's natural predisposition to play. Drama is not a new skill to be taught, but a natural process that often becomes blocked as the instinct to play gets buried under the cloak of academics, rational thinking, and socially acceptable behavior.

In looking at the show and tell example, the teacher might say: "Now that you've told us about your experiments with water, this time show us how water changes form. But do it without using real water. Think of yourselves as water, and through your movements show us how you would change shape if you were water." To avoid the performance orientation here, the teacher might ask all students to try this dramatic experiment together.

Show and tell would seem to be a most natural way to integrate drama within a busy school day. There is another time that drama can be valuable in the elementary classroom. It is a time of social confusion or crisis, one that cannot be scheduled into a curriculum guide or timetable. It happens for a variety of reasons: a fight between two students at lunch, unresolved feelings regarding an action of the teacher or principal, a political or social crisis in the community, and so on. If any of these issues are so pronounced as to impede the educational process, they must be dealt with in some fashion. The usual method is not dealing with them at all, as the teacher most often feels unprepared, and the principal most often thinks it is inappropriate for the school to deal with social and emotional matters.

Drama is one way of examining such issues. The danger of this application of drama lies, of course, in teachers who are not trained in role-playing techniques and who are generally uncomfortable dealing with emotionally charged issues. They might believe, also, that the classroom is off-limits for such explorations. Obviously, such teachers should not experiment with more social and emotional uses of drama. But for teachers who have learned the techniques of role-playing and have explored their own fears of leading such dramas, the charged situation can be defused and attention can be freed for other curricular matters.

In the elementary school role-playing experiences should be basic; for example, in exploring feelings of anger toward teachers, students may be asked to assume a teacher's role and answer questions put to them by other students. Through the processes of role-playing, where several children get the chance to take on the role of teacher and angry student, and role-reversal, where a girl in the role of angry student, for example, is asked to switch roles with a boy in the role of teacher, the volatile situation is explored dramatically. Following the demonstration, students are asked to discuss their feelings and insights.

These role-playing experiences usually have three phases: a warm-up phase, an action phase, and a closure. During the warm-up the teacher, who has recognized a clear disturbance within the group, might ask each student to verbally express how he or she is feeling at the moment. Or the teacher might ask each student to draw a picture or assume a body posture that represents a present feeling.

From there, assuming that the students are sufficiently sensitized to their feelings, the teacher can move into the role-playing, acting-out phase, carefully choosing students to assume roles and carefully orchestrating the role-reversals, so that the students can move toward an understanding of several points of view.

Finally, through group discussion, sharing of feelings and summing-up, the teacher can bring the group to a point of equilibrium, if not understanding. This is the phase of closure.

Role-playing in the elementary classroom is a modification of psychodrama and sociodrama developed by J. L. Moreno, who was very active in pioneering early forms of improvisational theatre.[1] We take a closer look at psychodrama later (chapter 7).

Drama, then, occurs in the elementary school as a method of educating. Teachers apply it to not only affective learning but cognitive learning as well. As we see below, many basic cognitive skills, such as attending, concentrating, and problem solving, are learned through drama. Also, subject-matter areas such as reading, writing, and history are also learned through the method of drama.

Much of elementary school drama, though, occurs at a specified time in the day, as a subject or activity in itself. There have been many books written about drama in the elementary classroom. Most of them, again, draw attention to the primacy of play and specify the various methods and techniques that have been used throughout this century. For the most part, the experts advise that drama work should begin with exercises in body movement, pantomime, sense awareness, voice, and characterization.[2] The beginnings of drama in the elementary schools, they believe, are in exercises and games, geared to develop the child's ability to relax, trust, concentrate, and begin to develop imagination and social and self-awareness.

The characteristics of the drama exercise, according to Gavin Bolton, a British educational drama expert, are as follows:

1. It is always short term.
2. It always has a specific goal.
3. It always has a cutting-off point.
4. The rules are usually clear.
5. Often it is easily repeatable.
6. It is not normally associated with a high degree of emotion.[3]

From the basic drama exercise, many experts suggest moving to improvisational work where, for example, the students are given some minimal information—who, what, where, and why—and are asked to create a brief, spontaneous scene. The next step suggested involves the use of stories and/or poems to dramatize. Finally, many experts recommend the development of a play to be presented to an invited audience.

Other experts, most notably from England, neither begin drama with exercises nor move progressively to play production. Rather, they work with an eclectic, less linear form that combines many elements, techniques, and aims of the drama experience. The work and thoughts of several leading educational drama experts from America and Great Britain demonstrate not only differences in approach, but also similarities in aims and techniques applicable to the development of a child's learning in the elementary classroom.

Coleman Jennings is an author, director, and drama educator at the University of Texas at Austin. In a recent workshop he demonstrated the dramatization of several Greek myths with a group of fourth and fifth graders.[4] In structuring his brief twenty-minute session, Jennings began with an imagination warm-up and then proceeded to the story dramatization. During the warm-up Jennings provided a "magic carpet" for students to sit on, thus separating the world of imagination from the everyday world of school. He presented the students with a number of common objects that had been altered, such as a bent fork, and asked them to imagine the object as other things. One girl, for example, saw the fork as a giraffe.

Jennings then brought over an imaginary box that, he said, was filled with little ducklings. Each child was asked to play with a duckling and watch it eat. Then he asked the students, themselves, to assume the roles of hungry, thirsty ducklings.

From there, Jennings asked the children to play the roles of larger birds and fly around in search of food. Having sufficiently warmed up his students to the imaginary experience of flight, Jennings then introduced the myth of Daedalus and Icarus. After all of the students became familiar with the story, he chose one scene to dramatize—the fatal flight of Icarus from Crete.

Jennings invited volunteers to portray Daedalus, Icarus, and the sun. The scene was then enacted: Icarus tests out his newly fashioned wings. His father, Daedalus, warns him not to fly too close to the sun, but he does. His wings melt, and he falls into the sea.

The scene is recreated several times, with different children playing different roles. Jennings took time to develop more depth of characterization, movement, and sound. Finally, he asked a group of several children to play the Daedalus role. They became a chorus who chanted their warning to Icarus in unison: "Icarus, don't fly so close to the sun. Your wings will melt."

Jennings directed a second dramatization of the myth of Pandora by assigning one child to play Pandora and several other children to play the various blessings in the box. The curious Pandora opened the forbidden box, and all blessings escaped, surrounding her in a swirl of creative movements and sounds, then disappearing. All escaped except Hope, who remained with Pandora and would stay in the world forever.

Following the dramatization, Jennings engaged the children in a follow-up discussion with questions such as "What happens to Pandora?"

In an interview discussing his work in creative drama, Jennings offered the following:[5]

Interviewer: What is story dramatization? Is this a technique used often in creative drama?

Coleman Jennings: Story dramatization is a very important part of creative drama. We are concerned primarily with telling the children a story and having the children create that story, not for an audience, but for their own enjoyment.

Interviewer: Let's talk about the beginning of story dramatization. We saw several minutes of a warm-up period.

Jennings: We were talking about "If this were not." I got the children going, using their imaginations. I continued the warm-up process with an idea I was going to use later in the dramatization, leading up to flying.

Interviewer: In creative drama do you always use a warm-up period?

Jennings: Yes. It can be physical movements, a poem, anything. I try to tie it around the main content presentation I am going to use. Then you go into your major activity. Finally, you have an ending, a calming session, an evaluation.

Interviewer: How do you go about evaluation?

Jennings: We sit and talk about it. What was the most exciting thing we did? What was the most fun? I think it's very important to take a positive attitude. You don't say: "What was wrong with that?" I might ask: "If we were to do it again, how might we do it?"

Interviewer: What are your main educational objectives for using story dramatization?

Jennings: I might tie it into creative drama, since creative drama and story dramatization are one. One thing is just to have fun. We are helping the children develop their imagination, their creativity, seeing life a different way. We are not concerned with doing a play. So many people think when they hear drama in the elementary classroom that we are concerned with putting these young people on stage. That's not what we're after. Sometimes we share our work with other children, but we are primarily helping in the development of the child. I see it also as a way of relating to the curriculum. Creative drama can be both curricular and extra-curricular. Sometimes my motivation might be: "Allright, we are going to do this social studies unit, and we're going to do a story dramatization of one of the events from the westward movement." I think we have to be careful not to say we are going to teach everything by creative drama.

Interviewer: Is there now a requirement in Texas for creative drama in the curriculum?

Jennings: Yes, along with art, music, and physical education. Drama is required in every elementary classroom. A lot of schools have extensive programs. Some others are still learning about it. The Texas Education Agency also has a handbook that has been prepared for every elementary classroom teacher in Texas on how to use drama in the classroom.[6]

Interviewer: What about teachers already in the field who have not been trained in creative drama?

Jennings: Some teachers who have been using creative methods say: "I've been doing that all my life. I just didn't call it creative drama." In the current colleges and universities, creative drama is an important course in teacher education. But for people already in the field, I see reading, going to workshops, and experimenting as important. All it requires are the children, the teacher, the space, and some ideas. It's thoroughly flexible. I can spend two minutes or thirty. I can do it at the beginning of the day, the end of the day, any time I want.

Interviewer: What is creative drama?

Jennings: Creative drama is a process activity. It is about the development of the child. We are not concerned with the final product, a production. We continually have to tell people we are not doing plays.

Note that Coleman Jennings stressed the importance of creative drama as a process, child-centered activity. He also underlined the importance of the warm-up and positive follow-up discussion. Finally, he maintained the flexible nature of creative drama as brief or extensive, curricular or extra-curricular.

In examining a different use of story material in elementary school drama, we turn to the work of Geraldine Brain Siks, professor emeritus at the University of Washington, author and pioneer in the development of

American creative drama practice. In a recent workshop with a group of nine through eleven year olds, Siks began with a physical warm-up exercise.[7] Students were led through a series of separation exercises, that is, a series of independent movements focused upon specific areas of the body such as fingers, wrists, hips, and legs. As they acted out their movements, she beat out a rhythm on a tambourine. Then with a bang on the tambourine, she called "freeze."

She asked: "If you were a person or thing different from yourself, who would you be and what would you be doing?" Children's responses included dancer, monster, and tree.

Next, she gave each child a flattened-out cardboard box and asked the child to move it around in space. Again, she froze the movement and asked the children to transform their cardboard boxes imaginatively into other objects suggesting a character and a place.

As they played with the cardboard, Siks asked them to use their imaginations and respond to the question: "If it were either a particular place or if you were a particular person in that place different from yourself, who might you be?" Ideas included a swing, spaceship, house, and weight lifter.

She then divided the children into small groups and asked each group to create a story with a beginning, a middle, and an end. Each story was to be based in the objects, places, and characters suggested by the cardboard. Each group was asked to respond to the following: Where are you? Who are you? What are you doing? How do you relate to one another?

Then each group acted out its story improvisationally to the other children who, as observers, were asked to decide who the actors were, where they were, and what they were doing.

When one child exclaimed: "I don't know what to do," Siks took the time to help her discover a character, an object suggested by the cardboard, and a setting. Through a process of question and answer, the child and her partner were able to proceed with their improvisation, an intricate one concerning a little girl who rides on the back of a bird. Her partner, who has transformed his cardboard into a pair of binoculars, spies the girl and calls the police to help rescue her from the bird. Another child, as policeman, shoots the bird. But according to the storyteller, the bird escapes and is hidden away safely in her closet when she returns home.

In a related exercise Siks used chairs instead of cardboard. The children were asked to push the chairs out in space until they discovered a character, a place, and an action. Ideas included a mother vacuuming the house, a father mowing the lawn, an old lady in a wheelchair, and a race-car driver crashing. Through questioning Siks helped the children develop a story; for example, an old lady in a wheelchair on her way to go shopping to Macy's has an accident. Several passers-by come to her rescue.

Following the exercises Siks asked the children to discuss their reactions. She led them to specify what appealed to them most and what they could extend to their everyday lives. She also offered positive feedback about what she liked best of each child's play.

Following the session Siks shared her thoughts regarding creative drama in the elementary school:[8]

Geraldine Siks: I could see some of their patterns. They're very verbal. They wanted to talk instead of do, which is very good, because it lends itself to writing and communicating in speech. Lots of times the ideas come when they use their whole organic selves.

Interviewer: What are your educational objectives for using the warm-ups and the story dramas?

Siks: I start with a basic idea of drama. Drama is the process through which the child imagines that he or she is a character in action, in a conflict/resolution situation. Emphasis is on the process, the process of imaging; and as they image they actually perceive, drawing upon all this reservoir of sensory impressions in their memory banks. They communicate this whole thing to themselves, then to their friends. They're learning as a playmaker, giving structure and form to what's in their minds. And as an audience they're beginning to appreciate this whole thing. The emphasis is on the processes of perceiving, imaging, forming or improvising, and communicating and then evaluating. That's the process. Along with the process I have in mind certain concepts that are very necessary for the child to understand, both in drama and in communication, and that will help him express and communicate in life and at the same time grow in his appreciation of drama. If we would use a learning objective, we would say: "The student is able to control and use his or her body in nonlocomotor movement, and so he would try to see how many ways he could get the body to bend." The next thing would probably be that the student is able to manipulate an object for the purpose of stimulating his imagination to figure out where he is, who he is, and what he's doing.

Interviewer: It is conceivable that you could break down what we have just seen into many objectives that we could all observe and use in our own classroom.

Siks: I was looking at it from two points of view: the drama teacher's point of view and also from the language arts teacher's. One of the objectives for the language arts teacher is that the child is able to attend and listen and follow directions. This is one of the things in the past that all of us, across the nation, in public schools have failed to do, to develop good listening skills.

Interviewer: Let's take a day in a third- or fourth-grade teacher's life. Would the teacher use drama best in the context of a language arts lesson or at some other time in the day?

Siks: The answer depends upon the teacher. The teacher will only use it if the teacher believes in it. And the teacher will only believe strongly in it if the teacher understands it and has had a certain amount of learning or experience in it. We all know that the big movement across the country is back to basics. If I were a classroom teacher, I would use this as a very strong art, a central art in the language arts learning process, simply because I've heard teachers say many times it's hard to get children to understand how to write a composition. But here they're actually writing it nonverbally. And we could say to them next, now you sit down and tell the story: "Once upon a time, there was a little old lady who lived in a nursing home, and she was in a wheelchair. And she dreamed and dreamed about getting a dress at Macy's." Pretty soon they have the whole thing figured out. They've got the conflict in the middle. They've learned sequencing and how to express themselves in probably three paragraphs. They've learned to communicate, and pretty soon we would go into new vocabulary: wheelchairs, ambulance, emergency. The children would see something in the Gestalt; they would see a reason for putting this all together. I think it has to be explicitly stated by us in the drama field to the language arts people through in-service and pre-service training that drama is the natural way the child learns. We go with the child instead of saying: "Leave all the drama outside; come in here and sit and intellectually go at this."

Interviewer: How would you characterize creative drama?

Siks: There's been a long evolution. Winifred Ward started it. The core of it is in playmaking. The pattern of it has been to take a story already created by a storyteller, and then the child actually dramatizes it, plays the story. The emphasis was on the process. We'd tell it and say: "Who wants to be the characters?" They'd talk a little bit about the characters, and then they'd start to play it. Sometimes the children were very embarrassed and shy, and they didn't know what to do. Well, now that I look at it from a concept point of view, I say the child creates a character from two particular aspects: physical aspects and dominant personality traits. So now we're reducing it down to what I call fundamental concepts of the art form—helping the child really learn to create form, to give form to his inner thoughts and feelings, the things he perceives.

Geraldine Brain Siks, like Coleman Jennings and other American creative drama leaders, emphasized the telling of a story with a beginning, middle, and end. But her approach is unlike the more traditional use of story dramatization, as we have seen in the work with the Greek myths. The children, themselves, generate the stories and characters they will dramatize.

Like Jennings, Siks emphasized the importance of a warm-up exercise and follow-up discussion and feedback session. Working within a theoretical model of dramatic processes and concepts, she emphasized the importance of precise learning objectives.[9] Furthermore, she stressed the crucial integration of drama within the language arts curriculum, a relationship that we explore later in this chapter in some detail.

A third example of drama exercise and story dramatization in the elementary classroom is in the work of Albert Cullum, drama educator and author. In a recent workshop and interview Cullum aimed at teaching his college students how to educate young children, four to six years old, through drama.[10] The lesson involved teaching the sounds of the English language. Remaining consistent to the principle that drama must be taught through demonstration, Cullum asked his students to assume the emotional reality of five-year-old children.

Cullum began, in the role of teacher, by asking his students: "Let's create a rainy day this morning. Do you think we have the power to create a rainy day?"

He then helped the students develop the sounds: pit, pat, pitter, and pitter-patter. Each student was responsible for creating one sound. As the leader, Cullum orchestrated the rainstorm, starting with a sprinkle and building up to a full-blown storm, which he modulated with directed gestures indicating speed and volume.

Cullum referred to the storm experience as a play. During the twenty-minute drama session, he created several more plays. For example, he assumed the role of an angry grown-up and called his play: "Don't do this and don't do that." After again assigning his students the roles of children, he began to accuse them of various domestic crimes, each of which represented a particular alphabet sound, in this case the letter "d." He admonished his students with: "Don't dunk the donuts," "Don't dump the dominoes," "Don't dig in the dirt," "Don't bother Daddy." The children in mocking tones replied: "Don't do this and don't do that."

Cullum later explained that not only do children learn the "d" sound in this kind of play, but through their mocking, angry response to the teacher, they are playfully and safely releasing their angry feelings toward an authority figure.

In a third play Cullum exclaimed: "I'm willing to wager that everyone in this room has a belly button. Find it. Let's talk to it, and we'll begin our belly button play. It seems a little silly at first, but it'll warm up."

Cullum then spoke, and the students repeated in unison: "Belly button, belly button, on my tummy wall, / Belly button, belly button, like a little ball, / It can't bounce, it can't bend, / And it follows me like a friend."

According to Cullum, this exercise not only teaches the sound "b," but also leads students to become more accepting of their bodies and, again, to release emotion through laughter. Furthermore, they are introduced to the art of unison choral speaking.

In his last two plays Cullum asked his students to imagine eating a large meal as they chanted: "Chew, chomp, chew and chomp"; then he asked them to imagine a consequence of over-eating, that is, upset stomachs. As they experienced the sound of "c" while they ate, they worked with "m" in their nausea: "We ate too much, much too much." He ended the plays by asking if they had ever thrown up and by receiving a response in sounds that suggested that unpleasant experience.

In an interview following the plays Cullum offered the following remarks:

Interviewer: How did you get started using drama in elementary education?

Albert Cullum: As an elementary school teacher for twenty years, I realized very early that children are theatre. Four, five, and six year olds carry with them a fantastic world of creating and make-believe, and I decided I should join them in this process of learning and in that way create an atmosphere where basic skills could be introduced through drama, classroom drama.

Interviewer: What would your objectives be for using this kind of work in an elementary school classroom?

Cullum: I would begin it in nursery school and kindergarten to introduce them to the sounds of the alphabet. In *Picnic of Sounds* we cover every sound of the English language.[11] When they are introduced to formal reading, they hear the sounds and connect with them. It's not an abstract thing to them. So many children have difficulty reading today in America, because they're not prepared for these sounds.

Interviewer: What is the process of drama all about?

Cullum: When children or anyone goes through this drama process in an honest way, it really is a rebirth of liking oneself. And to me, that is the foundation of learning. You have to like yourself first, and then there's room for other things to go in.

Some adults who witnessed Cullum's use of drama were shocked at the idea of children playing at throwing up or talking to their belly buttons. But the children's perspective is very different. Through the drama they are allowed to reexperience situations often not openly discussed, thus exploding the unpleasantness in a safe group setting. The fringe benefits are enormous: having fun, developing a sense of group cooperation, learning how to speak in unison, and, mostly obviously, learning how to pronounce and recognize the various sounds of the alphabet.

Like the work of Geraldine Siks, Cullum's exercises can be well integrated within the language arts curriculum. Like Coleman Jennings, Cullum uses scripted material to create his plays. One difference in his approach, though, is that he, himself, assumes a central role in the dramas. That role is no longer simply that of the director, but rather the participant who can make things happen from within the drama.

In the work of British drama educators we see how the notion of leader as player becomes an integral part of their work. We also see a deemphasis of the dramatic exercise and story dramatization, with a stress upon an extended, in-depth experience. Like their American counterparts, British educational drama leaders have worked for many years to demonstrate the developmental educational values in drama. Although their basic aims are similar, there is a difference in emphasis. Americans have traditionally emphasized the following goals and values: development of the imagination, thinking on one's feet, group cooperation, social awareness, healthy release of emotion, better speech habits, and an introduction to the theatre arts.[12]

Generally, British drama educators echo these goals, but some go further. For example, Gavin Bolton has written: "Drama is concerned with a change of insight.... For drama to be effective in these terms there must be some shift of appraisal, an act of cognition that has involved a change of feeling, so that some facet of living is given (however temporarily) a different value."[13]

Dorothy Heathcote wrote: "One of the broad aims of education is to help people achieve the fullest and most varied and subtle changes of register in relating to others.... It is in this field that dramatic activity is of most direct help."[14] Brian Way added: "In education, the arts ... are concerned with the development of intuition."[15] Insight, cognition, change of feeling, varied social interaction, and intuition—all are challenging aims.

In April 1977 Dorothy Heathcote conducted a four-day, eight-hour drama workshop with a group of fourth graders in Orange County, California. In contrast to an exercise approach, Heathcote's drama was an extensive experience in full and varied human relations, cognitive learning, clarifying values, and the development of intuition.

She began the first day warming up the students through an informal discussion. She introduced herself and then invited students to recommend topics for a drama. Taking her cue from the regular classroom teacher, she suggested that they all continue exploring a unit of work already in progress —that of futurism.

After suggesting a space journey and meeting with a favorable response, Heathcote assumed the role of a government official who must check the credentials of those about to embark upon a voyage into outer space. In doing so, she began to build the students' belief in themselves as astronauts.

Next, Heathcote presented the group with a series of cards, each labeled for a different function of the space ship, for example, take-off system, waste removal, or doors and apertures. She then instructed the students to choose, in small groups, one function that would be their responsibility throughout the journey. Next, she helped them determine their ranks onboard the ship, thus establishing a chain of command. Following that, she allowed each small group the time physically to set up its part of the ship, using the available classroom furniture, blackboards, books, and the like. Then she asked each small group to check out all systems in preparation for take-off. Since a group of adult observers was present, Heathcote brought them into the drama as engineers who must listen to the astronauts' reports and give their approval before take-off. Adult engineers were instructed to help the astronauts articulate their conceptions of the rocket systems, without actually telling them what do do. Permission to proceed was to be granted only when the engineers were convinced the astronauts had a clear conception of their area of responsibility. Following this phase of the drama, Heathcote, out of role, questioned the students about the quality of the adult engineers' judgments.

In a discussion with the adults later, Heathcote explained that it is not her intention to teach the children how to pilot a spaceship, but rather how to assume the role of an astronaut and demonstrate the ability to think and act like an astronaut. She called this process "the mantle of the expert," implying that a crucial function of educational drama is to give children permission to assume the role of an expert, to act as if they were astronauts.

On day two Heathcote asked the children questions to help them review the highlights of the previous day. Next, she asked them to check out their equipment and record its fitness in writing. To monitor each small group, she invented a walkie-talkie system and asked each group to call in and give her their reports. Then, still in the role of their supervisor, she called in her report to NASA on the general fitness of the spaceship. In her report she mentioned several weaknesses in the ship. She discussed her finding with the crew in an attempt to lead them into understanding the importance of anticipating problems and the implications of failing to plan thoroughly and carefully. She encouraged them to double-check their work. Finally, in role, she read them her final report. In doing so she was, in fact, providing students feedback about the learning they had been experiencing. She said:

1. The crew is not afraid to admit it does not know.
2. The crew tells what it knows.
3. The crew occupies itself meaningfully.
4. The crew concentrates on the job.
5. The crew tolerates interruptions.
6. The crew engages in research.
7. The crew believes in its craft.

She asked the students to strap themselves in and informed them that they were responsible for launching themselves. She waited. There was silence. After a pause of a minute or so, Heathcote said: "I'm thinking if things don't work out, we won't get home again."

But no one picked up on the cue. They were uncomfortable with the silence and eager to take off. Heathcote then explained the importance of silence as a time to think of what is about to occur and to experience one's personal feelings.

There was no dramatic take-off scene. Heathcote made it clear that a conventional count-down was unacceptable to her. The rocket was off when one girl said: "I can see the country, America, below."

The second day ended with a problem—mechanical difficulties on the outside of the ship. Heathcote led them into a problem-solving discussion. She also set up a log in which the crew would document daily adventures.

The third day began with a discussion of how to go about docking the ship. One crew member drew the docking mechanism on the blackboard, and Heathcote led him into a discussion of the docking procedure.

She asked them to name their spaceship, making clear that names have implications. "I wouldn't want to fly in a ship named "Death," would you?" she asked. The crew decided upon the name "Eagle 2000."

Heathcote then assumed the role of a crew member and announced that she had brought a taped message with her from NASA headquarters, explaining the purpose of the mission. She played the tape, pre-recorded by one of the adult observers, and asked the crew to "listen with implication."

Before they docked, Heathcote led them in a ritual. They all gathered around an imaginary wheel to be used for the docking operation. They stood close together in a circle, trying to experience their feelings at the moment, and then chanted a statement of hope in unison.

On the fourth day students entered a new land in outer space. Dorothy Heathcote assembled the crew before exiting and asked them to record their final thoughts into the log. One boy offered: "We have obeyed our orders." Heathcote then exited to the other side of an imaginary barrier. The others were asked to close their eyes.

Heathcote had pre-arranged for the adults to assume the roles of effigies, frozen in place, because they had abused the natural water supply and polluted their environment. Each adult wore a sign, upon which was written a poetic riddle, relating to environmental abuse, for example, "You may pass from this place when you can know and show the dance of the tree dying for need of rain." When the children opened their eyes, they saw the frozen effigies who whispered: "Help me if you can."

Heathcote informed them that the only way to free the effigies was through creative dance. The group spontaneously launched into a mock Indian rain dance, which Heathcote stopped immediately, exclaiming, out of role, that she would not allow them to mock a serious religious ritual.

The crew, then, broke up into small groups and focused upon individual adult effigies. Their movements became much more intense. They were creating something personal and authentic. Heathcote instructed the effigies only to respond when they recognized a searching, creative effort from each of the dancers.

Time was up. As a final touch, Heathcote asked the adults to comment upon what they now understood in light of the dancing. One man said: "I understand caring, the caring of three girls." The faces of the three crew members lit up noticably. Their journey was successful.

This experiment in educational drama is a powerful one that demands a great deal of time to prepare and execute. It transcends exercise in that it is more extensive in time and intensive in feeling; its goals concern insight, change of feeling, and varied social interaction; and it is not easily replicable. It is almost a full curriculum in itself since it draws upon skills of writing, speaking, and thinking; of science and technology; of art and dance. It is geared very much toward a full experience not only in acting in role, or "the mantle of the expert," but also in exploring a vital social concern of everyday life, in this case, the depletion of the earth's natural resources.

Gavin Bolton's work has been similar in scope. Through his workshops he has also created imaginary environments within which to explore social concerns, such as the relationship between men and women. In one instance Bolton led the participants into building new sets of laws, governments, and systems of education and family life. A whole new society was created from scratch. In creating a new world the participants were, in fact, recreating the old one. In so doing, they made many of the same mistakes that had been made before. But there were breakthroughs—times when they would see new ways of living together, sharing responsibility and power. This, of course, was the point of the extended drama—through recreation of everyday society in drama, we can be led to explore alternative ways to relate to one another. Drama creates a laboratory for human behavior that can be reflected upon, understood, and perhaps modified.

In a recent interview Bolton spoke about his work as a drama educator.[16]

Interviewer: Can you tell us about your current drama work in England?
Gavin Bolton: I work in the University of Durham, where my students are mostly experienced teachers who return to the university for in-service training. My responsibility is to help them either use drama in their teaching or teach drama at the elementary or senior high level.
Interviewer: If we were to walk into a room where you were leading a group of children in drama, what would we see?
Bolton: Chances are that immediately you would think that nothing was happening, because when I talk about drama in education, I don't necessarily mean a great deal of activity. The other way of looking at drama is to think of children rushing around all over the place, working very fast, doing lots of exercises, being very stimulated and in all kinds of directions, and that drama is very exciting. I see drama quite differently. I see it as a very thoughtful process, and so if you were an observer

of my work you would have to be very patient, and you would see a very slow approach to action and a great deal of reflection upon the action when it's over.

Interviewer: Could you describe a session that you have led recently?

Bolton: I was working with a class of mentally retarded children who wanted to do a drama about robbing a bank. Very often I give the children a choice of topic, and then when I know what the choice of topic is, I see how they approach it and decide how then I'm going to adjust the material so that they learn something from it. These were retarded children and children who had also committed some crime against the law. They were in a residential home. Age twelve. Their idea of doing a drama about robbing a bank was shooting each other, being dead, getting up again, and carrying on. So I persuaded one child to stay dead. The others were surprised but stepped over him and carried on with their drama. And I called it to a halt and said: "I think you've got a problem when I return next week. You've got a body on your hands. I don't know how people deal with bodies."

So next week when they arrived I said: "If you're this gang of robbers, what are you going to do with this body?" They took a long time discussing how they were going to get the body from where it lay to where they were going to hide it. As retarded children, their thinking level isn't very high. But all the time in my work I'm demanding more and more thinking from them, more and more precision in their thinking. So they went through a series of experiences of carrying that body in a way that didn't draw attention to themselves as they moved along the street. And I, as teacher in role, role-played various parts, for example, somebody who wanted to know where the station was. Then at the end of that lesson, I said: "You've got a problem for next week. Do you think that body is going to be missed by anybody? Who was he?"

They decided he was a policeman. The next lesson went through a series of my interviewing them, again in role, wanting to know whether they saw a policeman on duty that night, and who were they and what were they doing and what were their alibis. I had turned what started as a dramatic playing exercise into a language experience, because now they have to find the right words to answer the questions, and they can't anticipate what questions I'm going to ask. And according to which child I'm dealing with, I press harder and harder. If I'm dealing with a child who can only cope with yes and no answers, I ask that kind of question. But if I'm dealing with a child who could, if pressed, think more elaborately, I ask a more sophisticated question.

Interviewer: Did they choose the content?

Bolton: They nearly always choose the content. What I do is decide upon the theme. Very often they will choose a fantasy context, so it might be creating some primitive society that's never existed before, or it might be going on a space ship and living on Mars. Whenever I know the context, I then say: "What in that context can relate to their own lives? What conceptually is worth exploring?"

Interviewer: Is that the same as universal meanings in drama?

Bolton: Yes. If they were going to visit Mars the universal then may be facing dangers, may be the problem of working together as a team, may be the problem of the selection of a leader, may be the problem of having to leave somewhere knowing that you may never return. It may initially sound like fantasy. I'm going to make them look at very real problems. There are always two plays going on. There's the play for them and the play for the teacher who is always working on an educational plane. And if the teacher role-plays, he is never role-playing with them. He's always role-playing beyond them; so he is demanding they reach up to his level.

Interviewer: Generally, what is the teacher's responsibility in the kind of dramas you do? Can we explore the teacher's role in drama a little further?

Bolton: He can play many different kinds of roles. If you are working with a class who appear to not want to take the initiative, you may then take a leadership role. On the other hand, the most useful role a teacher can take is the contrasting one of being a follower, the one who doesn't know, the one who says: "I've got a terrible problem. You see, I've got this child who can't talk properly, who doesn't know the proper words to use. Can you—I may be talking to a six or seven year old—help this child to learn our language?" And you're the one who's treating the children in the class as experts. So they then draw on their "expertise" in order to solve this particular problem. In fact, using them as experts is very, very useful. Recently, I was working with a class of twelve, thirteen years olds, and they were very interested in sports. So I role-played being a representative from the Nigerian government, saying: "Nigeria wanted to do as well in the Olympic Games as any other country. We brought these experts over from America and Canada and England. Could you experts—talking to the kids—help us to train Nigerians? What skills will you train them in? Also, we need help in how you design gymnasia and that kind of thing." So in role, they are using their expertise, and very often they find they haven't got enough, so they rush to books. A great deal of my drama work is connected with the library. I don't know whether you have it in America, but certainly in England we have this move "back to basics." And it seems to me drama more than any other aspect of the curriculum can help children learn the basics. I use drama for reading, math, any concept, right across the curriculum.

Interviewer: Is drama a basic in itself?

Bolton: It's basic, because it's concerned with identification. And if you look at any aspect of the curriculum, whether it's history, geography, literature, or social studies, you are concerned with getting the child to identify with somebody else's situation. Now drama does this in a particular way. So it is a medium for helping the process of identification. So to the teacher, it's as useful as a blackboard or a picture or a video-tape.

Interviewer: Could you talk a bit further about identification? What is it?

Bolton: I suppose, simply, it's getting into somebody else's shoes. We want to help children through the process of education to understand how other people think. Drama does this particularly well, because it gets children on their feet to do it. So there is a physical and emotional way to approach that understanding. This is where it differs from sitting at a desk learning.

Interviewer: How do you train a teacher in drama? How do you get a teacher to be comfortable role-playing with children?

Bolton: One important thing for a teacher to realize is that drama does not have to last a certain length of time. Drama can last for two minutes. And it may be the elementary schoolteacher teaching literature or some other subject who imperceptably introduces into the classroom the use of role-play. If a teacher is not used to role-play, it is better that he role-play somebody that's like himself. So he can role-play being the head teacher or a teacher in another school, or he can role-play being himself as a stranger, and as a stranger in role, he says to his class of children: "Excuse me, I'm a stranger to this town. Can you tell me where the post office is?" And the teacher is really testing himself, and he's also testing how the children are going to react to his role-play. And when they accept it, he'll gain in confidence and move from there to more elaborate role-playing.

Interviewer: Do teachers have to be trained to role-play, or is it something they have to be ready for and simply work into?

Bolton: I think a mixture of the two. If they are given confidence in using it, then they will reach a certain level of work in doing it. If, in fact, they are given further training, then they will be more subtle in their use of that particular tool.

Interviewer: Getting back to using drama to teach basics, how might one incorporate drama in a math lesson?

Bolton: The other week I was asked by a kindergarten teacher to use drama to teach children the recognition of numbers between one and five. Some already recognized them; others didn't. So I role-played being a very stupid king with a bad tummy. And I got this pain, so the children advised me that I needed medicine from the doctor. I asked them to go to the doctor for me—that was the class teacher. And she gave them a bottle and wrote on it: "Take two teaspoons." They brought it back to me, and I helped myself to this medicine, taking three teaspoons. And they were astonished and said: "You've got it wrong."

And I said: "Well, how?" And they said: "Well, you should take two." And I said: "Well, how do you know?" And they said: "Well, it says it." And I said: "What do you mean, says it?"

And so they showed me how it says two. And my stomach gets worse, and they say: "No wonder." So they go back for different medicine. The teacher writes three on the bottle this time, and I still get it wrong, so they then take me round the classroom, because they realize by now that not only is this king in poor health, he's also stupid. And with some sense of frustration, they go around the classroom pointing out the various numbers, one through five. And they teach me to recognize numbers. Of course, what's happening is that they are either reinforcing what they already know, or the ones that didn't know those numbers are very quickly picking them up, because the motivation is there. And, here again, if the teacher plays a role that is inferior to where they stand, there's a good chance that they will really learn something.

Interviewer: What are the principles behind your work?

Bolton: Basically I'm concerned with refining concepts. Only secondly am I concerned with teaching about drama. The important thing to me is if you watch children play, the essential mode of that playing is spontaneous, existential playing. If you see a lot of drama lessons, they are made up of a series of exercises. Now, both these modes have their strengths and weaknesses. What I would like to see in drama is a combination of those two. So when I work in drama, I try to set up an opportunity for a playing mode, a mode of spontaneity, combined with the very tight structure of an exercise. So within the exercise structure they are playing and they can say: "It is happening now." We're not demonstrating that it is happening. We're not pretending it is happening. It is happening to us now. In that sense, it is existential, and I do believe that existential playing within the tight structure of exercise offers the greatest potential for learning.

Interviewer: And finally, what is the process of drama, as opposed to a more product-oriented theatre production?

Bolton: I think there are two orientations that pull in different directions. One is toward performance. One is toward experiencing. Now, performance has to encapsulate experience, and one of the problems is that we tend to invite children to encapsulate experience without allowing them to experience. So it seems to me a very important step is the process of experiencing. This may well be refined at some stage, depending upon the maturity of the class and the age group, by turning it into a product so they re-create an experience.

Here we see again an emphasis upon the teacher as player and the student in the role of the expert. We also see a connection between drama and the standard curriculum, in this case math. Furthermore, we see an integration of the structured exercise that can be repeated with different groups in varying circumstances and the more existential playing mode that would, by definition, vary from group to group. Finally, we find another extension of the goals of learning through drama—the refining of concepts.

Certainly, all of the above aims, techniques, and philosophical approaches are valid in educating children through drama. Many of the differences are of degree rather than kind, and most all educational drama specialists would readily admit to borrowing ideas and techniques from colleagues. Much of the most exciting and innovative work in educational drama occurs at the elementary school level, for the young learner is still very much open to the values inherent in role-playing, imagination, movement, and fantasy work. As we shall see, though, the aims, techniques, and values that are valid in the elementary classroom apply consistently throughout all subsequent schooling.

EDUCATIONAL DRAMA IN THE SECONDARY SCHOOL

In moving from elementary to secondary education, one change we find is in the external content of the dramas. A spaceship might not be an appropriate dramatic vehicle for a sixteen year old. Yet the universal issues that Dorothy Heathcote explored with nine year olds, such as social responsibility and leadership, could equally be explored with teenagers. It is only necessary to change the outer form, which must coincide with the students' interests, so that they will be motivated to enter into the dramatic experience.

At the secondary level drama is used frequently in three ways: as performance or formal theatre; as a method of teaching other subject areas, history and English, in particular; and as a means of enhancing social and emotional development.

In the area of social development drama can be applied to those situations where behavioral problems intrude upon academic achievement. Most secondary schoolteachers face some form of behavioral problems in the classroom: the acting-out student who always needs to be the center of attention, the student who is chronically shy and withdrawn, and the student who bullies or is bullied, to mention a few. During the course of a lesson, should these kinds of behaviors intrude upon the learning process, the techniques of role-playing, psychodrama, and sociodrama might prove useful. However, as we have seen above, most teachers have neither the training nor the confidence to use these techniques, which, as we see later (chapter 7), are used routinely in drama therapy.

When psychodramatic techniques are used with secondary school students, the setting is most often nonacademic. For example, several years ago Dr. Lewis Yablonsky, educator, author, and psychodramatist, led a series of psychodrama sessions with a group of teenagers from a Los Angeles high school. The purpose was an exploration of selected issues of concern to teenagers: relationships with parents, teachers, and friends; feelings about school, sex, drugs, racial tensions; and so on. The setting was a local television studio, and several of the sessions were aired in the Los Angeles area.

Although psychodrama is rare in a secondary school classroom, teachers aware of the value of drama for social development have experimented with improvisational and creative drama techniques. One outstanding example is in the work of Thom Turner, principal of the Street Academy, an extension of Boys and Girls High School in the Bedford-Stuyvesant section of Brooklyn. In a recent interview Turner explained the task of the Street Academy:[17]

> *Thom Turner:* Our major task is to work with youngsters who have not been able to manage the regular school day and the regular school system. We take these youngsters into the Street Academy and involve them in what we call an environmental and learning readiness program, where the emphasis is on the affective domain. We teach English and mathematics and social studies and health education, but the focus is on behavior. They stay in the school for six months to a year, and when we've been able to redirect some of the norm-violating behavior, they learn certain basic skills, and they take these skills back to Boys and Girls High School.

To teach these basic skills, Turner and his staff use drama activities that they call "CDRPs," Creative Dramatic Reality Practices. An example is "The Getover Rap," a dramatization of a situation where a student attempts to manipulate an authority figure. In a recent demonstration Turner chose a situation where two disruptive youngsters are reported to the principal by the teacher. The two improvise their confrontation with their teacher and then their conversation with the principal. They successfully manage to "get over" on him, that is, deny any personal responsibility for their disruptive behavior. Next, all concerned—teacher, students, and principal—discuss the dramatization out of role, focusing not only upon the effects of disruptive behavior and the need to take responsibility for one's actions, but also upon ways to rechannel the extremely well-developed communication skills of the students into more positive, socially acceptable directions.

Turner stressed his belief that many students never learn how to play their roles as students. The reasons include academic failures, weak adult role models who offer few controls, and poor human relations practices on the part of teachers and administrators. To solve the problems of social irresponsibility and disruptive behavior, each individual within the school system must learn to play his or her role appropriately and humanely in relationship to others in their roles. Through improvisational role-playing experiences, such as "The Getover Rap," students, teachers, and administrators can examine their behavior and try out alternative ways to break through the frustration of trying to learn or teach in a chaotic atmosphere.

Other CDRPs, such as "Respect Yourself," "The Line," and "The Winners and the Losers," also serve to teach positive social skills. Turner calls his social dramatic approach a process of learning how to learn, that is, learning and/or redirecting essential skills necessary for all further learning to occur. This approach is of very special importance in those inner city communities where teachers and administrators, often out of frustration, have neglected the primacy of social learning and positive self-concept building as the true basics without which all other learning is rendered meaningless.

There is another interesting social application of drama to the secondary classroom. Given a modern society that is often confusing and irrational, at best, the teacher may want to search for ways to help the student make sense out of the world he lives in. This act of making order out of disorder, sense out of nonsense, may well represent the most essential value in the dramatic experience. From our dramatic play as children to our viewing of the great plays from our dramatic literature, we continue to explore the crucial human concerns of meaning and mortality in a form that is managable, intelligible, and personal.

During the Great Depression in America, when the newspapers reported the grim statistics of unemployment and the preparations for an inevitable war, the Federal Theatre Project responded by dramatizing the news and provoking active discussion and thought.[18] The Living Newspaper, as it was called, which actually originated in the early experiments in spontaneous theatre by the psychodramatist J. L. Moreno, could just as well apply to the secondary classroom. In fact, this author modified the technique for use in the classroom.

Shortly after the assassination of Martin Luther King, the author, who was teaching at the secondary school level, was searching for a way to commemorate the death of the great civil rights leader. Working from a concept of trying to make sense of the recent past in terms of current events and feelings, he asked five students to select newspaper articles of interest from an assortment of daily papers. Then each was to find a personal space in the room and read his or her article with some care. A sixth student was chosen as a kind of stage manager, whose function was to begin and end the drama and to elicit responses from the others. The stage manager's text was simply the title of the drama: "Martin Luther King—1929-1968." He was the only one permitted to move around the room freely.

The five students were instructed to read portions of their articles aloud, randomly, one voice at a time. There was to be no prescribed order of readings and no prescribed way to read from one's article. Sentences or phrases could be repeated or deleted and presented in various tempos, rhythms, and emotional tones. The dramatic skills to practice included concentration, memory of emotion, listening, and responding.[19]

In practicing concentration the students were instructed to focus their attention upon the meaning of their words and the relationship between their words and the theme of the drama. In practicing memory of emotion the students were asked to recall their feelings at the time of Martin Luther King's death and to find a connection between those past feelings and the present feelings evoked by their articles. They were also asked to allow those feelings to be expressed through their readings.

Furthermore, students were encouraged to listen to the readings and be sensitive to the feelings expressed by the others in the drama and to respond appropriately, again, only using their articles as a text. Each student was instructed to respect the rights of expression of others, to share time and space, and to be sensitive to picking up cues and finding appropriate connections.

The stage manager began the drama by reading the title. As the drama proceeded, he would repeat the title to fill in silences or to cut off a speaker who might have gone on too long. Through his movement, he would also try to cue in the shy student or restrain the overly eager one. The play ended, again, at the discretion of the stage manager, with a reading of the title followed by a reading of the present date.

Following the drama the students would engage in a discussion with those who observed. Although this experience is, strictly speaking, a classroom activity, it has been "performed" to small audiences of peers and invited guests. The purpose of the follow-up discussion was to examine student feelings and thoughts concerning the death of Martin Luther King and to determine the relationship between a past event of much significance and current events of varying significance.

Questions raised included: is all contemporary data relevant in illuminating the world we live in? How does a subway mugging, a used car ad, a teacher's strike, the unsuccessful comeback of an old rock and roll star, and a war in Southeast Asia relate to the murder of Martin Luther King? Are there factors in our culture that provoke feelings of hate and violence? It is these kinds of questions, concretized and stimulated by the drama, that can lend depth and relevance to a lesson in the secondary classroom.

Carol Korty also deals with social and emotional concerns of secondary school students. As a playwright she dramatized a significant social and political event in American history, the Lawrence Mill strike of 1912, a revolt of thousands of ethnic workers, many of whom were women and children. Her play *On the Line* is a participatory theatre experience, involving secondary school students in the examination of the social and emotional events leading up to the strike.

As an educational drama leader, Korty often works to help students explore their feelings and personal concerns through drama. In a recent demonstration she worked with a group of junior high school students.[20]

Korty began with a discussion of wishing for superhuman powers. As they talked she discovered their concern with crime in the city. They were afraid of being robbed and wished they could do something about it.

Following this discussion Korty directed the group through an improvisation, determined entirely by the group. A boy is robbed on the street. He becomes angry and decides to take action. First, he puts his money in the bank. Then he endows himself with the power to become invisible. While at the bank he witnesses a robbery. Using his superhuman power he captures the robber and feels vindicated.

Following the improvisation, Korty offered the following:

> Educational drama is actually about some of the simplest aspects of human interaction—people talking to each other and working together. It's also about people knowing how to read each other, not having to be told how to do one particular thing and following along a single track. In that way I'd say it's the most sophisticated form of human behavior there is, because there's very subtle interaction. Everybody has his or her own space, respects each other's ideas, and takes the time to listen and to be heard.[21]

As mentioned above, a second application of drama to secondary education concerns drama as a method of teaching other subjects. We discuss the relationship between drama and language arts, history, and integrated arts below. For now, let us look briefly at the most common application of drama to secondary education—performance.

Generally, secondary schools that offer drama/theatre studies tend to stress performance, production techniques, and dramatic literature courses. Creative drama might remain in the transitional junior high school grades, but by grade nine or ten, it all but disappears. In the recently published *Theatre Arts: Framework for Grades 7-12*, for example, we find mention of dramatic storytelling, puppetry, mime, and improvisation in grades seven and eight. But by grade eight we also find introduction to stagecraft, audition procedures, play production, and acting techniques.[22]

In fact, the one comprehensive study of drama/theatre in American secondary education, Joseph L. Peluso's *A Survey of the Status of Theatre in United States High Schools*, only makes reference to performance and not to the more process-oriented creative dramatic activities.[23] It is interesting, though, that high school principals and teachers agreed that the two most important values in play production and theatre courses are to enable students to grow in self-confidence and self-understanding, and to provide experiences that will help increase the student's understanding of others.[24] Certainly, these values apply to all drama experiences, whether in play, creative drama, or performance.

In concluding his study Peluso noted that most United States high schools produce plays, but few actually offer theatre arts courses. Furthermore, the teachers assigned to direct the plays tend to be inexperienced in theatre or drama. Schools that do offer theatre courses, taught by teachers with some training in drama and/or theatre, tend to be large schools, primarily located in large urban areas. When we discuss the school play below, we explore several issues of theatre production and performance in both elementary and secondary education.

In the secondary schools of America and to a lesser extent in England, educational drama, when available at all, is most frequently taught as a subject called theatre arts or dramatic arts. Yet the examples of Thom Turner's CDRPs and the Living Newspaper point to ways that secondary school drama can be applied throughout the curriculum as a method of examining many social, emotional, and intellectual concerns.

In developing a dramatic curriculum for grade ten (fifteen year olds), Richard Courtney argued for a multidisciplinary approach that accounts for each student as unique; that encourages a sound learning experience in thinking, feeling, and experiencing; that recognizes the application of play to the continued growth of adolescents; and that provides for a "genuine encounter between teacher and student."[25] With these principles in mind, Courtney included within his curriculum the use of role-playing, improvisation, playmaking, dance, and speech in combination with more theatrical aspects of makeup, lighting, and performance. Although adolescents are developmentally ready and willing to perform to an audience, their more basic need to learn through play and spontaneous, informal drama remains intact.

EDUCATIONAL DRAMA IN HIGHER EDUCATION

At the college or university level, we find educational drama applied, for the most part, to the training of teachers. The same goals and values mentioned above apply equally to higher education and complement those goals generally associated with a liberal arts education.

Quite a few colleges and universities throughout the United States, England, Canada, and Australia are now offering courses in educational drama, although these courses often comprise a small portion of the more standard theatre arts fare of history and criticism, design and performance courses.

In a recent review of United States university programs offering courses in children's drama, defined as "a composite term referring to creative drama and children's theatre," Wendy Perks tabulated responses from forty-five schools indicating varying quantity of courses but common philosophical points of view, types of undergraduate and graduate course offerings, research concerns, and practical experiences in the field.[26] Among the most comprehensive programs identified include those at the University of Washington, Arizona State University, and the California

State University system, all offering diverse courses in creative drama and children's theatre. Recent specialized higher education programs include the development of interrelated comprehensive arts undergraduate training programs at Illinois State University and the University of Washington, among others; the refinement and implementation of state drama/theatre frameworks in California, Texas, and Washington; and the continuation of the successful summer study abroad program in educational theatre at New York University.

British and Canadian universities also offer a diverse range of courses in educational drama, although, like American universities, great emphasis still lies in the more conventional dramatic literature and theatre production areas.

In speculating about the training needs for the future, Dorothy Heathcote has suggested a possible new curriculum in educational drama to include two areas. The first, academic study and experiences, would include birth and origins of saga, myth, legend, and folk-lore; group dynamics; differences in dramatic form; anthropological studies of the place of drama and theatre; understanding of play and elaboration procedures; child development; and mental health. The second area, practical experience, would include self-discovery of teacher type and strengths and weaknesses; handling groups of all sizes in all types of spaces; studies in observation and analysis of self and others; skill in tension and confrontation; and learning to receive and listen.[27]

Richard Courtney has greatly influenced university curricula throughout Canada. During his tenure at the University of Calgary, he developed a curriculum in developmental drama, defined as "the study of human development through enactment."[28] The range of studies included two areas. The first, personal studies, concerned "individual human development through drama as role-playing (process) and drama as art (form)." The second area, cultural studies, included "human cultural development through dramatic activity in the child-rearing process and its effect on cultural similarities and differences in dramatic art forms."[29]

Whereas much of educational drama studies in America occur in theatre departments, the trend in England is toward colleges of education. One outstanding British program is headed by John Hodgson at the Bretton Hall College. Hodgson bases much of his training of teachers of drama in the techniques of improvisation and simulation. In a recent workshop and interview he demonstrated and spoke about his work:[30]

> *Interviewer:* You call your work improvisation. What does that mean to you?
> *John Hodgson:* It simply means—no script. There's an element of spontaneity always present. And we're demanding concentration and imagination from the people in response to each other at a given moment in time.

Hodgson begins much of his work with a game approach, which often develops into scene work. Both the game-playing and the scene study are focused in a common theme. An example is a recent demonstration centered in the theme of ownership and responsibility.

Hodgson began by asking four students to work in pairs. Each one had a coin and was instructed to try to snatch the other's coin. The students worked with open palms, nonverbally.

Then Hodgson moved into a verbal exercise. He asked each student to produce an object of some special personal value and to let the partner know what it is and what it means. Examples included family heirlooms and antique jewelry that had magical powers. Next, Hodgson asked that each try to persuade his or her partner to give up the object to the other for safe-keeping.

As Hodgson moved from objects to living things each student was asked to fashion a piece of cloth into a baby. As the baby cried students got into role by calming it down. Then an improvisation developed. Each pair became babysitters for a child left to their care by a friend. As the baby became agitated, the couple had to deal with the problem.

Following that, Hodgson took the theme of responsibility one step further. He asked one couple to act out their discovery of a baby at the doorstep. Then he switched focus from the couple who found the baby to the couple who abandoned the child, asking the deserting parents to act out their decision to reclaim the child.

After that, the first couple acted out their plans to raise the foundling child. Then the two couples were brought together. A passionate argument developed—explanations were offered, morality was debated, tears were shed.

Hodgson moved into another scene. Two men as arbitrators were to decide the fate of the child. Each of two women claimed to be the lawful mother. After the women stated their cases, the arbitrators conferred.

Following these improvised scenes the students were introduced to the text *The Caucasian Chalk Circle* by Bertolt Brecht, which concerns in part, the legal and moral conflict of ownership and responsibility in caring for a baby. The game and improvisational experience, then, not only led the students through the exploration of a significant theme, but also pointed toward an identification with and understanding of a dramatic text.

In a second workshop experience Hodgson demonstrated the technique of simulation as a way to explore a social problem and to prepare for the study of a dramatic text. The situation to be simulated was set in a valley with a lake in the center. Two community groups lived nearby. One looked after goats and made cheese; the other tended the vineyards and made wine. The valley was sketched on a piece of paper, and a story was created by Hodgson: The goatherders had been occupying the valley for some time. During a recent war they were driven out. But now they wanted to return. Their village had been damaged during the war but was reparable. The vineyard community also wanted to move into the valley, because it was a fine location for their crops, given the natural resource of the lake water. They believed they could develop the land fully.

Hodgson asked the students to discuss the question of who had the right to live in the valley. He divided the group into vineyard farmers, goatherders, and government officials. The students assumed specific roles, for example, from the goatherders, a village elder and a village woman who doesn't want to be displaced; from the vineyard farmers, a small vineyard owner who represents the commercial needs of the village; from business, a representative from a large corporation who is courting the village farmers; and from the government, an official who represents a peacemaking position, determined by which group operates most definitely in the national interest.

Hodgson then set up a public meeting to determine a solution to the conflict. Following a debate at the public meeting, the simulation ended. A follow-up discussion ensued, comparing the simulation to real political and moral conflicts, such as the conflict in the Middle East that, at least in part, concerns land ownership. Finally, Hodgson introduced a dramatic text, again Brecht's *Caucasian Chalk Circle*, which the students were now ready to explore, having, in essence, simulated the first scene of the play.

After the workshop Hodgson offered the following:

John Hodgson: Simulation is something which can have considerable value in helping people understand situations, because if you get in someone else's shoes like that, at least you begin to understand what the problems are and try and see them from another point of view. It would have been possible, had we had the time, to change round and to argue the opposite case instead of sticking to one side. That way they would see that the other side has its own valuable ideas.

Interviewer: Is simulation taking on another person's point of view, taking on another role?

Hodgson: Yes. You actually argue from another set of positions and attitudes. In a simulation exercise drama can come to the aid of understanding another attitude and thereby, hopefully, help you to see your own prejudices and limitations.

Interviewer: What kind of preparation do you need for simulation?

Hodgson: I was trying to work on two levels, both to explore a situation and to involve us, perhaps, in opening up a text. This is actually based on Brecht's *Caucasian Chalk Circle*. They have actually enacted the first scene of the play. Not in Brecht's words, but Brecht's ideas. That is the preparation, in a sense, for the next phase. They can read the text and understand it much better, because they've actually tried to live through the situation.

Interviewer: Is simulation always a preparation for a text?

Hodgson: No. It's a preparation for anything, really, for some further development or understanding. You can take any situation from a play or the newspapers and help people to understand it. In Britain a short time ago we had a fireman's strike. I got a group of students to take a newspaper cutting and to see the various attitudes and the various factions that were involved. And we reenacted certain areas of that through an imaginative reconstruction. We all understand that situation far better, because we actually approached it and related to it.

Interviewer: Would you use simulation in a classroom?

Hodgson: Very much so. We didn't use much movement here. If you have fixed desks, it's a very useful means of getting people involved, both emotionally and imaginatively.

Interviewer: What scripts are most appropriate to work with through simulation?

Hodgson: Any script where you want people to appreciate a situation that is not only something of the past, but something real. *King Lear*, for example, seems a very remote thing about a king and his daughters. But if you say it's a father concerned with his children and you want to understand the fact that he's getting old and giving all his money away, then you begin to get a greater understanding of that situation, and off you go into a look at *King Lear* from a different point of view, because you see a human being and the relevance of the story.

Interviewer: Is simulation a form of improvisation?

Hodgson: Yes. Simulation is one aspect of improvisation. For me, *improvisation* is a big word covering many aspects of drama work. It simply means that what we're doing is not scripted. We are developing the ideas as we go along. *Improvisation* is an all-embracing term. Simulation is one way of employing it.

With the work of John Hodgson and Albert Cullum in training teachers, we find a most creative application of educational drama to the college or university classroom. Certainly, in both instances we find a connection between drama and the language arts—in Cullum's work, the learning of sounds; in Hodgson's work, the learning of a literary text. In fact, most of the above workshop examples indicate an interrelationship between drama and the academic curriculum.

EDUCATIONAL DRAMA AS A METHOD OF TEACHING OTHER SUBJECTS

Drama and the Language Arts

Drama and the language arts are very closely interrelated. In fact, long before drama became an academic discipline in its own right, it was taught by English teachers as part of the language arts curriculum.

But as English once was the basis for teaching drama, drama can now be seen as the basis for teaching English. In a recent book concerning the essential function of drama within the language arts curriculum, John Stewig wrote:

> Because of the widespread view among linguists that language is primarily a spoken art, language programs which do not give children chances to talk should be viewed by teachers as inadequate. It is my contention that the addition of spontaneous dramatics to the language arts curriculum can provide the necessary opportunities for development of language and language related abilities.[31]

But the strongest case for drama as an essential way to teach language arts was argued by James Moffett, who has devised an entire language arts curriculum, grades kindergarten through thirteen, based heavily in essential principles and techniques of drama.[32]

Proceeding from an understanding of drama as the moment of direct experience, as "what is happening," Moffett wrote:

> I would like to argue here that drama and speech are central to a language curriculum, not peripheral. They are base and essence, not specialties. I see drama as the matrix of all language activities, subsuming speech and engendering the varieties of writing and reading.[33]

In a recent interview, exploring the interrelationships between drama and the language arts, Moffett offered the following:[34]

> *Interviewer:* What is it about drama that is so essential for the learning and teaching of language arts?
> *James Moffett:* I think the means to language arts goals are social and often physical or nonverbal. They're dramatic in the sense that communication has a concrete context—that is, the speaker, the listener, the purpose, the circumstances are all quite clear. A theatre play is a good model for this, in that you know who's talking, who's listening, who's present or absent.... What actually gets said, the discourse, is right there and has great emotional impact. It teaches you the basic lesson in rhetoric, which is that one person is trying to get effects upon another person through the use of language. I think when this is all incarnated for you on the stage, or when you, as a participant, are taking a role in a scene, this basic lesson in rhetoric really gets across. As students become more involved in the disembodied communications or messages in books and so on, the author may be dead several centuries. In drama they don't lose the feeling, the rhetorical relationship, the I-Thou relationship that Martin Buber talked about.[35] It's a spiritual notion of a kind of communion, as well as communication.

Interviewer: So we're talking about language arts as relationship.

Moffett: Very much. As interaction, ongoing relationships.

Interviewer: You mentioned the I-Thou relationship, which Buber calls dialogue. You refer to dialogue in *Teaching the Universe of Discourse* as a very basic way that language is learned. Could you talk some more about dialogue.

Moffett: This interview is, to some extent, a model of that. It's not completely planned. We're acting under the impact of each other's statements. You ask me something or I say something, and I prompt something else from you. It's giving yourself to the situation, without insisting that you control it from one end. There is the give and take and the interaction. In learning terms this is the basis of the process of expatiating, of expanding, of collaborative discourse, where people build ideas and images with language concepts together, so that they advance from where they began. In other words, there's a basic growing, a learning process that is the heart of dialogue. If we use it well, admittedly, there can be very bad dialogues and very good ones. And part of the methodology for good dialogues, for good dialectic, is the interplay of minds—minds and hearts. I think Buber had that in mind when he talked about dialogue in the sense of existential relating. You relate to the other as a ''Thou,'' not as an ''It.'' An ''It'' is removed, remote. These are abstract conceptualizations. But the two parties that are interacting are alive and collaborating together.

Interviewer: Could you make some distinctions between the three kinds of speech you mention in the chapter ''Drama, What Is Happening''—dialogue, monologue, and soliloquy.[36]

Moffett: One reason I think drama is a good base or matrix is that the learning to monologue derives from dialogue. It was in the Greek plays. There's a dialogue going on, and then somebody begins to monologue out of that. Or there's a situation going on and the messenger comes in, and there's a long monologue of how somebody died—Hippolytus, for example. This is expository. A monologue can go any direction—it might be expository; it might be narrative; it might be emotional-descriptive. But the point is the speaker has to sustain a discourse by himself for awhile. And he no longer has the continued prompting, the cuing, the interacting. It's easier, I feel, to dialogue with somebody than monologue. It's much harder work to keep the monologue going. You don't get feedback. You just have to have faith that you're making sense, that this continuity is spinning out there and is going to connect. But I think the way you learn how to do that well—and it certainly ties into writing, because writing is monologue—is by internalizing the dialogue. You internalize this information if you've had good conversation experiences. More and more you know ahead of time what your listener needs, what he's going to relate to and understand, when he's going to need explanation, how implicit or explicit to be, what kind of language to use, and so on. You get this from conversation experience. Soliloquy is inner speech, but we externalize it to benefit an audience.

Interviewer: What is inner speech?

Moffett: Inner speech is, for the most part, going on all the time within everyone. We're talking to ourselves inside. Interior monologue is really interior dialogue, different voices and persona and roles that we have.

Interviewer: Do you see inner speech as a dramatic process?

Moffett: Well it is. It has been since Greek and Elizabethan theatre. The idea of simply externalizing thought so that you could sample the inner life for the benefit of the audience has become a major stage device. I'm happy to see the convention stays alive today in the musical, where you can have somebody externalize his or her inner speech, usually in song. Inner speech is just a realistic psychological process. First it's external and then the child shunts it inward as he realizes that some of the things he says are just for himself. But then as you internalize dialogue, it becomes part of your inner dialogue. This is why I think outer conversation is extremely important in developing inner mental processes that occur as a person sits down alone to write. I'm currently working a lot on the notion of relating inner speech to the writing and composition process. It seems to me that anything a person writes can only be some kind of excerpted, edited, and revised version of his or her inner speech at a given moment. So when you sit down to write on a particular topic, you are exerting fairly tight control over your inner speech for the moment. I'm interested in meditation techniques, and I'm trying to interest teachers in learning to meditate and teach meditation techniques to their students, because I think meditation is essentially controlling inner speech.

Interviewer: How do children learn language? Can this be seen as a dramatic process?

Moffett: Their own speech development, of course, goes with the interactive, dialogical approach. This can occur with peers, elders, other people. I think the more heterogeneous a classroom is, the more kids learn. In other words, the more differences there are in student temperament, background, language experiences, vocabulary, the more valuable it is for the learner.

Interviewer: Why is that?

Moffett: People who don't understand you too well initially are the best people to talk with, because they are the ones who will feed back in the most useful ways, in saying they don't understand this or that. Or you find out your use of language doesn't mean anything to them. One reason for getting the kids out of the house and into school is that Mommy and Daddy understand them too well. You have to get them with people who can't anticipate what they're thinking or who go more than half way in understanding them. So talking across differences is a vital learning process. It doesn't always take a language specialist or an adult. Any peer or group of peers can teach one another just because their natural dialogical processes or feedback help them grow in their communication.

Interviewer: You're saying there must be heterogeneous classroom groupings.

Moffett: I don't think there is any question about it. In fact, I would be in favor of having mixed age groups and grades as some alternative schools have done. My daughter for a while was in a school that grouped grades seven through twelve together. This is even better, because you have to talk across differences in ages, as well as background, social class, and so on. For enriching the language, this is where the child acquires a richer language than the one he hears in his own environment.

Interviewer: We spoke earlier about children who have performed *Uncle Vanya*, the Chekhov text, and you had some questions about the emotional content, but not about the language itself.

Moffett: I think it's good for kids to work with languages of other periods and other styles. I'm not one who thinks that relevance means just use of street language, of the peer language. They get plenty of that already. School should give them something they don't get. You say, "OK, give them a lot of reading input." But suppose they're not into reading yet? And they won't go off by themselves to read a book. Then I think drama is tremendously useful. In other words, they get into books and texts and the richer literature surrounding their own language community by performing texts, and this is a nice group social activity. They work with partners, and the texts they perform don't have to be scripts. I try to encourage teachers to have students see any text as a possible performing item. I don't care if it's a label off a soup can. It could be a poem. It could be excerpts. One of the things I like about reader's theatre is that they draw their material from any source—it could be ads, bits of biography, diaries. They piece these together, collage them. Students like finding their own texts. They read extensively in order to find their material. And once they find some material they read it intensively together, in order to find out how to render it, how to perform it. They don't have to memorize it, as long as they've worked it up to their own satisfaction.

Interviewer: There's another technique you use called chamber theatre. What is that?

Moffett: Robert Breen developed this at Northwestern.[37] I guess it's like a subclass of reader's theatre. It's done only for narrative. The narrative could be either fictional or biographical. It features the narrator. You can dramatize a relationship between the narrator and his characters in either third or first person. The performers decide together which lines are going to be delivered by characters in the action and which lines by the narrator.

Interviewer: Is this improvisational or scripted?

Moffett: They take an actual narrative, a short story, such as a William Carlos Williams short story or a Thurber fable—one scene. They don't write a new script. They use the story as it was written.

Interviewer: This reminds me of story theatre.[38]

Moffett: We've worked with story theatre too. I like story theatre very much, because there are so many options for students. You could have a group or an individual deliver certain lines; one the narration, others the dialogue. Others could pantomime the action. You can divide it up many ways. In deciding which way to divide it up and render it, students, in effect, analyze the text in a natural way, in an enjoyable way. I think it takes them well into those issues of comprehension and interpretation that we always worry about in reading terms.

Interviewer: Given our emphasis upon back to basics, are English teachers still free to use chamber theatre and other techniques based in your work?

Moffett: Since the Dartmouth seminar, many have come out so strongly in favor of drama and tried to present some methodology for using it in both secondary and elementary schools.[39] You can measure this kind of thing by the amount of programs, conferences, and articles in professional journals. But I find today that there is not as much going on in the classroom as one would think, looking at those sources, for a couple of reasons. For one, very few teachers have had the training that would help in this direction. But even those who feel confident to use drama in the classroom are not often free to. I think we're in an era where the control of the curriculum is getting farther and farther outside the classroom.

Interviewer: What about a more conventional technique, such as show and tell, which teachers certainly are free to use. How can show and tell be made more dramatic?

Moffett: I think you have to break a classroom down into small groups and teach the kids how to question each other about the objects that are brought in. Part of the history of the object is what you want them to ask about. This leads to little narratives and how-to-do-it descriptions of process, an excellent kind of expository development of monologue. It can be emotional, such as: "How do you feel about the object?" Once kids get the idea of interrogating each other in an honest way and finding out more, they get the speaker to elaborate more on what he initially said. The teacher can sit in on each group and model the role of the interested responders. But she should not sit in the group all the time.

Interviewer: You've also written about the use of pantomime and movement in the early grades as a way to approach language learning.

Moffett: I think for the small child, language is a mode of communicating. It's not isolated out as something special in his mind. To him, this is part of body behavior. I think drama leads verbal and nonverbal communication right together and this makes sense to kids. They can spin off verbally more and more, but from a nonverbal base where they can use body language.

Moffett's thoughts of drama as present-oriented, living language, as "one person trying to get effects upon another person through the use of language," have been translated into many dramatic techniques in language arts classrooms, kindergarten through university. In fact, a series of teaching guides, called the Interaction Series, has been developed to help teachers implement many of his ideas.

Two areas of drama and the language arts that have been heavily influenced by Moffett are the teaching of writing and reading through drama. Recently, there has been a lot of attention to the reality that people do not write acceptable English—all people: children, adolescents, and adults. One solution has been a back-to-basics approach, implying more attention to grammar, sentence structure, and vocabulary. The assumption is that if we know the rules and know the words, we will have the tools to write. But writing is not necessarily a skill to be learned through sharpening the right tools, but rather a part of one's natural use of language. It is another manifestation of speaking, which is, from a developmental point of view, the first kind of language that we all use. We speak before we reason or write or read. Our first speech and certainly our first use of dialogue can be seen as dramatic in that it is truly spontaneous and playful. It depends upon the language and sounds that we have internalized from others in our immediate environment, and it is representative of what is happening at the moment it is spoken. The reason young children cannot sustain long narrative stories is that they are not developmentally ready to move from the dramatic orientation of the present to the narrative orientation of the past. Young children live and think in the present, and thus their speech is present-oriented and dramatic.

Moffett's work in teaching writing through drama is extensive. One of his basic techniques concerns the use of dictation—a speaker dictates his spontaneous flow of thoughts or impressions to a recorder, who writes down the speech. This device is helpful for a child who feels comfortable speaking but inhibited when it comes to writing. The technique is equally applicable to a writing-blocked adult. After the piece is spoken and transcribed, it is read back to the speaker. This is an effective way to show the connection between oral and written language and to demonstrate that if one can speak spontaneously, one can write.

Speaking can also be expressed in nonverbal modes. The speaker can act out or pantomime thoughts while a recorder transcribes what he or she sees. The point is that the mechanical act of writing down is preceded by the dramatic act of producing or acting out a spontaneous flow of speech and/or movement.

When moving from two people, one acting out and one writing down, to a single person writing, the procedure is similar. Teachers would begin by creating a context for the writing, often in the form of a drama exercise. Then they would ask their students to verbalize their experience. Next, they would ask them to write down the experience. Finally, the writing would be read back to them and discussed with them.

An example of a drama experience that can begin the writing process involves a sensory-awareness exercise. Students are asked to look around the room and identify as many objects and shapes as they can. Then they are asked to focus their attention on the space immediately surrounding their bodies and to identify what they see. Next, they shift attention to one of their hands and study it in some detail. Finally, they are asked to close their eyes and visualize the inside of their body—the brain, for example. "What do you see?" the teacher asks. Following the exercise, the students externalize their images in speech and transform their speech into writing.

This exercise can be done in pairs, where two students share their images with each other and write down either their own thoughts or those of the other. Or the exercise can be done individually, where each student, having had the experience, immediately writes down his or her thoughts and images freely, that is, nonstop for a limited period, without paying attention to syntax, grammar, or self-imposed censorship. Only later does the student edit his or her work while developing subsequent drafts. For the student working alone who needs a mediating step between having the experience and writing about it, another creative method is to ask the student either to draw a picture expressing the experience or to create a pantomime capturing the feelings of the experience.

From a dramatic point of view writing can be seen as a kind of linguistic improvisation where a flow of internal thoughts and images, generated by an experience, are externalized and given form in language. The initial first-draft writing is particularly improvisational in that it is spontaneous and unprepared. Later drafts take on more characteristics of formal theatre in that they depend upon the preparation and development of a script that will be viewed and re-viewed by an "audience" of readers.

The teaching of writing, then, is not necessarily based upon elaborate rules, but rather upon a person's natural, developmental use of language. The source of language usage, according to Moffett, among others, is in drama, the moment of direct experience.

In teaching reading we appear to shift our attention from the use of our own language to the use of another's words. But in dramatizing literature students are asked to translate the author's words into their own words, movements, and images. To do this students must understand the author's intentions, a process that fosters the development of reading comprehension and interpretation skills. Furthermore, through dramatization, students personalize a text and thus learn to find direct meaning in it.

In his discussion of reading Moffett explained the value and process of dramatization:

In order to dramatize or discuss a text, pupils have to think about the meaning of it and follow out implications. Enacting a story or poem is translating a text into voice, movement, and space. Characterization, sequence of actions, mood, setting, build-up, and climax have to be grasped in order to be rendered by the children. Disagreements in interpretation have to be discussed. Inventing details of action and dialogue and extending stories are based on implications and potentialities of the text. They help pupils render future texts in their own minds.[40]

Story dramatization, as an approach to motivate a student's acquisition of basic reading skills, has become one of the most widely used drama techniques in American education. From the early work of Winifred Ward, to the more current ideas of Nellie McCaslin, we find a growing bibliography of stories, poems, and tales to dramatize that have proven successful in many elementary and secondary school English classes.[41] Even Shakespeare's plays have been modified for dramatization in elementary classrooms.[42]

Another dramatic technique of some popularity in teaching reading is reader's theatre. Shirlee Sloyer, professor of speech arts and sciences at Hofstra University and expert in the use of reader's theatre, explained it this way:

It's not a play. There are no stage sets, no elaborate costumes. There's no need to memorize lines. Actually, it's a minimally staged interpretation of dramatized literature. It takes the form of one story or one scene from a play or one poem, or a compilation of many entities organized around a theme which could express an idea or create a mood.[43]

In an interview Sloyer continued her discussion of reader's theatre:[44]

Interviewer: How did you first get started in reader's theatre?
Shirlee Sloyer: Kids were just not taking books out of the library. They were not reading recreationally. As a result, we decided to help by taking our interpretive readers and developing a story theatre, bringing the story theatre into the libraries and the elementary schools within the community, displaying the books from which we were utilizing stories, reading the stories dramatically, then having the children take those books out and meet old friends again.
Interviewer: Is reader's theatre always performed by children or could anybody do it?
Sloyer: Anybody can do reader's theatre.
Interviewer: Where does reader's theatre take place?
Sloyer: It can take place in a small space, a little square in the front of a classroom, for instance. It could take place in a lunchroom. The best

place for reader's theatre is in the library, among the books.

Interviewer: When is reader's theatre rehearsed?

Sloyer: In truth, reader's theatre is an adjunct to the language arts curriculum. It really actively engages the children in the process of reading, writing, speaking, and listening.

Interviewer: What literature is appropriate for reader's theatre?

Sloyer: E. M. Forster said in *Aspects of the Novel* that a good plot or story has the "and then" quality—and then what happened? This implies a taut plot, compelling characters, image-forming language. Fairy tales are great. A good example is "The Fisherman and His Wife." It starts off with: "Once upon a time there was a fisherman and his wife. They lived in a hovel by the sea. One day he went out fishing. He threw a line into the water and drew out an enchanted flounder." There you have it. All the characters are present. The story is underway in just a few sentences. That's a good story.

During a workshop led by Sloyer a group of fourth and fifth graders from Long Island, New York, demonstrated the steps in the process of reader's theatre: selecting, writing or adapting, staging and rehearsing, and presenting.[45]

From the general idea of "Fairy Tales without Fairies," the children selected the specific theme "showing how silly the bluebloods were." The story they chose to exemplify the theme was "The Princess and the Pea" by Hans Christian Andersen.

First, Sloyer asked the children to tell the story in their own words. Then she asked them a series of questions to explore the reasons why Andersen wrote the story. Through the question and answer period Sloyer helped the children clarify Andersen's intentions as well as determine how they intended to transform narration into dialogue.

Following the question and answer phase Sloyer moved directly into the writing session. During this phase the children began to transform the story into a script. They deleted lines, added their own lines, and divided much of the narration among characters, while leaving some narration for an actual narrator. Finally, they produced a script true to both the spirit of Andersen and their own sense of satire and playfulness.

Then with script in hand Sloyer led the children into a discussion of staging and visual elements including costumes, props, and movement. This was followed by a discussion of the vocal requirements for each role. Next, she focused the discussion on the technical aspects of the reading, including the use of narration, dialogue, choral speaking, and sound effects.

Following the staging and rehearsing phase the children presented their reader's theatre version of "The Princess and the Pea," complete with minimal costumes to represent character types, simple percussion instruments to represent required sounds, choral speeches to stress important thematic points, and good humor to represent their ironic attitude toward the bluebloods.

Following the presenting phase, Sloyer noted, a discussion with the viewers helps clarify the intentions of both the storyteller and the young dramatists.

Generally, an audience does attend a reader's theatre presentation, although it is a small one of peers and others involved in the process of teaching and learning reading through drama.

Drama and History

In teaching history through drama there are, generally, two approaches. The more personal approach implies that history comprises a series of decisions made by numerous individuals at given moments in time. It is the teacher's responsibility to help the students find ways to identify with historical characters, understand their motivations and conflicts, and assume their roles in order to make decisions.

In her article "Dramatizing History" Joanna Halpert Kraus wrote:

> The drama inherent in decision making is the substance of human history. The study of history should reflect more than external events, for the study of man is the progression of attitude changes on basic issues. ... If a student is to receive any illumination from a survey of conquests and battles, he needs to conjecture on the motivation propelling actors of certain historical scenes. He needs to comprehend the indecision, the ambivalence, the vacillating opinions that existed, for example, on the eve of the American Revolution.[46]

In applying this approach teachers generally adhere to the techniques of creative drama and do not depend upon more than minimal costumes, properties, and other theatrical elements. Although a historical moment, such as the eve of the American Revolution, is explored with some attention to the philosophy, culture, and customs of the day, the main focus is upon the individual struggling to make a decision that has certain ethical consequences. It is the dramatic elements of identification and role-playing, of personalizing a historical moment, that motivates the student to enter the drama of history. Teachers proceed, then, from the inside out, from the person to the event.

A second approach to teaching history through drama is more external and intellectual. Rather than beginning with the individual, teachers begin with the age. They lead their students toward an understanding of the social, political, and intellectual aspects of the age. They introduce them to the costumes, foods, dances, literature, architecture, and other cultural aspects of a chosen historical moment.

Having begun from the outside, teachers then work inward toward a role-playing situation that sometimes takes the form of a historical improvisation and sometimes takes the form of the examination of a dramatic text, such as an Elizabethan or Restoration play.

A good example of this approach can be seen in the work of the New York University Program in Educational Theatre Study Abroad Program at Bretton, England. Professors Nancy Swortzell of New York University and John Hodgson of Bretton Hall College, leaders of the program, recently filmed some of their work in teaching university students the history of Elizabethan and Georgian England.[47]

In explaining his philosophy Hodgson said:

> The general philosophy behind the work is that drama is doing, and that the best way to remember things is by understanding them. So we try to give the students an opportunity to discover a method as well as a period. In this example, we're looking at the Elizabethan theatre and the Elizabethan drama. We'd like to show you some of the techniques we employ in trying to give the students a real appreciation through experience of a period which we hope, though it's 400 years ago, isn't quite as remote as they may have thought at first. And so the idea is to give them an historical perspective which will enable them to understand something of the ways of human beings in this and other ages.[48]

Through an exploration of actual Elizabethan costumes, the students in the film are led through a series of movements and dances very much determined by the clothing and body postures of the period. Through song students are introduced to the rhythms and lyrics of the age.

Furthermore, the history and architecture of the Elizabethan theatre are explored. From a lecture by the Shakespearian scholar C. Walter Hodges, the students learn of the design of the Elizabethan stage and how that design implied a certain kind of stage movement. With this understanding in mind students are led to play scenes from Shakespeare's *Midsummer Night's Dream.*

Nancy Swortzell later clarified the point that this approach toward teaching history does not at all have to culminate in a formal production. It can occur in any classroom with any age group willing to study history through recreating characters from a dramatic script or from everyday life who dress, move, speak, eat, and generally behave in ways consistent to their historical period.

In the second part of the film we see an exploration of seventeenth- and eighteenth-century England through the clothing, food, transportation, and ideas of the Georgian period. During one long sequence students dress up in costume and parade through the streets of town, transporting the queen in a sedan chair. They arrive at a ballroom, where they sing, dance, and dine, all in eighteenth-century fashion.

John Hodgson called this kind of work in drama and history "anthology." In a discussion between Swortzell and Hodgson at the end of the film, he explained his method of teaching history through anthology:

Nancy Swortzell: What does an anthology mean and how is it used?

John Hodgson: Anthology really is a collection of authentic material from a period like the Georgian or Elizabethan. It can be music, poetry, prose, plays, any form of actable, livable, presentable, communicable idea or sound or facility.

Swortzell: What about people in history?

Hodgson: It's all about people in history. It's about the people living in an age, what they did, what they said to each other, what they thought about each other, what they wrote to each other and about each other.

Swortzell: Is anthology a learning experience? A process? Or is it an entertainment for an audience?

Hodgson: It should really be all those things if it's being done properly. It should start as being a learning process for the people involved, and then it should go to being developed, performed, communicated. It can be brought together in a living situation, which could be an entertainment both for the people in it and those watching it.

Swortzell: If you're going to begin with this learning experience, what sorts of things go into it and how do you approach it?

Hogdson: I think you can approach it from many different points of view. You can start with a play and work out. Or you can start with the material and work in towards the drama.

Swortzell: What sorts of material would you begin with, regardless of the age you are working in?

Hodgson: Something which is accessible is the first thing. If it's a group who seems to enjoy singing, I begin with the music of the age. If it's a group which is very keen on poetry, I take some verse of the period. If it's a group that likes a story, I pick a story of the period, anything that will get to the minds and interests of those you're involving.

Swortzell: This seems like an integrated arts experience. What about art and architecture?

Hodgson: Sure. In certain ages art and architecture are of primary interest. In, for example, the Georgian period it is the architecture which is the great interest. If it's another age it might be through portraits or through other kinds of painting. That's an excellent way of beginning.

Swortzell: But people are going to say: "How does art relate to drama?"

Hodgson: It relates to drama, because it's the same kind of people expressing themselves in a different medium.

Swortzell: Is it possible to discover character?

Hodgson: Undoubtedly. It's undoubtedly possible to discover the character of an age. Does that age wish to show itself as flamboyant, or does it want to present itself much more in terms of something restricted, limited, or even secret?

Swortzell: Can art then be extended into dance and movement?

Hodgson: Very much so, because I think through dance and movement, through the way in which we present ourselves, we communicate an awful lot about ourselves. And every age has its particular characteristics.

Swortzell: If we were going to do a project in dance, could this be related to an anthology?

Hodgson: Very much so, because dance is one element of that movement quality. In any age we have our own particular jiving sessions, as in the twentieth century. Others present their dance in a more formal way. The Georgians are very formal. Elizabethans are very vigorous. You can capture something of the spirit of any age through its dance.

Swortzell: When an anthology is extended through study of sources in music, dance, art, social conditions, then where does it go?

Hodgson: It ought to go somewhere. The important thing about all of this is, it goes toward a culminating point, an activity where you draw all the things together. You'd want to draw together your music, song, poetry, dancing, movement quality, costume, and you'd find something that is appropriate to the age.

Swortzell: How do you stimulate people to do this?

Hodgson: It would arise from the study previously done, no matter what the age. For example, in the Georgian period the great thing was the ball, often the masked ball. And so people would arrive at that ball. Everything would happen at that time.

Swortzell: Your implication is that it's not only an intergated arts experience, but that it's all world expansive. How does this relate to a production, and does the anthology lead to a production?

Hodgson: It doesn't lead to a production in the sense of a play, though it can. You can work either way. You can have anthology used to understand Shakespeare's plays. Or you can have an anthology which is the end product in itself—starting with the play and leading out from the play to an understanding of an age. Whatever you're doing, you can use the age to be either your foreground in terms of a great production, a ball, for example, or you can use it to help you get underneath the skin of the characters in a play and the author's attitude.

Swortzell: In an anthology presentation versus a script presentation, doesn't the individual have a great right to choose his own material and do his own thing?

Hodgson: That, I think, is one of the advantages of anthology work. It doesn't restrict you to people having to play a small part, because there's only a small part in the play for them. In anthology, you can give everybody a reasonable amount of involvement, and they can, as you suggest, be involved in the way that interests them the most.

Educational Drama as Interdisciplinary

From the many examples above of drama and the language arts, history, math, and interrelated arts of dance, music, architecture, and the like, a total picture begins to emerge. Drama can be seen as a bridge between several disciplines. When Geraldine Brain Siks asked her students to move cardboard and chairs in space, she viewed her work as a language arts experience. When Gavin Bolton took on the role of a stupid king who couldn't read the numbers on his medicine bottle, he viewed his work as a math lesson. When Nancy Swortzell and John Hodgson presented their students with costumes, songs, and foods, they viewed their work as a history lesson.

As we have seen, the anthology method of dramatic education involves many disciplines: all of the arts, history, literature, and philosophy. Just as well might Gavin Bolton have used his dramatic math lesson to teach history. After all, he assumed the role of a king who at a given point in history had certain responsibilities and powers that could be explored with students.

We have also seen, in the example of Dorothy Heathcote, how an extended dramatization can include the study of many disciplines such as art, dance, science, and technology. In using the example of space travel, or flight in general, the teacher has a great choice of disciplines to draw upon. We saw how Coleman Jennings applied the physical experience of flight to the study of Greek mythology in the story of "Daedalus and Icarus." Certainly, a teacher could explore the connections between many representations of flight, taken from mythology, biology, history, literature, science, and technology, all disciplines that can be drawn together not only by a common theme, but also through a common method, that of drama. The dramatic method of education, unlike the lecture or discussion method, is one of direct experience, identification and role-playing, and recreating or representing, in microcosm, a concern from everyday life, history, or literature, so that it can be assimilated and understood.

Educational drama is not only a bridge connecting disciplines, but also an interdisciplinary field in its own right. Richard Courtney, in setting forth his understanding of the intellectual background to drama in education, identified the following disciplines as related to the larger field of dramatic education: educational philosophy, depth psychology, sociology and social anthropology, cognition and psycholinguistics, and theatrical disciplines.[49] Several years later this author narrowed those fields down to four: theatre, language arts, humanistic education, and social psychology. He claimed that the aims and techniques implicit in these disciplines reflect those practiced by drama educators.[50] Both Courtney and this author went on to say that this vast, interdisciplinary field implies a process of learning that applies to all subject matter in all disciplines.

In a recent book Courtney offered a new model of an integrated dramatic school curriculum.[51] His model is truly interdisciplinary, drawing upon areas such as reading, writing, speaking, listening, physical education, math, science, art, crafts, and music. Behind this interdisciplinary model is the assumption that all learning is by nature interrelated and interactive. One needs to read, reason, draw, speak, and listen in all studies. In embracing this philosophical perspective, teachers and administrators can truly realize the educational values inherent in the interdisciplinary nature of drama, a process that in many ways underlies all human learning.

NOTES

1. See J. L. Moreno, *Psychodrama*, 3 vols. (Beacon, N.Y.: Beacon House, 1946, 1959).

2. See, for example, Geraldine Brain Siks, *Drama with Children* (New York: Harper and Row, 1977); Ruth Beal Heinig and Lyda Stillwell, *Creative Drama for the Classroom Teacher*, 2d ed. (Englewood Cliffs, N.J.: Prentice-Hall, 1981); Nellie McCaslin, *Creative Drama in the Classroom*, 3d ed. (New York: Longman, 1980); and Brian Way, *Development through Drama* (New York: Humanities Press, 1972).

3. Gavin Bolton, *Towards a Theory of Drama in Education* (London: Longman, 1979).

4. WCBS-TV, *Sunrise Semester*, "Drama in Education: Story Dramatization" (September 28, 1979).

5. Ibid.

6. Texas Education Agency, *Creative Dramatics in the Elementary School* (Austin, Tex., 1978).

7. WCBS-TV, *Sunrise Semester*, "Drama in Education: Getting Started" (September 24 and 26, 1979).

8. Ibid.

9. For a full description of the process/concept approach, see Siks, *Drama with Children*; and John Manley et al., *Drama/Theatre Framework for California Public Schools* (Sacramento: California State Department of Education, 1971). For a full discussion of behavioral objectives in creative drama, see Ann M. Shaw, "A Development of a Taxonomy of Educational Objectives in Creative Dramatics" (Ed.D. diss. Columbia University, 1968).

10. WCBS-TV, *Sunrise Semester*, "Drama in Education: Training Teachers Through Drama" (October 15, 1979).

11. Albert Cullum and Lillian A. Buckley, *Picnic of Sounds: A Playful Approach to Reading* (New York: Citation Press, 1975).

12. See McCaslin, *Creative Drama*, pp. 12-17; and Winifred Ward, *Playmaking with Children: From Kindergarten through Junior High School*, 2d ed. (New York: Appleton-Century-Crofts, 1957), pp. 3-9.

13. Bolton, *Towards a Theory of Drama*, p. 41.

14. Dorothy Heathcote et al., *Drama in the Education of Teachers* (Newcastle upon Tyne, Eng.: University of Newcastle upon Tyne, n.d.), p. 21.

15. Way, *Development through Drama*, p. 4.

16. WCBS-TV, *Sunrise Semester*, "Drama in Education: An Interview with Gavin Bolton" (October 15, 1979).

17. WCBS-TV, *Sunrise Semester*, "Drama in Education: Drama in an Inner City School" (October 8, 1979).

18. For a discussion of the Federal Theatre Project, see Hallie Flanagan, *Arena* (New York: Duell, Sloan, and Pearce, 1940).

19. For a discussion of emotion memory, see Constantin Stanislavski, *An Actor Prepares* (New York: Theatre Arts Books, 1956), pp. 154-81.

20. WCBS-TV, *Sunrise Semester*, "Drama in Education: The Child as Playmaker" (October 1, 1979).

21. Ibid.

22. Texas Education Agency, *Theatre Arts: Framework for Grades 7-12* (Austin, Tex., 1979).

23. Joseph L. Peluso, *A Survey of the Status of Theatre in United States High Schools* (Washington, D.C.: U.S. Department of Health, Education, and Welfare, Office of Education, Bureau of Research, 1970).

24. Ibid., p. 9.

25. Richard Courtney, *The Dramatic Curriculum* (New York: Drama Book Specialists, 1980), pp. 96-98.

26. Wendy Perks, "Children's Drama 1976: A Review of University Programs in the United States," *Children's Theatre Review*, 25, 3 (1976): 6-12.

27. Dorothy Heathcote, "Training Needs for the Future," in John Hodgson and Martin Banham, eds., *Drama in Education: The Annual Survey*, vol. 1 (London: Pitman, 1972), pp. 81-83.

28. University of Calgary, Department of Drama, "Developmental Drama, a Report," mimeograph, November 1973.

29. Ibid.

30. WCBS-TV, *Sunrise Semester*, "Drama in Education: Improvisation" (October 10, 1979).

31. John Stewig, *Spontaneous Drama: A Language Art* (Columbus, Ohio: Charles E. Merrill, 1973), p. 4.

32. James Moffett, *A Student-Centered Language Arts Curriculum, K-13* (Boston: Houghton-Mifflin, 1968).

33. James Moffett, *Teaching the Universe of Discourse* (Boston: Houghton-Mifflin, 1968), pp. 60-61.

34. WCBS-TV, *Sunrise Semester*, "Drama in Education: Teaching Language Arts through Drama" (October 22, 1979).

35. The philosopher Martin Buber wrote many books relevant to an understanding of human communication, among them *I and Thou* (New York: Scribner's, 1937); and *Between Man and Man* (New York: Macmillan, 1948).

36. James Moffett, "Drama, What Is Happening," in Moffett, *Teaching the Universe of Discourse*; this chapter is also published separately as a booklet, James Moffett, *Drama, What Is Happening* (Urbana, Ill.: National Council of Teachers of English, 1967).

37. See Robert Breen, *Chamber Theatre* (Englewood Cliffs, N.J.: Prentice-Hall, 1978).

38. See Paul Sills, *Story Theatre* (New York: Samuel French, 1971).

39. The Dartmouth Seminar refers to the Anglo-American Conference on the

Teaching of English, held at Dartmouth, New Hampshire, in 1966. The use of drama in the teaching of English was a prominent topic. See Douglas Barnes, *Drama in the English Classroom* (Champaign, Ill.: National Council of Teachers of English, 1968).

40. Moffett, *A Student-Centered Language Arts Curriculum*, pp. 103-4.

41. See Ward, *Playmaking with Children*; and idem, *Stories to Dramatize* (Anchorage, Ky.: The Children's Theatre Press, 1952). See McCaslin, *Creative Drama*.

42. See Albert Cullum, *Shake Hands with Shakespeare* (New York: Citation Press, 1968).

43. WCBS-TV, *Sunrise Semester*, "Drama in Education: Teaching Reading through Drama" (October 26, 1979).

44. Ibid.

45. Ibid.

46. Joanna Halpert Kraus, "Dramatizing History," in Nellie McCaslin, ed., *Children and Drama* (New York: Longman, 1981), pp. 128-29.

47. The film was aired on WCBS-TV, *Sunrise Semester*, "Drama in Education: Teaching History through Drama" (October 17 and 19, 1979).

48. Ibid.

49. Courtney, *Play, Drama, and Thought*.

50. Robert J. Landy, "Dramatic Education; An Interdisciplinary Approach to Learning" (Ph.D. diss., University of California, Santa Barbara, 1975).

51. Courtney, *Dramatic Curriculum*.

BIBLIOGRAPHY AND RESOURCES

Books and Dissertations

Alington, A. F. *Drama and Education.* Oxford: Basil, Blackwell, and Mott, Ltd., 1961.

Allen, John, et al. *Drama: Education Survey 2.* London: Department of Education and Science, 1967.

_____. *Drama in Schools: Its Theory and Practice.* London: Heinemann, 1979.

Barnes, Douglas. *Drama in the English Classroom.* Champaign, Ill.: National Council of Teachers of English, 1968.

Barnfield, Gabriel. *Creative Drama in Schools.* New York: Macmillan, 1971.

Bolton, Gavin. *Towards a Theory of Drama in Education.* London: Longman, 1979.

Breen, Robert. *Chamber Theatre.* Englewood Cliffs, N.J.: Prentice-Hall, 1978.

Coger, Leslie. *Reader's Theatre Handbook.* Chicago: Scott, Foresman, 1967.

Cook, H. Caldwell. *The Play Way.* New York: Stokes, 1919.

Courtney, Richard. *Drama for Youth.* London: Pitman, 1964.

_____. *The Dramatic Curriculum.* New York: Drama Book Specialists, 1980.

_____. *Play, Drama, and Thought.* New York: Drama Book Specialists, 1974.

_____. *Re-play: Studies of Human Drama in Education.* Toronto: Ontario Institute for Studies in Education Press, 1982.

Crosscup, Richard. *Children and Dramatics.* New York: Scribner's, 1966.

Cullum, Albert. *Push Back the Desks*. New York: Citation 1967.

———, and Lillian A. Buckley. *Picnic of Sounds: A Playful Approach to Reading*. New York: Citation Press, 1975.

Dodd, Nigel, and Winifred Hickson, eds. *Drama and Theatre in Education*. London: Heinemann, 1971.

Duke, Charles R. *Creative Dramatics and English Teaching*. Urbana, Ill.: National Council of Teachers of English, 1974.

Ehrlich, Harriett, and Patricia Grastry. *Creative Dramatics Handbook*. Philadelphia: School District of Philadelphia Instructional Services, 1971.

Fines, John, and Raymond Verrier. *The Drama of History*. London: New University Education, 1974.

Fitzgerald, Brudette. *World Tales for Creative Dramatics and Storytelling*. Englewood Cliffs, N.J.: Prentice-Hall, 1962.

Gallagher, Kent G., ed. *Drama Education Guidelines: A Curriculum Guideline for the Theatre Arts in Education in the State of Washington*. Olympia, Wash.: Office of the State Superintendent of Public Instruction, 1972.

Goodridge, Janet. *Creative Drama and Improvisational Movement*. Boston: Plays, Inc., 1971.

Haggerty, Joan. *Please Can I Play God?* London: Methuen, 1966.

Heathcote, Dorothy, et al. *Drama in the Education of Teachers*. Newcastle upon Tyne, Eng.: University of Newcastle upon Tyne, Institute of Education, n.d.

Heinig, Ruth Beall, and Lyda Stillwell. *Creative Drama for the Classroom Teacher*. 2d ed. Englewood Cliffs, N.J.: Prentice-Hall, 1981.

Herron, R. D., and Brian Sutton-Smith. *Child's Play*. New York: John Wiley, 1971.

Hodgson, John, and Ernest Richards. *Improvisation*. New York: Grove Press, 1979.

Hodgson, John, ed. *The Uses of Drama*. London: Methuen, 1972.

Hodgson, John, and Martin Banham, eds. *Drama in Education: The Annual Survey*. 3 vols. London: Pitman, 1972, 1973, 1975.

Hoetker, James. *Dramatics and the Teaching of Literature*. Champaign, Ill.: National Council of Teachers of English, 1969.

Johnstone, Keith. *Impro*. New York: Theatre Arts Books, 1979.

Kase, Robert. *Stories for Creative Acting*. New York: Samuel French, 1961.

Kennedy, Carol Jean. *Child Drama: A Selected and Annotated Bibliography, 1974-1979*. Washington, D.C.: Children's Theatre Association of America, 1981.

King, Nancy. *Giving Form to Feeling*. New York: Drama Book Specialists, 1975.

Klock, Mary Eileen. *Creative Drama: A Selected and Annotated Bibliography*. Washington, D.C.: Children's Theatre Association of America, 1975.

Landy, Robert J. "Dramatic Education, An Interdisciplinary Approach to Learning." Ph.D. dissertation, University of California, Santa Barbara, 1975.

Lazier, Gil, and E. J. Karioth. *The Inventory of Dramatic Behavior: A Content Analysis Technique for Creative Dramatics*. Tallahassee, Fla.: Theatre Science Laboratory, Florida State University, 1972.

Lowndes, Betty. *Movement and Creative Drama for Children*. Boston: Plays, Inc., 1971.

Maley, Alan, and Alan Duff. *Drama Techniques in Language Learning*. London: Cambridge University Press, 1978.

Manley, John, et al. *Drama/Theatre Framework for California Public Schools*. Sacramento: California State Department of Education, 1974.

Maclay, Joanna Hawkins. *Readers Theatre: Toward a Grammar of Practice*. New York: Random House, 1971.

McCaslin, Nellie. *Creative Drama in the Classroom*. 3d ed. New York: Longman, 1980.

_____. ed. *Children and Drama*. New York: Longman, 1981.

McGregor, Lynn; Maggie Tate; and Ken Robinson. *Learning through Drama*. London: Heinemann, 1977.

Mearns, Hughes. *Creative Power*. New York: Dover Press, 1958.

Moffett, James. *Interaction: A Student-Centered Language Arts and Reading Program*. Boston: Houghton-Mifflin, 1973.

_____. *Teaching the Universe of Discourse*. Boston: Houghton-Mifflin, 1968.

_____, and Betty Jane Wagner. *Student-Centered Language Arts and Reading, K-13: A Handbook for Teachers*. 2d ed. Boston: Houghton-Mifflin, 1976.

Ontario Ministry of Education. *Dramatic Arts Guidelines for Secondary Schools*. Toronto, Ont., 1976.

Peluso, Joseph L. *A Survey of the Status of Theatre in United States High Schools*. Washington, D.C.: United States Department of Health, Education, and Welfare, Office of Education, Bureau of Research, 1970.

Piaget, Jean. *Play, Dreams, and Imitation in Childhood*. New York: W. W. Norton, 1962.

Polsky, Milton. *Let's Improvise*. Englewood Cliffs, N.J.: Prentice-Hall, 1980.

Popovich, James E. "A Study of Significant Contributions to the Development of Creative Dramatics in American Education." Ph.D. dissertation, Northwestern University, 1955.

Prokes, Sister Dorothy. "Exploring the Relationship between Participation in Creative Dramatics and Development in Imaginative Capacities of Gifted Junior High School Students," Ph.D. dissertation, New York University, 1971.

Robinson, Ken. *Exploring Theatre and Education*. Exeter, N.H.: Heinemann, 1979.

Rockefeller, David, Jr., et al. *Coming to Our Senses*. New York: McGraw-Hill, 1977.

Scott, Graham S. "A Survey of Selected Approaches to the Teaching of Creative Drama in the United States and England." M.A. thesis, University of Calgary, 1972.

Selected and Annotated Bibliography for the Secondary School Theatre Teacher and Student. Washington, D.C.: Secondary School Theatre Association, 1976.

Shaw, Ann M. "A Development of a Taxonomy of Educational Objectives in Creative Dramatics." Ed.D. dissertation, Columbia University, 1968.

Siks, Geraldine Brain. *Children's Literature for Dramatization: An Anthology*. New York: Harper and Row, 1964.

_____. *Creative Dramatics, An Art for Children*. New York: Harper and Row, 1958.

_____. *Creative Dramatics for Children*. New York: Ginn and Company, 1961.

_____. *Drama with Children*. New York: Harper and Row, 1977.

_____, and Hazel Brain Dunnington. *Children's Theatre and Creative Dramatics*. Seattle: University of Washington Press, 1961.

Slade, Peter. *Child Drama*. London: University of London Press, 1954.

_____. *Experience of Spontaneity*. London: Longman, 1968.

_____. *An Introduction to Child Drama*. London: University of London Press, 1958.

_____. *Natural Dance*. London: Hodder and Stoughton, 1977.

Sloyer, Shirlee. *Reader's Theatre: A Guide to Story Dramatization in the Classroom*. Urbana, Ill.: National Council of Teachers of English, 1982.

Spolin, Viola. *Improvisation for the Theatre*. Evanston, Ill.: Northwestern University Press, 1969.

Stake, Robert. *Evaluating the Arts in Education*. Columbus, Ohio: Charles E. Merrill, 1975.

Stewig, John. *Spontaneous Drama: A Language Art*. Columbus, Ohio: Charles E. Merrill, 1973.

Texas Education Agency. *Creative Dramatics in the Elementary School*. Austin, Tex., 1978.

_____. *Theatre Arts: Framework for Grades 7-12*. Austin, Tex., 1979.

Van Tassel, Katrina, and Millie Greimann. *Creative Dramatization*. New York: Macmillan, 1973.

Wagner, Betty Jane. *Dorothy Heathcote: Drama as a Learning Medium*. Washington, D.C.: National Education Association, 1976.

Ward, Winifred. *Creative Dramatics: For the Upper Grades and Junior High School*. New York: D. Appleton Company, 1930.

_____. *Drama with and for Children*. Washington, D.C.: United States Department of Health, Education, and Welfare, 1960.

_____. *Playmaking with Children: From Kindergarten through Junior High School*. New York: Appleton-Century-Crofts, 1957.

_____. *Stories to Dramatize*. Anchorage, Ky.: Anchorage Press, 1952.

Way, Brian. *Development through Drama*. New York: Humanities Press, 1972.

Witkin, Robert. *The Intelligence of Feeling*. London: Heinemann, 1974.

Journals and Periodicals

Children's Theatre Review. American Theatre Association (CTAA division), 1000 Vermont Avenue, Washington, D.C. 20005.

Creative Drama. Educational Drama Association, Drama Centre, Rea Street South, Birmingham B5 GLB, England.

Design for the Arts and Education. 4000 Albemarle Street, N.W., Suite 100, Washington, D.C. 20016.

Discussions in Developmental Drama. Department of Drama, University of Calgary, Calgary T2N IN4, Alberta, Canada.

The Drama Review. MIT Press, 28 Carleton Street, Cambridge, Massachusetts 02142.

Dramatics. 3368 Central Parkway, Cincinnati, Ohio 45225.

Empirical Research in the Theatre. The Center for Communications Research, Bowling Green State University, Bowling Green, Ohio 43403.

Secondary School Theatre Journal. American Theatre Association (SSTA division), 1000 Vermont Avenue, Washington, D.C. 20005.

Theatre (formerly *Yale/Theatre*). Box 2046 Yale Station, New Haven, Connecticut 06520.

Theatre Crafts. 250 West 57 Street, New York, New York 10019.
Theatre Journal (formerly *Educational Theatre Journal*). American Theatre Association, 1000 Vermont Avenue, Washington, D.C. 20005.

   Films and Video-tapes

Creative Dramatics. Video-tapes.
    Agency for Instructional Television
    Box A
    Bloomington, Indiana 47401
    Eight sets of creative drama lessons, plus a teacher's guide.
Creative Dramatics: The First Steps. 16mm film.
    Northwestern University Film Library
    Evanston, Illinois 60201
    Creative dramatics demonstration with a group of fourth graders.
Dorothy Heathcote Talks to Teachers, Part I and Part II. 16mm film.
    Northwestern University Film Library
    Evanston, Illinois 60201
    Dorothy Heathcote explains her educational drama theories and techniques.
The Human Images: Private Faces, Public Masks. 16mm film.
    CBS
    383 Madison Avenue
    New York, New York 100017
    Exploration of dramatic role-playing in everyday life.
Improvised Drama, Part 1 and Part 2. 16mm film.
    Time-Life Films
    100 Eisenhower Drive
    Paramus, New Jersey 07652
    John Hodgson demonstrates his improvisational techniques with groups of adolescents.
Three Looms Waiting. 16mm film.
    Time-Life Films
    100 Eisenhower Drive
    Paramus, New Jersey 07652
    Dorothy Heathcote is seen at work with children.
Sunrise Semester, Drama in Education. Video-tapes.
    WCBS-TV
    518 West 57 Street
    New York, New York 10019
    Forty-eight half-hour programs, broadcast September 1979 through January 1980.

2
THEATRE-IN-EDUCATION: THE TRANSITION BETWEEN EDUCATIONAL DRAMA AND EDUCATIONAL THEATRE

In recent years a new form has developed that can be seen as truly representative of both educational drama and educational theatre, process and product, playing and plays, improvisation and performance. It is called theatre-in-education or TIE and is most widely practiced in England. Like educational drama, TIE often occurs in schools and provides a connection to and interrelationship with standard curricular subjects. Through TIE students can study history, language arts, science, and other subjects.

Like the more performance aspects of educational theatre, TIE often involves the presentation of a scripted play by trained actors to an audience. Unlike a more conventional production of a school play, however, the TIE program often involves active participation on the part of the students.

Although TIE appears to be the perfect pedagogical bridge between drama and theatre, its form and format is highly changeable. At times TIE teams produce plays that are indistinguishable from other educational theatre experiences. At other times TIE teams will work through creative drama techniques with various classroom groups.

Yet the very nature of the TIE team is that it can move comfortably between improvisation and performance, meeting the educational goals of each. Its members are trained both as theatre artists and as teachers. What makes it unique is its commitment to perform and teach a part of the curriculum that is often neglected during the school day. Examples include the history and development of labor unions, sex stereotyping, racism, violence, and vandalism.

Having available a wide range of improvisational and theatrical techniques, the TIE team has the freedom and expertise to apply the most appropriate methods to any given educational situation in order to help students grow in their understanding of a crucial issue.

In a recent interview Professor Nancy Swortzell of New York University discussed the history and practice of TIE:[1]

Interviewer: What are the origins of TIE?

Nancy Swortzell: It all began in Coventry, England, about twenty-five years ago. A man named Gordon Vallins had the idea to do curricular programs dramatizing subjects that would help teachers in schools.

Interviewer: Is there a history in England of using drama in the curriculum?

Swortzell: Yes, but this is quite different. England has always used drama—for example, in the study of Shakespeare. About twenty years ago drama became a part of almost every school curriculum. TIE, however, is quite different. Gordon Vallins was a teacher, but he was also a professional actor, and he thought that to bring really professional theatre to the teachers to help them learn was a dynamic idea.

Later, David Pammenter took over the Coventry Theatre and TIE Company in 1965 and trained most of the major TIE representatives in England.

Interviewer: What is a TIE team?

Swortzell: A TIE team is made up of either an actor-teacher or a teacher-actor. In England TIE teams are paid through the education board. Therefore, they have a teacher's contract and are certified as teachers. However, they are also Equity members, which means they are fully trained as professionals in the skills of theatre—acting, directing, scene design, etcetera. Therefore, some companies have actor-teachers, because they were Equity first and then certified. Other groups have teacher-actors, which means they first achieved certification and then took special training in theatre.

A TIE team is a democratic organization. Most teams are composed of from six to twelve members, all paid. At Coventry, for example, they have eight actors. They have one scene designer and one paraprofessional who works with the schools and with the team. They have one stage manager who is also the research director on projects. The research director and the paraprofessional determine the needs of the local education authorities. The team at that point choose what they want to bring to children, whether they are historical issues, literary issues, moral issues, or whatever. The team votes on the projects they will do. Coventry used to do twelve programs a year, which is tremendously ambitious.

Interviewer: Does the choice of content come from a need in the community or school, or is it something that comes from an interest within the team itself?

Swortzell: Both. Some theatres, for example, the Curtain in London, do predominantly curricular projects. There a teacher can call in to the TIE team and say: "I'm having a terrible time with children who don't read.

Will you make a show for me?'' And the TIE team goes to the school. The research assistant researches the problem. Out of this issue came a very successful program called "E-Man." "E-Man," a British Super-man character, was made to teach the use of the silent "E." The team dramatized all the ways "E" could be used for six to nine year olds. They put the youngsters into participation after they'd seen the theatre program.

Interviewer: Let's explore this notion of participation. You said that the participation came after the children viewed the theatre.

Swortzell: Any theatre experience involves the participation of the audience member. Therefore, children's theatre, which is not TIE, involves the participation of the spectator in what's going on onstage. Participation theatre means a structured play through formal means, which at various points will call for the child's active participation, whether verbal, physical, or intellectual, in decision making or in carry-ing out the course of the play.

It all began with *Peter Pan*. When Peter calls out: "Do you believe in fairies?" in order to save Tinkerbell's life, I've been tempted to call out: "Boo. No." I think this is one of the dangers of participatory theatre. Unless the action of the child is a vote in structured, creative, and tested terms, the child can be forced into action he doesn't really wish to participate in and which does not influence the flow of the sequence of plot, character, etcetera.

Interviewer: So we've actually defined two kinds of participation. One is the conventional situation of viewing a play and intellectually participat-ing in its message. Another is an actual break in the production where the audience member influences the progression of the action. But I think TIE presents a third kind of participation, doesn't it, in terms of follow-up.

Swortzell: It's more than a follow-up, because usually the teams prepare materials for the teacher, which may include preparation through read-ing, research, field trips, etcetera. Then an actor may come in and work with the children in improvisation before the program is presented. Then the program is presented. After the program, the actors may come back and lead discussions with the children. They also give the teacher follow-up materials so that she can carry on this sort of activity in her class-room.

TIE may be a forty-minute program. It can also be a four-day program.

Interviewer: Could you give us an example of an extended program.

Swortzell: One of the four-day programs centered about the Parliamentary Act of 1830, in a working-class town in Bolton. It was called "Poverty Strikes." It was for nine to eleven year olds. The issues were working conditions, property rights, and voting rights. An actor first prepared the children by coming into the classroom and making it into a sweat shop, where the children had to grind out material. Then the actors performed.

The next day the children and actors performed together. On the third day they built town and family groups in the hall, which is equivalent to an all-purpose room in an American school. Then the actors involved the children in a carefully structured plot where a child actually died, because there was insufficient money for medicine.

Interviewer: Was the role of the dying child played by one of the students?

Swortzell: That role was played by an actor who guided the emotional reactions of the children. At the same time, the children were reading all of the laws, history, and social conditions of the time with their teacher.

On the fourth day the children held their meeting and wrote a song of protest. It was a dreadful, rainy day, and they marched throughout a five-block area with their signs of protest. In the end they passed a new law defining working hours and granting privileges of voting in 1830.

Now, this play is very pertinent to Bolton, because it's predominantly manufacturing and immigrant, with children who relate very much to these problems.

The Creative Arts Team of New York University has done a program that is really about a New York problem—subways. It's couched as a musical comedy, but biting musical comedy.

Another example is a program about ecology, called "Where's Earth?" which considers a small town on the seacoast of Japan. The children in the town are maimed and crippled, because a fertilizer factory is dumping its mercury wastes into their river. It's beautifully performed in Kabuki style.

Interviewer: Who created that play?

Swortzell: David Pammenter.

Interviewer: Wasn't there a series of photographs, taken by Eugene Smith, concerning the same issue?[2]

Swortzell: They took their research, in part, from some of his photographs.

Interviewer: Where can one get TIE scripts?

Swortzell: It is because of the democratic team spirit of the TIE team that each team develops its own material. If it becomes a script, it's usually because it's tape-recorded, typed up by a secretary, and then subsequently printed.

Interviewer: Then it's the concept that we want to replicate, as opposed to the exact text.

Swortzell: Yes. A great deal of ideas come from improvisational drama and simulation. For example, the Inner London Education Authority sponsored a program at the Curtain Theatre. They brought fifty to sixty teenagers in for what they called "factory." The TIE team were all costumed, one in morning clothes as the president of the company, another in white coat as foreman of the shop. The factory made decals to hang on car mirrors, which were little clowns put together by pieces of concentric felt.

The children were divided by being given a red chip or a blue chip, as management and labor. Labor went upstairs. An actor playing the foreman said: "You've got to turn out more. Come one, you've made a mistake here. Get these out."

In an hour they made fifty decals, and the kids started to complain. There were telephones hooked up to management in a different part of the theatre. Management sat drinking their morning tea, saying that labor had to work harder. Labor said: "We want shorter hours and better conditions." Management hung up on labor.

Management was then served a beautiful lunch on white plates. Labor went down to the basement of the theatre and had a brown bag lunch. After lunch, it happened—labor mutinied. Then the decision-making part came where the actors guided the children through a structure that was formalized in theatre text, but involved participation of all as to deciding upon the working conditions they would accept.

Interviewer: Could you talk about the relationship between TIE and the curriculum—science, for example.

Swortzell: A marvelous TIE, also done by the Curtain, was a full-day production of *Darwin*, in which they examined the origins of evolution. Darwin was played by a professional actor. The team used slides, music, even sails. When they crossed the equator, a child was physically dunked, which was great fun.

Even sex education can be done. The original TIE script is called *Sweetie-Pie.* It is really an examination of birth control, contraception, and women's rights. When it was first done and went on tour, it achieved the distinction of being banned by the Edinburgh, Scotland, Board of Education Authority. It is now quite accepted as being one of the best means of examining these subjects. Another text is "Love and Marriage," which the Watford Team did, examining the nature of relationships, marriage, and teenage pregnancy.

TIE is a sensitive, creative source for education, better than any computer. The teacher can rely on the TIE team as the greatest audio-visual aid available.

Although the concept and practice of TIE originated in England, it has migrated to America in recent years. One outstanding example is the Creative Arts Team, based in New York University. For the past eight years the Creative Arts Team has been involved in workshops for students, teachers, and community groups, as well as the performance of theatre programs involving issues such as strip-mining, violence, vandalism, and racism. They have also devised special workshops for adolescents with behavioral problems.

In a recent televised presentation the Creative Arts Team, or CAT, demonstrated the process they use in planning a workshop dealing with disruptive behavior.[3] One topic chosen by artistic director Laurie Meadoff was that of peer pressure. To develop ideas around that theme, Meadoff set up several improvisational scenes. For example, two friends meet on a playground. One has missed an important basketball game, because he was studying for a history test. The other ridicules him for not being "cool" and demands that he join the group and stay away from the exam.

As the conflict built to a peak, Meadoff called "Freeze." She then asked the full team to suggest ideas for resolving the conflict. Several endings were acted out in movement, words, and song. This technique of acting out alternative endings to a conflict situation is used often in CAT's work with students labeled disruptive who, in the actual workshops, are the ones to suggest the alternative endings. CAT team members discussed their experiences in using this and related techniques in the classroom:

Interviewer: What happens if a student comes up with a very unexpected ending after the freeze?
Laurie Meadoff: That's happened to us a lot. We are very well versed in improvisational techniques. Part of our training includes being able to handle whatever the audience throws out. A lot of our research and discussion is about what people do in conflict situations. A lot of focus in our workshops is on how we deal with the kids and open them up to other possibilities.
E. Dexter Locke: For example, we were at a school, and we were dealing with violence in the home. An actress, playing the mother, had a knife and was going to stab her husband. We froze the scene there and asked the kids what they would like to see happen in the scene, how they would like to see it resolved. They said: "Kill, make sure that she kills him. Kill that dude."
Interviewer: How did you deal with that?
Meadoff: I don't usually let things go that far. I said: "OK, let's play it out." We played out a real violent ending. There wasn't one word spoken. No one laughed; no one said anything. Then we played out an alternative ending of one couple getting together, so the students could see both sides of the issue.
Ben Epps: One particular student that we all became very fond of had a very bad problem with substance abuse. So I played him. He was jailed, arrested while loitering on the street. It was a very touching scene. I think it might have been the first time that he ever came in close contact with his feelings.

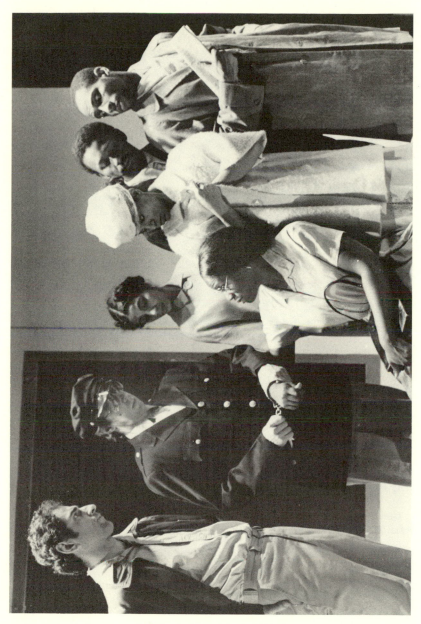

1. The Creative Arts Team of New York University in Jim Mirrione's *Rosa Parks: Back of the Bus.* Courtesy of CREATIVE ARTS TEAM.

2. The Creative Arts Team of New York University in Jim Mirrione's *Saloogie*. Courtesy of CREATIVE ARTS TEAM.

3. The Creative Arts Team of New York University in Jim Mirrione's *Saloogie*. Courtesy of CREATIVE ARTS TEAM.

Meadoff: To add to that, at the end of our residency with these kids, we asked them to write letters to themselves. What do they want to see changed? What kinds of changes do they want to make? The person Ben mentioned asked us to read his letter and share his feelings about needing to change.

Interviewer: How else do you follow up this kind of workshop?

Meadoff: We're very concerned with follow-up. Before we go to a school, we do teacher-training workshops on how to use drama in the curriculum. Whenever possible, we deal with parents in parenting workshops. Follow-up work is involved with getting the teachers and the community people involved in developing drama clubs and rap sessions for the kids concerning their feelings and discussing ways to bring the kids into some kind of peer leadership position in the school.

Interviewer: What is the most essential purpose of your workshops?

Lynda Zimmerman: I really feel that in our educational system we have spent too long looking at the arts as a fringe activity. It's only through activities such as drama that we can develop the total child, not only the cognitive level, but also the affective level. I really see the value of our work as being in creative personal growth.

Along with their commitment to working through improvisation and creative drama within various classroom situations, CAT also engages in a considerable performance schedule. Recently, they toured schools, community groups, and theatres with two pieces written by their resident playwright James Mirrione: *Rosa Parks: Back of the Bus*, a play about racism and the beginnings of the Civil Rights movement in the United States, and *Saloogie*, a play commissioned by the New York State Division for Youth and the New York City Youth Board, dealing with violence and vandalism in schools. Lynda Zimmerman, executive director of CAT, noted that the difference between such scripts and more conventional children's theatre scripts, for example, is that the TIE program aims to provoke discussion and promote communication among the viewers.

An outstanding example of a piece reflecting these aims was CAT's production of Mirrione's *Tower of Babble*. Zimmerman spoke of the genesis of this project, and the CAT team demonstrated their approach to developing the material in a recent presentation.[4]

Interviewer: How did the idea originate for *Tower of Babble?*

Lynda Zimmerman: About four years ago we were asked by the New York Urban Coalition's Education Department to dramatize a problem that's prevalent in today's educational system—the lack of effective communication between constituencies that work in a school system. Administrators, principals, teachers, custodians, and paraprofessionals are not communicating effectively. The result is that the child suffers in the end. We did a lot of research in the schools and in the city. We looked at newspaper articles and everything we could find to tell us what was going on in the New York City educational system. We improvised upon that material, and then our playwright completed a script based upon our work.

Interviewer: Is that your usual way of working?

Zimmerman: Yes. That is the way a TIE company works in that we do our research, then improvise upon that research, and then develop it further into a final scripted play.

Interviewer: Is there a follow-up to the performance experience?

Zimmerman: In most cases when we're performing, we follow up with classroom discussion or general group discussion. The performance is a catalyst. We're saying: "This is a problem. What can we do about it?" That's the focus—to provoke a discussion.

In demonstrating the way CAT develops a scene improvisationally based upon its research, Laurie Meadoff led the following:

Laurie Meadoff: The last couple of weeks we spent our time interviewing teachers, administrators, principals, people in and out of the school system, as well as kids. And now it's time to brainstorm on ideas. How can we take our information and put it into some kind of metaphor? Let's role-play. You are a principal and I'm the teacher, and we have a rope between us. We're having a tug-of-war. I might say: "What's the matter? Why are my classrooms so overcrowded?"

Principal: It's because you're not an efficient teacher.

Teacher: But they don't give me any time to get any different kind of training.

Principal: You ought to get more experience. Why don't you go back to school.

Other ideas are offered, for example, a tightrope walker on a balance beam and a pinball machine. The team then settles on the idea of a pool game. Two actors choose the roles of a young teacher and a principal and improvise the following:

Teacher: Your shot first, please.

Principal: How long you been playing here?

Teacher: I just started last September—two months.

Principal: You're new at this, huh? Well, you got a lot to learn.

Teacher: I guess so. I'm playing with the expert.

Principal: I'm going to make that shot over in the left-hand corner. This is your raise for next year, which I'm going to veto. (He makes the shot.)

Teacher: It went in! I have a group of bilingual students in my class, and I'd like to get more books. . . .

After improvising on the pool game the pinball idea is implemented. Roles are again taken by the team: child, parent, teacher, and so on. As the child bounces around from character to character, an improvised dialogue occurs:

Parent: Go to school.

Teacher: You're late.

Teacher: What are you doing here? This isn't your class.

Parent: What do you mean you got an F on your report card?

Teacher: This is the teacher's lounge.

Parent: You failed again!

Teacher: Where are your books today?

Teacher: Go back into that homeroom class!

Parent: Why can't you be like your brother?

Teacher: Cover those books!

Principal: Where's your pink slip?

Parent and Teacher: You never listen to me!

From these kinds of exercises the script is developed into a first draft and then presented to various groups of students and colleagues for feedback. The script is then reworked into subsequent drafts until a final text is completed. As mentioned above, TIE programs usually involve pre-performance and/or post-performance workshops with teachers and other relevant personnel to examine ways of relating the material to the school curriculum.

A TIE script focuses on issues. It tends not to be as concerned with developing substantial characterizations. For example, in Mirrione's scripts, *Tower of Babble* and *Saloogie*, there are no individualized characters, but rather types representing administration, staff, students, researchers, abused children, and so on. One actor will often play multiple roles, again focusing attention on ideas rather than fully developed characters.

In this sense TIE programs reflect Bertolt Brecht's notion of alienation in that the aim of the playwright is to provoke thought and social awareness, rather than to allow an easy emotional identification between actor and audience.[5] In using theatrical devices such as slides, music, puppets, and stylized movements, CAT's work remains in the tradition of didactic theatre that seeks to alienate in order to educate.

But just as Brecht was immensely successful by virtue of not fully realizing his philosophical and political aims and, in fact, creating human, identifiable characters, so, too, have TIE teams created accessible characters. In one of Mirrione's scripts, for example, the protagonist Rosa Parks, who sparked the Civil Rights movement in the 1950s by refusing to sit at the back of the bus in Alabama, is portrayed as a fully developed, heroic character. With this script, the aim is twofold: both an emotional identification with the central character and an understanding of the issues surrounding racism in the 1950s as well as in the present.

It is difficult for any theatre company to draw both feelings and insights from the same audience. But that seems to be the aim of many TIE teams who employ their expertise as theatre artists to draw an audience into the lives of the characters portrayed and equally to use their talents as educators to help their audiences and students understand the political, social, economic, and moral conditions that determine the quality of the characters' lives.

NOTES

1. WCBS-TV, *Sunrise Semester*, "Drama in Education: Theatre-in-Education, Principles and Practices" (October 29, 1979).

2. W. Eugene Smith and Eileen M. Smith, *Minamata* (New York: Holt, Rinehart, and Winston, 1975).

3. WCBS-TV, *Sunrise Semester*, "Drama in Education: Theatre-in-Education, Practical Application in Schools" (October 31, 1979).

4. Ibid.

5. For a full discussion of Brecht's alienation effect, see John Willett, *Brecht on Theatre* (New York: Hill and Wang, 1964).

BIBLIOGRAPHY AND RESOURCES

Books, Articles, and Published Scripts

Ball, Hilary, "TIE: Mapping Its Growth in England." In John Hodgson and Martin Banham, eds. *Drama in Education 3*. London: Pitman 1975, pp. 12-22.

Bradby, David, and John McCormick. *People's Theatre*. London: Croom Helm, 1978.

Chapman, Roger, and Brian Wilks, eds. *Snap Out of It: A Programme about Mental Illness*. London: Methuen Young Drama Series, 1973.

Education Survey No. 22: Actors in Schools. London: Department of Education and Science, HMSO, 1976.

Hunt, Albert. "Education as Theatre: Turning the Tables." *Theatre Quarterly* 17 (1975): 55-60.

Jackson, Tony, ed. *Learning through Theatre, Essays and Casebooks on Theatre in Education*. Manchester, Eng.: Manchester University Press, 1980.

Murphy, Eileen, ed. *Sweetie Pie: A Play about Women in Society*. London: Methuen Young Drama Series, 1975.

Newham Drama, Issue Nine, Monega Drama Centre, Autumn 1980.

O'Toole, John. *Theatre in Education*. London: Hodder and Stoughton, 1976.

"Production Casebook: Three TIE Entertainments." *Theatre Quarterly* 17 (1975): 74-94.

Robinson, Ken, "Looking for TIE." In John Hodgson and Martin Banham, eds. *Drama in Education 3.* London: Pitman, 1975, pp. 23-33.

Schweitzer, Pam, ed. *Theatre-in-Education, Five Infant Programs.* London: Methuen Young Drama Series, 1980.

_____. *Theatre-in-Education, Four Junior Programmes.* London: Methuen Young Drama Series, 1980.

_____. *Theatre-in-Education, Four Secondary Programmes.* London: Methuen Young Drama Series, 1980.

_____. *Theatre-in-Education Directory, 1975-1976.* London and Los Angeles: TQ Publications, 1975.

Vallins, Gordon. "Drama and Theatre in Education." In J. R. Brown, ed. *Drama and the Theatre: an Outline for the Student.* London: Routledge and Kegan Paul, 1971, pp. 161-84.

Wyatt, Stephen, and Maggie Steed, eds. *Rare Earth: A Programme about Pollution.* London: Methuen Young Drama Series, 1976.

Some Prominent TIE Teams

Bolton Octagon TIE
1 Gorton Street
Bolton, England

Cockpit TIE Team
Gateforth Street
London NW8, England

Coventry TIE
Belgrade Theatre
Corporation Street
Coventry, England

Creative Arts Team
New York University
733 Shimkin Hall
New York, New York 10003

Curtain Theatre Company
26 Commercial Street
London E1, England

Looking Glass Theatre
P.O. Box 2853
The Casino, Roger Williams Park
Providence, Rhode Island 02907

Theatre Centre Ltd.
Victor Road
London NW10, England

Theatre of Youth Company
681 Main Street
Buffalo, New York 14203

3
THE SCHOOL PLAY

THE EDUCATIONAL SIGNIFICANCE OF THE SCHOOL PLAY

The school play is undoubtedly the most widely practiced form of drama and theatre in education. Most American, British, Canadian, and Australian schools, kindergarten through twelfth grade, including those that neither schedule drama as a subject nor practice drama as a method, still predictably produce school plays. The school play, in its most conventional form, is used to celebrate a holiday, perpetuate an assembly program tradition, serve as an extracurricular club activity, or satisfy an adult assumption that plays are educationally sound activities for children.

As noted in Joseph Peluso's survey, most directors of secondary school plays tend to be inexperienced in drama and theatre.[1] Very often an English or social studies teacher takes on the responsibility of directing, assisted by the art and music teachers, who design the set and orchestrate the music.

It is difficult to generalize about the motivations of well-intentioned administrators and teachers who perpetuate the ritual of school plays. For many, it is undoubtedly equivalent to an athletic event, where students try out for a team, practice hard, and early on become aware of their status on the squad. Finally, the big game is played, a sense of group spirit is generated, the heroes are rewarded, and the game is recounted and embellished upon at various social functions; then everybody goes about his or her business as before.

Like the athletic event, the school play has a prescribed structure: auditions, casting (with its inherent caste system), rehearsals, performance, ensemble interaction, award ceremony, cast party, and so on. Yet the analogy implies that the school play is competitive, encouraging a hierarchy of players and a team spirit based upon a common enemy.

There is, of course, an alternative vision of the school play that is more in line with the goals delineated by Peluso: growth in self-confidence, self-understanding, and understanding of others. This vision is one that, like educational drama work, is noncompetitive; that promotes a fully developed characterization for each actor, no matter how sizable his or her role; and that leads to an ensemble effort based upon a common purpose, the realization of a creative promise. Unless this vision is operative the educational significance of the school play will be severely minimized.

There are many potential educational values inherent in the experience of preparing the school play. On a personal level student actors are learning to expand their own repertory of roles through taking on the role of another. They are learning, also, to overcome performance anxiety and experience a sense of personal accomplishment. On a social level students are learning to listen, share space and praise with others, take risks in relation to their peers and their audience, and share responsibility for creating an artistic product within a limited period. On an intellectual level students are learning not only to understand a dramatic text, but to translate that understanding into verbal and physical action. They are potentially developing their language skills and their understanding of human behavior and motivation.

Emotionally, students learn through empathy, through entering into the life or world view of another. If the dramatic experience is successful on an affective level, students will identify with the tension and conflict within a character and find ways to present that tension in terms of their own experience.

On a physical level students learn how to move, speak, and gesture like their characters, thus expanding their own capacity for movement and speech.

All of these values apply not only to student actors but to student designers, writers, and directors. Student audience members, too, can participate in a similar process while viewing the school play.

THE RELATIONSHIP BETWEEN EDUCATIONAL DRAMA AND THE SCHOOL PLAY

It is often said that educational drama is a student-centered activity, involving a learning process, whereas the school play, an experience in educational theatre, represents a product that is audience-centered. As we have seen, educational drama is, in fact, student-centered, spontaneous, and open-ended. It is indeed intended as a learning process.

When we speak of the school play, though, it is too simplistic to refer to the experience of rehearsal and performance merely as a product. A *product* implies something complete in all of its parts that is, in a sense, packaged and ready to be consumed by the public at large. It is the end result of a process or procedure. One who creates a product is not concerned with unknowns, but with known ways to arrive at a point of completion.

A *process*, on the other hand, is incomplete and open-ended. People who engage in a process often do not concern themselves with the outcome or result of their play or work. To play on a familiar American advertising slogan, in educational theatre "process is our most important product."

Rehearsing is a process. Performing to an audience is a process. A live play can never be a product to the degree of a video-tape or film. The tape fixes time. With each showing the actors perform in exactly the same way. In live theatre each performance varies and each action varies, no matter how often the play has been rehearsed. Yet many directors and/or teachers still stress elements of product during rehearsals—attention to end results and elimination of unpredictable actions. These elements must be adhered to if the rehearsal stage is to proceed to the production stage.

In speaking of the school play, then, it probably makes most sense to talk in terms of the relationship between product and process within the educational experience. That is, it is important to view both the spontaneous play aspects and the more controlled performance aspects in relationship to each other within the experience of rehearsing and performing a play.

For the most part, undue emphasis upon either extreme of product or process does not lead to the most fully realized educational experience. The product extreme would imply a situation where the adult director has prepared, in detail, all of the blocking, line-readings, character motivations, and interactions and simply leads the actors through the motions, like so many puppets. The process extreme would imply a structure where the actors are given permission to improvise at will, to "do their own thing," and to read their lines and move according to their whims at any given moment.

A more balanced approach to the school play would draw upon the ideas of the student actors in relationship to the ideas of the director, designer, and playwright. It is now common for directors to use improvisational techniques in their rehearsal process, as it is common for many educational drama instructors to make good use of scripts, stories, costumes, makeup, and other more fixed, theatrical elements.

To avoid the pitfalls of a product orientation, the director of the school play must allow the element of play to be firmly rooted in the rehearsal and performance experience. Since play implies spontaneity, experimentation, and process, these aspects must also be present in the school play experience.

Many educational drama and theatre experts frown upon play production in the elementary school. We have noted above that Peter Slade, for one, cautions against a performance orientation before the age of twelve, fearing that it will divert the children's attention from learning about themselves to pleasing an audience. Given a competitive society that over-values applause, that glorifies the star and ignores the supporting player, that rewards the everyday performer who gives people what they expect, it is easy to see how children might automatically learn to pander to their audiences and thus miss the opportunity to experience educational theatre on a deeper level.

As we have mentioned above, educational drama does not necessarily lead to a theatrical experience. Not all students need to be cast in school plays. The school play is the art form of educational drama and theatre and, like the music and dance recital, should be performed by those who are ready to perform and who are motivated to express themselves through their chosen art form. Educational drama is a much more populist activity. Like child's play, it is for everyone.

Aside from the assumption that showcasing child actors is educationally unsound, how much do we really know about school plays? Is there a dramatic literature appropriate for performance by elementary, secondary, and university students? Are there ways to incorporate the school play within the curriculum so that it becomes more than the spring rendering of a tired Broadway musical comedy?

CHOOSING SCHOOL PLAYS

Despite the warnings of performance before age twelve, most elementary schools produce plays. As a student in a large urban school, this author acted in *Hansel and Gretel*, *Chicken Little*, and an original play based upon "The Night Before Christmas," all before he was eight years old. The choices were based upon a teacher's conception of plays suitable for child actors to perform during special occasions.

Many elementary schoolteachers will consult various catalogues of publishers that stock specialized plays—for example, Anchorage Press, Plays, Inc., New Plays, Dramatic Publishing Company, Pioneer Drama Service, Baker's Plays, Samuel French—and make their choices based upon their particular needs. In Baker's table of contents, for example, we find a listing of specialized needs such as holiday plays, junior high plays, juvenile plays, pageants, and teen-age plays.

Other teachers will tap known educational theatre sources, such as the adaptations of classical plays by Albert Cullum, for example, *Shake Hands with Shakespeare* and *Greek Tears and Roman Laughter*. Some will turn to folk tales, fables, and mythology for inspiration. Many of these sources have already been dramatized by educational theatre experts, for example, Carol Korty's *Plays from African Folktales* and Albert Cullum's *Aesop in the Afternoon*. Some teachers begin without a dramatic script but use a more reader's theatre approach in transforming narrative literature or poetry into drama.

On the secondary level a wider choice of plays appears to exist. But in that the adolescent is in a transitional stage of development, he or she will often feel uncomfortable playing roles that are either too immature or too mature. In scanning the play publishers' catalogues, there are very few plays of substance with substantial roles for adolescents. *West Side Story* is one, but it is expensive and has been played to the point of exhaustion. The various versions of *Tom Sawyer* and *Huckleberry Finn* are others, but both include substantial adult roles, and many high school students associate these classics as appropriate to child actors and audiences. George Kaufman and Moss Hart's *You Can't Take It With You* is an old secondary school standby but again calls for many adult actors.

When playwrights have attempted to write for adolescent actors, the results have often been mediocre, at best, as in Ed Graczyk's *To Be*, a sentimental and vapid updated version of *Hamlet*.

But why *To Be* when *Hamlet* is available? Why *West Side Story* when *Romeo and Juliet* is available? In a recent article Julian S. Schlusberg discussed his award-winning high school production of *Othello*.[2] Schlusberg convincingly argued that Shakespeare's language and concerns are universal and highly motivating for high school students. But even though Shakespeare's plays are consistently produced in schools throughout the world, many high schools will not produce Shakespeare because of the difficulties of casting and working within the Elizabethan style and language.

The principles that govern choices of high school plays tend often to be based upon extraneous factors such as commercial potential, wholesomeness and lack of controversy surrounding the theme, and suitability to students and curriculum.[3] But as Patrick Gouran, associate professor at Iowa State University, claimed:

> In educational theatre we often become schizophrenic in that we attempt to present a totally "artistic" event, fill the coffers at the box office, please the audience, mollify the administration, and contribute significantly to the artistic and personal growth of the students.[4]

To solve this dilemma secondary school theatre directors must be willing to make some real choices based upon their own philosophies of education, knowledge of the dramatic literature available, and the needs and interests of their students.

In 1979 the Secondary School Theatre Association compiled a list of criteria governing play selection that might provide guidelines for choosing appropriate plays from the classical, modern, or contemporary dramatic literature.[5] Items identified include:

1. Characters worth doing—challenging to the performers
2. Theme worth expressing—of lasting value to the audience as well as the cast and production staff

3. Lines worth learning—good literary quality
4. Suitable cast size
5. Audience appeal
6. Capable of production within the budget and with the facilities

Other items include the appropriateness of the material to the varied interests, abilities, and maturity levels of all involved as producers and viewers and the provision for presenting opposing viewpoints on controversial issues.

Again, this list sounds like an attempt to be all things to all people. Searching for a play that is appropriate for everybody concerned, with balanced viewpoints, universal themes, and suitable cast size, might just lead a high school director to the safe, tried and true titles that have been perpetuated for years, such as *Arsenic and Old Lace*, *Bye Bye Birdie*, and *Oklahoma*.

Doug Finney of the International Thespian Society claimed that the hope to move beyond the over-produced high school conserve of plays lies in the vision of those excellent high school theatre arts teachers who are willing to take chances and who have the talent and dedication to direct excellent productions of, for example, *Marat/Sade*, *One Flew Over the Cuckoo's Nest*, and original student work. The coffers of the box office might not be as full and the local clergy might not be as happy, but if the director and students meet their goals in exploring issues, characters, and world views as presented in a dramatic text, the educational experience will be rewarding.

Similar considerations abound in choosing plays for production at the college or university level. Most theatre departments deal yearly with the conflicts of classical versus contemporary plays; box office draws versus more risky, lesser-known titles; quantity of women's roles versus men's roles; and so on. As budgets are further cut, many may well feel the need to produce safer, more popular choices with a view to ticket sales as the way to pay the bills. On the other hand, budget cuts can have a positive effect upon university theatres in that financial restraints can lead directors away from perseverating upon the most expensive aspects of production, such as sets, costumes, lights, and royalties on the current hit musical, toward the more basic and human aspects of educational theatre, that is, the actor, director, playwright, and designer in relationship to one another.

A fully educational theatre experience is one where the choice of the school play is based upon human and artistic considerations, rather than financial anxieties and assumed audience expectations. School plays can be produced with a minimal budget. All one needs is a space, a group of motivated students, a director-teacher and either a new play or a royalty-free play.

Many would doubt the educational and artistic value of producing new plays, especially those written by children. But for those teachers skilled in helping students develop their experiences in dramatic form, the potential rewards are great. One example is in the work of Gerald Chapman, who has been inspiring children to write plays first at the Royal Court Theatre in London and more recently through the Young People's Playwriting Program of the Dramatists Guild in New York. Chapman visited twenty-two public schools in New York City, helping children express their experiences through the art of playwriting. He candidly admitted that 90 percent of the plays are not very good, but "We are looking for the 10% whose courage leads them (the children) to say, loud and clear, 'Look, the emperor has no clothes.'"[6] In the spring of 1982, ten of the plays Chapman developed were produced at the Circle Repertory Theatre Company's Young Playwright's Festival in New York.

Given a teacher with the resourcefulness and talent of Chapman, that 10 percent might be discovered again and again within many schools and add new life and new value to theatre programs that all too often produce plays without considering the deeper needs of the players.

THE SCHOOL PLAY AND THE CURRICULUM

Generally, the school play is separated from the curriculum. Because so much energy is expended in the production of a school play, the teacher has little time or energy to consider its application to the curriculum or to consult with other teachers about ways they might teach related topics. Also, in that so many school plays are pedagogically trivial, any attempt to interrelate academic studies could well be frivolous.

Yet there are exceptions. In connection with a recent production at New York University of "The Padrone," a new play based upon Horatio's Alger's *Phil, the Fiddler*, concerning child labor and the pursuit of the American Dream, several junior high school groups discussed the script in class and applied it to their study of the history and social conditions of late nineteenth-century America. The classroom work occurred before they saw the play. After the play the students further discussed their experience with the production and wrote papers based upon their developing understanding of the issues presented.

Also on the university level a season of plays may be planned to coordinate with related courses within the theatre, English, and/or history departments. To meet the needs of design classes, styles of acting and directing classes, literary history classes, and the like, a theatre department might well choose a bill of plays from varying historical periods, requiring various set, costume, and movement elements, so that students will be exposed to a diverse learning experience concerning style, design, and history.

Furthermore, in researching theatrical elements through qualitative and quantitative research methodologies, professors and students have turned to their colleagues in statistics and the social sciences for methodological aid, offering them in return exposure to an aesthetic method of inquiry and fostering a dialogue between academic disciplines that more often than not remain equal, but separate.[7]

The school play can also be integrated into an elementary school curriculum, especially when it evolves from a class project in history, English, or science. But often those teachers who use a project approach to education, that is, basing the entire curriculum for a limited time upon a theme or topic, such as ancient Greek civilization, space travel, or problems of living in a big city, tend to be unprepared to locate, write, or direct a play. They might invite other classes to observe their model city or simulated space journey. But this kind of sharing experience is different from mounting a production, based upon the project, on the stage in the school auditorium.

Yet given a teacher who has training in educational theatre and who is working through a project approach, there can be much value in moving toward production, if the students are so motivated. One unusual example occurred recently at P.S. 75 in New York City. It is unusual not only in that the school play evolved from a class project in creative writing, but also in the choice of the play, Anton Chekhov's *Uncle Vanya*.

The instructor, Phillip Lopate, had been an artist-in-residence, working with a group of fifth and sixth graders for some time. In a recent interview he described the genesis of his elementary school production of *Uncle Vanya*.[8]

Interviewer: How did you decide to use Chekhov with ten and eleven year olds?

Phillip Lopate: I really started off with just a scene from *Uncle Vanya*, because I was trying to get the kids to write dialogue. Their dialogue was a little flat. I wanted them to get a strong sense of how sometimes people talk to each other without necessarily saying right off what they mean. The conversation can exist at several levels. So I brought in a scene from *Uncle Vanya* about unrequited love. A is in love with B; B is in love with C; and nobody seems to be getting together. I thought it would probably bore them, but I tried it out anyway. They were surprisedly interested. So then I thought, what would happen if we all read the play as a study group? I still hadn't planned to put it on. I just wanted us to study a large piece of literature. Usually in schools you study little slivers of literature. You never get a chance to study a whole novel. I wanted to sink my teeth into a large work. It just so happened that I loved *Uncle Vanya*. I had been spending years doing what the kids wanted—comic books, vampire plays, Superman.... So I said: "Forget what the kids want to do. This is what I want to do. And I'm curious to see what the kids will make of it, whether they'll see any connections between the life of the Chekhov play and their own lives." I really had no idea how it was going to turn out.

PRODUCING *UNCLE VANYA* AS AN ELEMENTARY SCHOOL PLAY

The outcome in producing *Uncle Vanya* was extraordinary. Indeed, a group of fifth and sixth graders created all of the roles in the Chekhov classic and dramatized the very unchildlike themes of unrequited love, despair, and hopelessness. But are these themes appropriate for an elementary school play? Can a child of ten or eleven relate to Chekhov's existential musings? How does such an experience affect a child's home life and school life?

It will probably take all concerned—student actors, director, teachers, and parents—many years to answer these questions, if they can really ever answer them at all. However, several months after the experience Lopate and two of his leading actors viewed a video-tape of the performance and reflected upon the experience. The discussion, in part, follows:[9]

Interviewer (to Angus Johnston, who played the role of Uncle Vanya): How did you feel when you first began the experience of *Uncle Vanya*?
Angus Johnston: At first we just thought it was going to be a school play and not such a big deal.
Interviewer: What about the idea of performing Chekhov? Did *Uncle Vanya* seem appropriate to you?
Johnston: I though it was a bit grown-up, and I didn't think we were going to pull it off this well.
Lisa Cowan (who acted the role of Sonya): Most of us didn't know who Chekhov was, so it wasn't that impressive that we were doing Chekhov. But when you tell people: "We're going to do *Uncle Vanya* in school," they are really impressed, and that impresses you.
Johnston: At first, when I told my mother, she was really taken aback, and I didn't see what it was, because I hadn't read the play. I didn't even know who Chekhov was and what the play was all about.
Interviewer: Would it have made a difference if you were doing Shakespeare?
Johnston: If we were doing Shakespeare, I would have thought: "It's impossible. We can't do it."
Interviewer: When you were performing on stage, were you just wrestling to get the lines out, or were there some feelings going on? Do you remember?
Johnston: I knew my lines very well. Right before I went on, I put myself in his place, how I would feel if I were Uncle Vanya. When I was doing that, I was acting as if it was something that had been going through my mind for awhile and as if it was really happening to me.
Interviewer: How could you put yourself in Uncle Vanya's place? How could you understand someone whose experience is so different from your own?

Johnston: When I was studying my lines with my mother, she would ask me: "What do you think he's thinking now? What do you feel about Uncle Vanya?" By answering the question, I could get a certain picture of what he was like. Then I tried to make myself into him when I was onstage.

Cowan: You don't think of the characters being older than you, because you're playing them. You just think of the whole play as ten, eleven, and twelve year olds. You feel like the people when you're acting. I don't think about myself at all. When I'm rehearsing, I'm just Sonya. When I'm not, it's me. I can't think about us both together.

Lopate: I remember the struggle to get the kids past the point of embarrassment and self-consciousness to express true feelings. I think a lot of time when drama is done with kids, they have a way of giggling and acting like: "No, no, it's not happening to me. This is all a joke." They want to tip off the other kids in the audience that it's not so important and it's not real. I remember the scene between Sonya and Elena. At first, the two girls didn't want to touch each other. We kept going over that again and again. I said: "This is a real friendship. Can we have a little tenderness in this scene instead of jokey tenderness?" There was a real struggle to let sadness come in or any real emotion. It really wasn't easy. But we spent most of the time on the emotions and on the lines of the play. We didn't spend as much time on stage business or movement. Most of the movement was invented on the spur of the moment by the actors.

Interviewer (to the students): Did you feel comfortable about that, or did you want to be told exactly where to stand and move?

Johnston: Phillip gave us ideas and we combined that with what we felt at the spur of the moment. It was like we were in the character's place and we were moving as they would.

Interviewer: What kind of problems did you encounter during the process, from rehearsal to performance?

Cowan: Some of the actors didn't get around to memorizing their lines, and so everyone would be yelling at them and whispering their lines to them.

Interviewer: Do you think that's because the lines were so difficult?

Johnston: No. It's just because we were lazy. We were too busy doing other things. It would have been the same thing if we did *The Princess and the Pea* or *Peter Pan.*

Lopate: But it is a full-length play. Everytime they would master one act, I'd say: "OK, you've got Acts I and II; now you've got to go on to Act III." They would want to stop at Act II.

Johnston: Yes. We would want to stop at Act II and wait for awhile and then go on. It was first a feeling of accomplishment, but then we remembered there are two other acts.

Interviewer: So line memorization was a problem. What were others?

Cowan: When we would feel frustrated, because something wasn't going right, Phil would yell, and we would get really angry and let all our frustration out on him and on each other.

Interviewer: Was any of that frustration coming from the fact that you were doing a difficult play?

Johnston: A bit of that. We were angry with ourselves, because we weren't sure of our lines. Then Phil would get angry at us, and we'd feel even more angry at ourselves, and we'd let it out. So what was supposed to be a tender, sweet scene turned out to be an angry scene. We only did that in rehearsals, though.

Lopate: When you get involved in a theatrical production, all your manners go, and before you know it, everyone's letting it all hang out. People get very emotionally wrought up. If you are doing something like *West Side Story*, you have a song, then a few lines of dialogue, then a song. You keep having releases. The thing about Chekhov is that there is no release, except in a very subtle way. It's a problem for the actors and for the audience. You don't have these attention-grabbing things. It's all subtle.

Interviewer: Would you do Chekhov again? Was it worth it?

Johnston: In the end it turned out to be great. But it was really hard along the way.

Cowan: I'm glad that we did this, but if Phil is going to do *The Cherry Orchard* or *The Three Sisters*, which I think would be a stupid idea, I wouldn't do it.

Interviewer: Why?

Cowan: If you did it twice it wouldn't be the same thing.

Johnston: This was, for most of us, the first time we did a play. Part of it was fun, because it was the first time. Because it was hard, we really had a sense of accomplishment.

In taking another look at the affects of the production upon the students' academic and domestic lives, a second discussion occurred with Michael Tempel, the student actors' regular classroom teacher, and Joan Johnston, Angus's mother:[10]

Interviewer: Can we put the *Uncle Vanya* experience in the context of the school where it was performed, P.S. 75?

Michael Tempel: The school is on the west side of Manhattan. It is an innovative school. A lot of outside experts come in, particularly in the arts. The idea of somebody coming in and doing a play like *Uncle Vanya* is not new in itself. The idea of a project approach to learning is usual in this school. We don't have a rigid set of subject periods, so something like this can be worked into a school day without too much trouble.

Interviewer: How did you feel when you first heard that *Uncle Vanya* was going to be performed by fifth and sixth graders?

Joan Johnston: I took the whole thing with a grain of salt initially. Angus came home and said: "I have to learn my lines." So we started reading the play. I was not very familiar with *Uncle Vanya*. When we started reading it, I asked myself: "Why are they doing this? It's all talking. There's no action."

Interviewer: Did you have an answer at that point?

Johnston: I spoke to Phillip about it, and he explained how it had become a fact very gradually. I think that's the reason it was so successful. If he'd said: "OK, we're going to do *Uncle Vanya* in three months," everybody would have gone crazy.

Interviewer: Michael, what were your expectations at the beginning?

Tempel: When Phillip told me he wanted to do this, my first reaction was that he was crazy. But since we've done a lot of major projects before, I figured that it was something that he wanted to do, and I was willing to go along with it. I wasn't too involved with it at first.

Interviewer: In the last scene of the play, the characters talk of suffering, death, afterlife. Are these appropriate themes to explore in a play acted by children?

Johnston: I think they are. It's much better to challenge them than to give them baby food. I think that a lot of the themes in *Uncle Vanya* made Angus think about things and changed his ideas about things. It certainly changed my perceptions about him, because he was able to struggle through it. It was a struggle but also a growth experience.

Interviewer: Did the experience of the play change him in any way in terms of his home life?

Johnston: I'm not sure it changed him very much. At the beginning, most of it was just learning lines. I was playing it down, because I didn't want to make a big deal out of it and then find it was going to be a total disaster. After I saw him on the stage, I couldn't believe it was Angus. He's never shown any signs of having acting ability or being interested in doing this kind of thing. He's very articulate, but he's not the type of child who tends to show off in the sense of going up and performing. So it gave me a totally new view of Angus. In that respect it probably did change our relationship to a certain extent.

Interviewer: Michael, do you think these themes are appropriate for children to deal with through drama?

Tempel: Yes. I think the question is how much you can challenge children. The only problem can be that it's too far beyond what they're familiar with. Then the connection isn't made. I think that for most of the children involved in this, there were connections. They wouldn't have been able to do it if there weren't. They didn't really learn their lines that well. They learned their characters. That was the way Phillip directed it.

There were two performances, the first during the school day for the children. It seemed to go very smoothly, only it felt short. During the evening performance, I realized whole sections had been dropped. They kept it going, made the connections, and picked it up. So they did understand what they were doing. Learning lines was a big burden.

Interviewer: What about the audience's point of view? The first performance was to third through sixth graders. What was their reaction?

Johnston: It was very interesting. They were extremely attentive. They laughed and applauded and sighed in all the right places. We all felt that they couldn't possibly understand more than one-tenth of what was going on. And yet there was no fooling around. They really took it very seriously.

Tempel: It was clear this was not your everyday children's play. The main reaction I got from the cast after the first performance was: "We did it!" It was a very high risk operation, the whole thing. It's not what you usually get in school, which is a very controlled situation. The risk was that it could have flopped.

Interviewer: What do you mean by "flop"?

Tempel: I don't know. I've never gone to one of these that has flopped. I could speculate. It could have been really devastating. It would have been a major experience with failure.

Johnston: But it was very much a group effort.

Tempel: There was a tremendous mutual support during the performances.

Interviewer: I wonder how much the play *Uncle Vanya* contributed to this group cohesiveness. Wouldn't it have been there if the play had been *The Princess and the Pea?*

Johnston: I think the fact that it was *Uncle Vanya* made them take it a lot more seriously. I think there would have been a lot more fooling around if they were doing a children's play. They realized that there was this possibility of failure, and so they took it very seriously.

Interviewer: Could you speak about casting the play?

Johnston: Angus really got involved because Phillip asked him to. He didn't come and say: "I want to be in *Uncle Vanya*."

Tempel: The process of casting was interesting. You can't really take volunteers, if you really think about it. Who wants to be in *Uncle Vanya*? Who knows what it is? It really was a matter of Phillip and I deciding who would be good for it and who was interested in being a part of a play. This raises the question: "How much were these kids drawn into something that they really didn't understand?" We felt one boy was under a lot of pressure and should have been given the chance to get out.

He didn't and, I think, was glad in the end.

Interviewer: Could you speak about the social implications of this project for the class.

Tempel: My involvement grew. About one-third of the class was involved. We had two groups then—those who were doing it and those who were not. At first, that's not too important, because the play wasn't too important. As it grows, then the issue gets a lot heavier. One group is involved in something major, and the rest of the class is not. That presents a serious division in the class, created by Phillip and I. In the standard school plays, you have roles for everybody. Towards the end we had the necessity for involving everybody else in scenery, lighting, and so on. So it did become very much a class involvement, but not everybody together on an equal level. In most instances, that's the case anyway. It's just not so explicit. Socially, then, it worked out well.

Interviewer: Would you encourage other teachers to do a similar project?

Tempel: Not without someone like Phillip around. That's another thing about the standard class play. It has to be fairly nondemanding if you're also expected to do everything else. The time involved, especially toward the end, is just too much. Another question is how does the school play fit into the regular classroom curriculum? It doesn't very well. The way I run my classroom is to have an overall theme or themes which deal with all subjects. Something like *Uncle Vanya* could be part of a larger theme, but it's not the easiest thing to work in. Turn of the century Russia is not a big thing in the elementary curriculum. It could be done. It could be connected to history and a social context, a whole group of related areas that would increase the children's understanding of the play. But that wasn't done for two reasons: one, this came up in the middle of the year when I was heavily into other projects; and also, this was so hard to do. Had it been Greek tragedy, it would have been easier. Ancient Mediterranean civilization can be studied in the school curriculum. But this doesn't change the fact that it's a challenging project to do. It can be planned for.

Interviewer: Should children perform in plays to an audience?

Johnston: I think that this type of thing is preferable to the regular children's plays, because I don't think they're performing to the same extent. I think they're involved in the play in a very different way then when they're up on the stage doing their little number in a class play where you see thirty-two kids all in the play. I would rather have my child in something like this, because I think it's a much better experience. I don't want him to go on the stage or be a movie actor, but I think this type of thing has the potential for being a much more growth experience than the regular children's theatre.

Tempel: I agree with that. The other alternative is drama that comes out of children's own writing experience, which I think is also very valuable. Given the choice between the usual low level school play and this, I would absolutely chose something like this. No regrets.

Uncle Vanya proved to be a difficult, demanding, and risky project for all involved. At the end of a paper summarizing his experience, Phillip Lopate quoted Michael Tempel as saying:

> Educationally, *Uncle Vanya* was very inefficient. It was labor-intensive, took too many hours from other work, only involved a part of the class, and never was really integrated into the curriculum. It went against everything you're supposed to to. All the same, it was probably the single greatest educational experience those kids ever had.[11]

There did indeed seem to be qualitative differences between choosing Chekhov as opposed to a more conventional play for child actors. Lopate pointed out that the experience increased the children's vocabulary and reading skills and taught them an appreciation for dramatic literature and Russian history.[12] The choice of Uncle Vanya also implied a greater intellectual and emotional challenge and a greater attention to subtle human behavior than most other conventional choices would have provided.

But it will take time to evaluate many of the residual benefits. In fact, it is extremely difficult to evaluate the effects of a school play or, for that matter, any educational drama or theatre experience. Because the participant is living within the subjective realm of symbols and feelings, imagination and fantasy, many of our known objective means of evaluation appear to be fruitless. Those of us charged with making decisions about the appropriate plays to be enacted or situations to be improvised must, then, make our decisions based not only upon the limited data available, but also upon our knowledge of human learning and our philosophy of education, in general. If, like those involved in the *Uncle Vanya* project, we aim to challenge our students intellectually and emotionally; if we respect their potential for dealing with complex issues; if we are able to give ourselves permission to work with material that first excites us; and if we approach a vision of a product through encouraging a thoughtful, developmental process, then we are engaged in the kind of educational theatre work that, although often arduous and risky, can never be regrettable.

NOTES

1. Peluso, *Survey*.
2. Julian S. Schlusberg, "Shakespeare on the High School Stage," *Secondary School Theatre Journal* 20, no. 2 (Winter 1981): 2-5.

3. See "Viewpoints: The High School Play," *Secondary School Theatre Journal* 20, no. 2 (Winter 1981): 7-13.

4. Ibid., p. 9.

5. Ibid., p. 12.

6. Jeffrey Sweet, "Gerald Chapman's Talk on the Progress of Young People's Playwriting Program," *The Dramatists Guild Quarterly* 18, no. 1 (Spring 1981): 48.

7. See the journal *Empirical Research in the Theatre*, The Center for Communications Research, Bowling Green State University, Bowling Green, Ohio 43403.

8. WCBS-TV, *Sunrise Semester*, "Drama in Education: Children Perform the Classics" (November 5, 1979).

9. Ibid.

10. WCBS-TV, *Sunrise Semester*, "Drama in Education: The School Play" (November 7, 1979).

11. Phillip Lopate, "Chekhov for Children?" *Sunrise Semester*, "Drama in Education," *Newsletter No. 1*, New York University, Office of Off-Campus Programs, October 1979, p. 14.

12. Ibid.

BIBLIOGRAPHY AND RESOURCES

Books and Playscripts

Beck, Roy A., et al. *Play Production in High School*. Skokie, Ill.: National Textbook Company, 1977.

Birner, William. *Twenty Plays for Young People, A Collection of Plays for Children*. New Orleans: Anchorage Press, 1967.

Cohen, Robert, and John Harrop. *Creative Play Direction*. Englewood Cliffs, N.J.: Prentice-Hall, 1974.

Cullum, Albert. *Aesop in the Afternoon*. New York: Citation Press, 1972.

_____. *Greek Tears and Roman Laughter: Ten Tragedies and Five Comedies for Schools*. New York: Citation Press, 1970.

_____. *Shake Hands with Shakespeare*. New York: Citation Press, 1968.

Chekhov, Anton. *Four Great Plays*. New York: Bantam Books, 1958.

Chilver, Peter. *Staging a School Play*. New York: Harper and Row, 1967.

Courtney, Richard. *The School Play*. London: Cassell, 1966.

Dezseran, Louis John. *The Student Actor Handbook*. Palo Alto, Calif.: Mayfield Publishing Co., 1975.

Evans, Bernard. *Teaching Shakespeare in the High School*. New York: Macmillan, 1966.

Franklin, Miriam A. *Rehearsal: The Principles and Practice of Acting for the Stage*. Englewood Cliffs, N.J.: Prentice-Hall, 1972.

Kamerman, Sylvia E. *Dramatized Folk Tales of the World*. Boston: Plays, Inc., 1968.

Korty, Carol. "On the Line." Unpublished playscript, 1979.

_____. *Plays from African Folktales, with Ideas for Acting, Dance, Costumes, and Music*. New York: Scribner's, 1975.

_____. *Silly Soup*. New York: Scribner's, 1977.

Kraus, Joanna. *The Dragon Hammer and the Tale of Oniroku*. Rowayton, Conn.:
   New Plays, 1978.

Landy, Robert J. "The Padrone." Unpublished playscript, 1980.

Lopate, Phillip. *Being with Children*. New York: Doubleday, 1975.

McGaw, Charles. *Working a Scene*. New York: Holt, Rinehart, and Winston, 1977.

Motter, Charlotte. *Theatre in High School: Planning, Teaching, Directing*.
   Englewood Cliffs, N.J.: Prentice-Hall, 1970.

Secondary School Theatre Association. *A Selected and Annotated Bibliography for
   Secondary School Teacher and Student*. Washington, D.C.: American
   Theatre Association, 1975.

Swortzell, Lowell. *All the World's a Stage*. New York: Delacorte Press, 1972.

_____. "Five Plays: A Repertory of Children's Theatre to be Performed by and for
   Children." Ph.D. dissertation, New York University, 1963.

Play Publishers

Anchorage Press, P.O. Box 8067, New Orleans, Louisiana 70182

Baker's Plays, 100 Chauncy Street, Boston, Massachusetts 02111

Coach House Press, 53 West Jackson Boulevard, Chicago, Illinois 60604

Dramatic Publishing Company, 4150 North Milwaukee Avenue, Chicago, Illinois
   60641

Dramatics (magazine), 3368 Central Parkway, Cincinnati, Ohio 45225

Drama Book Specialists, 150 West 52 Street, New York, New York 10019

Heinemann, 4 Front Street, Exeter, New Hampshire 03833

New Plays, Box 273, Rowayton, Connecticut 06853

Pioneer Drama Service, 2172 South Colorado Boulevard, Denver, Colorado 80222

Plays, Inc., 8 Arlington Street, Boston, Massachusetts 02116

Plays Magazine, 8 Arlington Street, Boston, Massachusetts 02116

Samuel French, 25 West 45 Street, New York, New York 10036

Theatre Arts Books, 153 Waverly Place, New York, New York 10014

PART **II**

THE COMMUNITY AS AN ENVIRONMENT FOR EDUCATIONAL DRAMA AND THEATRE

INTRODUCTION: THE DRAMA OF THE COMMUNITY

In shifting our attention from the school to the community, we find a most natural environment in which to study educational drama and theatre. Any group of people in any given historical, cultural, or geographical locale dramatize their lives. In the language of the sociologist Erving Goffman, people present themselves in everyday life much the same way as the actor presents a character in the theatre.[1] Implicit in Goffman's thought is the notion that human beings are nothing more than actors who play social roles in relation to others within their various communities. The community, then, becomes a stage upon which everyday actors perform their social dramas.

In the work of the symbolic interactionists we find further theoretical evidence to suggest that people learn to understand who they are through a dramatic process of role-taking.[2] For example, children learn the role of child by taking on or internalizing the role of their parents and consequently acting toward themselves as the parents act toward them. According to George Herbert Mead:

> It is just because the individual finds himself taking the attitudes of others who are involved in his conduct that he becomes an object for himself. It is only by taking the roles of others that we have been able to come back to ourselves.[3]

Not only are our personal dramas artifacts of ourselves, but our social dramas are artifacts of our communities. Any community, past or present, primitive or industrialized, Occidental or Oriental, can be characterized by the nature of its drama. The dramatic activities of a community include play, worship, work, family life, and street life. These activities are dramatic, because they involve basic dramatic processes such as ritual, identification, and role-playing; they occur in present time; and they are symbolic actions representing the values and expectations of the larger society.

The child plays with a doll family to understand better her position within her real family. The celebrant worships in church to affirm his or her shared sense of belonging to a larger spiritual community. The man and woman work to support a family and maintain a sense of self-worth and respectability within their community. A family group sets rules of propriety that generally reflect an understanding of community expectations. Many subcultural street groups—clubs, cliques, gangs, and various organized crime elements—act out roles that consistently reflect certain prescribed standards of behavior.

There are other areas of community life where drama is evident. In the cultural life of a community we certainly find the obvious drama of the performing arts and the visual media. But less obvious is the potential drama in the museums, for example. Paintings, photographs, sculptures, scientific and technological exhibits, are all potentially animate and dramatic, since viewers discover something of themselves and their history in these objects. Like puppets and masks, all museum objects and artifacts live through the projection of the human imagination.

In the area of mental health we find still another reflection of community drama. Given overcrowded communities throughout the United States, for example, where powerlessness and anger are so often acted out through violence and assault, citizens become confused and frightened. The violent real-life dramas of the past twenty years overshadow their fictionalized counterparts on television and in films, plays, and novels. As a composite picture of the contemporary assassin begins to emerge—the loner, the drifter, the unstable and alienated individual—we look at that image for clues about ourselves, our own violent feelings, and the world we live in. Even if we do not identify at all with those we consider disturbed, alienated, and violent, we are, at the very least, a kind of audience to their actions. In 1981, after the assassination attempt on Ronald Reagan, for example, the television network programs broadcast the shooting literally hundreds of times, from every conceivable angle and with every conceivable video device —stop motion, slow motion, replay. With the omnipresence of the media, it becomes almost impossible for us to escape our audience role. Whether in the streets or at home with the television, we must at least attempt to make sense of the drama of violence, so that we can effectively function within our communities.

There has always been an interest in the overtly abnormal individual as a measure of our own sanity or physical well-being. Throughout the centuries freaks in sideshows have been the actors exposing themselves to the wonders of their viewers. In eighteenth-century Europe it became fashionable for certain of the nobility to frequent the local insane asylum, as if it were a theatre. Today, we go to the movies or theatre for contemporary entertainment such as *The Elephant Man*, *Equus*, or any of a number of related presentations of deviant or abnormal behavior.

But we have also learned to question the existence of dehumanizing institutions that tend to perpetuate deviant behavior. Given a more enlightened sensibility, educational drama and theatre practitioners have begun to bring their expertise into mental institutions and community organizations. Through the role-playing and improvisational techniques of drama therapy and the performance techniques of educational theatre, many emotionally disturbed, physically and developmentally disabled, and other special populations are receiving a new form of treatment that continues to make a difference in their lives and the life of the community as a whole.

So, too, have educational drama and theatre experts applied their methods to many institutions within the community: to the museum, the church, family life, mental health, and inner city life. Their purpose, like that of all who practice educational drama and theatre, is to help find ways to make the institution more accessible, immediate, and joyful and to help those who use it to understand the relationship between the inner life of an institution and the outer life of a community.

The drama of the community, then, can be seen both in terms of indigenous activity—such as play, worship, family, and street life—and imposed, planned activity—such as the application of improvisation to the museum and drama therapy techniques to the mental health clinic. This paradigm of indigenous and applied drama also holds true in our former discussion of educational drama and theatre in schools. Through indigenous dramatic play and other forms of improvisation, fantasy, and role-play, individuals learn language, thought, affect, and movement. Through drama and theatre techniques applied to the curriculum, students learn the same basic processes as they relate to subject matter content.

Richard Courtney has spent a great deal of time researching the drama of community life throughout the world. In the following discussion Courtney presented some of his views of community drama:[4]

Interviewer: What interest does a drama educator have in communities?
Richard Courtney: I think the essence of your question lies in what is a particular community and what is the need of that community. Let's take the example of Toronto. We're a very curious community. We have two federal government policies which are affecting our lives. The first is biculturalism and bilingualism: English and French are the official government languages. The second policy is called multiculturalism: the federal government puts funds into the cultural life of our Ukranian citizens, our Italian citizens, German, Vietnamese, and so on. I have a house in Toronto in the Hungarian quarter. There are nine great Hun-

garian restaurants nearby. There's a Hungarian publisher down the street. There's also Hungarian dancing going on. These cultural activities are funded by the federal government. It funds two types of need: the need for cultural expression of the ethnic group usually from their old country and the need for expression as Canadians. The drama of a community is one of the bases for the development of their cultural growth as human beings and their growth as both members of ethnic groups and as Canadians.

Interviewer: Do you see a distinction between a natural drama indigenous to the community and the kind of dramatic activity a community leader might use in a planned way?

Courtney: Yes. For the ease of discussion, let's distinguish between dramatic activities, on the one hand, and theatre, on the other. It seems to me that theatre is the tip of the iceberg and that dramatic activity includes all meaningful human actions. One can lead from the play of young children to improvisation through the role-play of adults and move into theatre, if one so wishes. Any particular community has needs at all these levels. There are needs for play, the play of children, and the play of adults. How do we play as adults? My first course for all my graduate students is for them to play. If thirty- or forty-year-old people are no longer able to play, there's something desperately wrong. We all have play needs. How does the community answer those play needs? We also have role-playing needs. How do we learn to play roles productively in life? Some few of us have needs to play theatrical roles as well, although not all of us need to be performers in theatre. All of us have to be performers in life, though. If the community and the authorities in a community don't service that need, then there's something wrong with the community.

Interviewer: How do communities encourage adults to play?

Courtney: I can give you some instances from other cultures. Dr. Louis Miller is working in Israel with kibbutzes that are breaking down socially. He uses certain kinds of dramatic activities. He and a team go into the community, and they improvise their problems and their concerns. The community then starts to play out their problems. Once this begins and they feel confident, they need to put it together as a show. Then they want to demonstrate it to other communities. From their play level they've moved into a theatrical level. Another example is the work of Bruce Kidd in Botswana, one of the enclaves within South Africa which recently became independent. They have enormous cultural problems, because many of the men in the communities go back into South Africa for their jobs and only return to Botswana occasionally. Bruce has been running spontaneous dramatic activities in the community to find out what the community wants. The community improvises its own problems and its own concerns in a form of social drama. They call it "education," because one community demonstrates to another what they have learned. That's two examples. How one copes with these problems in downtown Toronto or New York depends entirely upon identifying the needs of that community.

Interviewer: Let's talk more about indigenous cultural groups. You've traveled in Australia recently where you met with a particular aborigine, I believe?

Courtney: That was a very exciting meeting for me. I was in Canberra for only a day and a half. I was doing a seminar at the Curriculum Developmental Center. My host knew of my interest in shamans and North American Indians. She must have prepared something, because while I was in the Aboriginal Research Institute checking up some facts with an archeologist there, there was a tap on my shoulder. My hostess said: "There's a gentleman outside who wishes to see you." I walked out and there in the far distance on the green sward of Canberra was an Australian aboriginal, stark naked, with spear, shield, and fully painted. Evidently, he was in Canberra on behalf of the Australian government to bless a hill on which they needed to build a new Parliament building. We met and bowed. Then he saw this silver cross around my neck—a North American Kwakiutl cannibal mask. From round his neck, in his beads, he brought out his totem. We shared totems. From that moment, it was a most extraordinary experience for me. I said very little. I didn't ask any questions. Yet he knew the questions I wanted to ask: Is the dramatic activity of North American Indians similar to that of Australia and in what ways? He talked for an hour or so about all the kinds of things I wanted to know about dramatic activity amongst aboriginals. And I assure you, I wanted to know everything he said.

Interviewer: Is there a connection between the drama of such indigenous cultural groups and our own Western drama? Are there certain commonalities, certain shared forms or ways of using drama that justifies the kind of research you are doing?

Courtney: It appears as though all human beings have a deep need to dramatize their existence. In psychological terms this is "as if" thinking. I think "as if" I'm somebody, and then I have to be that somebody. D. W. Winnicott's book *Playing and Reality* talks about play as being "mediate" between the inner and outer world. The purpose of human play, he says, is to understand the external world. That starts when we're born and never finishes until we die. One of the ways that some, more traditional peoples have of doing this is what's known as shamanism, the ancient religion. This is still practiced all over the world. Interestingly, for Europeans, it was known as paganism. You and I, as ex-Europeans, had ancestors who were quietly celebrating shamanism all over Europe centuries ago. Christianity and other modern forms of religion developed from that.

The shamanic religion is fundamentally one where there are spirits in everything—there's a spirit in a tree, a salmon, a wolf, and in people. For Indians in the Northwest Coast, you and I are "spirits in the clothing of men." The shamans in Australia would agree with that. Being a "spirit in the clothing of a man," one is in a sense a spirit pretending to be a human being. If you're up on the Northwest Coast of America and you catch your first salmon, you cut off the flesh of the salmon and put it on one side. Then you take the bones and you slip them back into the sea, because the spirit of the salmon is in the bones. They have to go back into the sea so that the next year the spirit will come back again and provide us with the flesh of the salmon. This is a dramatic existence.

If I can, I will just move that idea over to some commonalities within modern religions. Take, for instance, ancient Jewry. We now know from the studies of the scholar Wijngaards that it may well be that the story of Moses in the Old Testament was actually a dramatization: a description of a ceremony that took place at Shechem when Joshua crossed the Jordan.[5] The character of God was the protagonist with his assistants Moses and Aaron; Pharoah was the antagonist, with the assistance of the court. And the antiphonal chorus of the people was on each side of the hill. That play was a development of ancient shamanic rituals. This illustrates the fundamentally dramatic way by which we all understand existence through our beliefs and rituals.

Interviewer: Can you make a comparison between the magic that is practiced by a shaman and the magic that's practiced by a child?

Courtney: If there are spirits in things, then you believe that everything around you, not just you and I, but the chairs we sit in and so on, has its own spiritual existence. If you're two years old and you're crawling past the table when you knock your head on it, you're liable to turn round and blame the table for hitting you. That's what is known as *animism*. The child is assuming that there's a life in all things around him. That's common to children and hunting peoples. Also, we are liable to treat everything anthropomorphically. For example, someone might say: "There, dear," when talking to the dog as if it were a human being. Yet a dog is a dog is a dog. If you project human qualities onto a dog, what you've got is another human being. But it isn't. It's a dog. That happens too amongst both hunting peoples and young children.

Interviewer: So all of us really engage in common forms of dramatic activity, no matter what community we live in?

Courtney: Exactly. In order for me to understand you or you to understand me we have to try to put ourselves in each other's shoes. We dramatize each other. You're trying to understand me from my point of view, and I'm trying to understand you from your point of view. This is where drama is so valuable in the community. It breaks down stereotyping. For instance, if you have a multicultural problem in a classroom and you dramatize things, they all try to get to know how the other person thinks, try to get into the skin of the other person. And if that happens stereotyping starts to break down. That's very important for social cohesion.

Interviewer: By playing the role of the other person, we're also getting closer to a true conception of ourselves as well.

Courtney: That's right. G. H. Mead said that there's a relationship between "me" and "not me" when one's very young.[6] How do you distinguish between the "me" and the "not me" when one's a baby? By what happens to you. Other people tell you things about yourself: "There's a good boy; there's a good boy." That increases your status and makes you feel good. When they say: "Don't be naughty!" your status gets smaller and smaller. The point is that the feedback you get from your community provides you with your image of yourself. If you try to get into their skins and they try to do the same with you, you get productive social growth and productive personal growth at the same time.

Interviewer: So through this reciprocal process of role-taking and role-playing, we become more integrated within our communities as we acquire a clearer conception of ourselves.

NOTES

1. Erving Goffman, *The Presentation of Self in Everyday Life* (New York: Doubleday, 1959).

2. See, for example, George Herbert Mead, *Mind, Self, and Society* (Chicago: University of Chicago Press, 1962); and Charles H. Cooley, *Human Nature and the Social Order* (New York: Scribners, 1902).

3. George Herbert Mead, "The Genesis of the Self and Social Control," *International Journal of Ethics* 35, no. 3 (April 1925): 251-73.

4. WCBS-TV, *Sunrise Semester*, "Drama in Education: Drama in the Community" (November 9, 1979).

5. J.N.M. Wijngaards, *The Dramatization of Salvific History in the Deuteronomic Schools* (Leiden, Holland: E. J. Brill, 1969).

6. Mead, "Genesis of the Self."

4
DRAMA AND THEATRE IN THE MUSEUM

The museum offers fertile ground for drama and theatre. It seems that the very purpose of displaying collections of arts and crafts, natural history, and technology is dramatic. It is dramatic, because the museum exists, in part, to make the past or future present and alive for the viewer; to demonstrate that inanimate objects can live in the imaginations of viewers; to invite emotional, intellectual, and physical participation on the part of the viewer who can, then, review things past or preview things future. Like all drama spaces, the museum offers a representation of the world as it was, as it is, and as it could or should be. In understanding this representation viewers are, in fact, attempting to make sense of the larger world outside.

To mitigate against the conception of the museum as a mausoleum, as a storehouse of dead, lifeless things locked away in untouchable glass cases, many museum educators have adopted the planned application of drama and theatre techniques. One outstanding example is in the work of those at the Brooklyn Museum who, for the past fifteen years, have presented puppet shows, films, creative drama experiences, storytelling sessions, and formal performances to foster a direct and living relationship between children and many of the museum's collections.

In a recent interview Tom Cahill, a theatre and visual artist, spoke of his work as a museum educator at the Brooklyn Museum:[1]

Tom Cahill: The museum is an ideal place to apply drama in education. The role of a museum educator is to find ways to open up the museum to the public, to make the art objects more accessible. Drama is one way to get people actively involved in viewing art. Uses of drama in the Brooklyn Museum's educational programs include storytelling, improvisation, and performance. For example, museum visitors choose a scene in a painting, analyze the setting, and imagine what might happen if it were a real-life situation. The storytelling and improvisational theatre games focusing on different cultures and mythologies enable children to see the art and the people who made it as related to their own experience, rather than as something foreign.

In 1970 the film *Statues Hardly Ever Smile* was produced at the Brooklyn Museum. The initiator of the project was Duncan Cameron, then the director of the museum, who believed that through drama and theatre children would be better able to experience fully the life of the museum. Cameron invited Jonathan Ringkamp, director of the Everyman Theatre Company in New York, to develop drama workshops in the museum for the children of the community and to direct the film, based on the workshop experiences.

Throughout the film, which was focused on the museum's Egyptian collection, Ringkamp maintained a creative dramatic, improvisational approach with the twenty children involved in the six-week project. His exercises included movement, pantomime, transformation of objects, and experiments with sound, for example, building from a very small group sound, such as "ah," to a powerful roar that echoed throughout the entire hall.

The most significant work related directly to the Egyptian collection itself. Children were encouraged to create dramatic movements suggested by the forms of the statues. As they carefully observed the ancient sculptures, they began to assume the roles of the stone figures in action.

Through their drama the children explored the cultural experience of ancient Egyptians and their own experiences that reflected the Egyptian sensibility. They created rituals using chanting, choral speaking, and highly stylized movements. They also used story material, such as the myth of Osiris, to motivate improvisations. To heighten the mythic and cultural elements of these improvisations, Ringkamp used drums, played in a distinctly rhythmical fashion, that reflected both the mysteries of an ancient civilization and the more familiar rhythms of Brooklyn streets on a warm summer's night.

In discussing the values of the kinds of dramatic experiences demonstrated in the film, Cahill pointed out that in such work children have the chance to be involved in not only a valuable artistic experience, but also a productive social experience. They make friends in the museum. They exchange ideas about culture and discover new ways to look at and relate to art and artifacts. They begin to understand that different people see the same object in different ways. Given this personal relationship with the museum, children return year after year to an institution they now view as alive and relevant to their lives.

In further discussing his work with drama in relation to Egyptian culture, Cahill noted:

Tom Cahill: A lot of my work with the Egyptian collection was about finding ways to interpret art history through drama. I would take the gestural qualities of sculpture, for example, and explore them dramatically and visually through drawing. I would work with profile, with the idea of how it feels to stand in profile. If you work with kids and try to explain that profile is a certain way of standing, that's very abstract. But if you try to get the children into the postures and gestures of the sculptures, then they extend themselves to it. This also improves the quality of their drawings. I've worked with the mythology of the Egyptians. It is very rich and lends itself to all kinds of storytelling.

Interviewer: You used puppets, too, I understand.

Cahill: Right. I like puppetry; it's a blend of visual art and performance. I directed a company at New York University called GATE (the Group for Art and Theatre Education). Our project was based on the story of the Egyptian god Osiris. Our use of shadow puppets reflected the Egyptian representation of mythological characters. Through the shadow puppet play and participatory workshops in drama and art, we explored Egyptian culture, their gods, and their land. We used improvisation to explore texture and landscapes, the importance of the Nile, and the quality of Egyptian life to explain concepts like profile. This helps the children understand that when they see Egyptian art that it's part of a history and a culture.

Interviewer: How can we encourage other museums to follow the model of Brooklyn? How do we spread the word?

Cahill: I think the word's beginning to spread. The collections of museums are just waiting to be interpreted. The stories of different cultures are there and are really in need of exploration. The public has to put more energy into funding this kind of work. Money, of course, is always a problem. Also, we must educate museum people not to be afraid of letting kids become physically involved with a collection. Because we value art so much, we tend to put it up on a shelf. But there's actually very little, if any, destruction when the children are actually involved in a collection. If you begin to cherish something, you usually don't want to vandalize it.

In recent years the Brooklyn Museum Education Department has applied drama and theatre in exploring various cultural traditions related to their many collections. In 1977, for example, they produced a shadow puppet play with and for children, "Shadows of the Thunderbird," based upon the Northwest Coast Indian culture. In 1978 they produced the short play "African Odyssey," exploring African village life through music, movement, and dramatization. In 1979 Wendy Aibel-Weiss, their senior drama instructor, directed elementary school children in "Can You Hear the River Calling the Moon?" a program of Chinese music and mythology, relating to the museum's Chinese collection.

As a recent extension of their work with the Egyptian collection, the museum produced the shadow puppet play "Catching Shadows Across the Nile." All of these experiences in theatre include participatory activities for the children, including puppet making, creative dramatic experiences, and mask making. During the summer of 1981 the museum produced another series of participatory workshops in conjunction with the shadow puppet play "The Enchanted Calabash," based, in part, upon their traveling exhibition "African Furniture and Household Objects."

Within the tradition of the Brooklyn Museum, other museum educators also subscribe to the notion of the museum as a participatory environment. Several museums around the country are adapting this dramatic philosophy, especially the children's museums. Outstanding examples include the Children's Museum in Boston and the Manhattan Laboratory Museum in New York City. At The Manhattan Laboratory Museum the exhibits are designed for viewers to experience directly the objects through their senses. If there were directive signs on the walls, they would no doubt say: "Please Touch!" Many of the exhibits are larger than life in scale and are built with movable parts. There are three thematic areas: "Looking at Ourselves," an exploration of personal perception; "Looking at Family and Culture," an exploration of local cultural traditions; and "Looking at our Natural Environment," an exploration of urban wildlife.

The Manhattan Laboratory Museum is organized to accommodate groups of school children, pre-school to eighth grade. Within the museum's Center for Art Education, the children participate in art, music, and drama workshops, and their teachers learn how to integrate the arts within their school curricula. Recent dramatic activities at the museum have included a participatory theatre version of *Alice in Wonderland*, mask and makeup workshops, and creative dramatic experiences.

In a descriptive flyer the writers specified that the focus of the Manhattan Laboratory Museum is on "how we see and what we bring to our seeing— our past personal experience and our shared cultural expectations."[2] If the museum experience, in general, can be defined in these terms, educational drama and theatre can play a most vital role in museum education. The dramatic experience is very much about looking at the world from a personal point of view that is very much developmentally, socially, and culturally determined. As we have already seen, the educational drama leader aims to sharpen the personal and the social/cultural vision of each student, whether working with a mythological character, a piece of cardboard, a group of newspapers, or statues.

Drama education and museum education are closely related. Both aim toward the development of the ability to see artifacts of the world outside in relation to the inner world of the self, which grows in understanding and awareness through the interaction. The museum is one environment that underlines the transformational nature of drama. Not only are inanimate objects animated, but human beings transcend their limited roles and experiences through simple flights of the imagination.

NOTES

1. WCBS-TV, *Sunrise Semester*, "Drama in Education: The Museum as a Source of Drama Education" (November 12, 1979).

2. "Manhattan Laboratory Museum: Internships," a publicity brochure.

BIBLIOGRAPHY

Aibel-Weiss, Wendy, and Bernadette Brown. "A Theatrical Solution to the Problems of Summer Day-Camp Groups in an Urban Museum." *Curator* 22, no. 4 (December 1979): 271-80.

_____. "Theatre in the Gallery." *Museologist*. Spring 1980, no pagination.

Shadows Hardly Ever Smile. A 16mm. film produced by Chamba Films, N.Y., 1972.

5
DRAMA AND THEATRE
IN THE CHURCH

It was during the Medieval Period that the first church dramas began to appear. As Richard Courtney pointed out:

> The Mass itself of course has the seeds of drama—chanted dialogue and a theme of action—but not the essential quality of impersonation.
>
> Impersonation began with the trope sung during the night before Easter. A trope was an extra chant written to accompany church music on special occasions. . . . In the Mass, the trope had been sung by the choir. When repositioned, it became a separate little scene performed at Matins on Easter morning; much like a tiny opera, three people impersonated the Marys and one the angel before an improvised sepulchre.[1]

Eventually, the small-scale tropes evolved into more complex dramatizations of Easter and Christmas stories. The Bible stories were enacted in the church by priests. As these plays achieved a wide popularity, the dramas began to be written in the vernacular and performed outside the church proper, although still on the church grounds. Through this linguistic and spacial separation, the church dramas became more secularized. Eventually, the dramas were produced and performed by laypersons, guild members who would enact cycles of miracle plays based upon biblical stories and the lives of the saints. These plays included many secular elements of farce and mime that appealed to the medieval audiences.

Given this history, it is no wonder that the church continues to be a most natural environment for drama and theatre. During the 1950s and the 1960s, at the beginnings of the Off-Broadway avant-garde movement in New York City, several churches provided homes for gifted theatre artists.

Perhaps the most notable was the Judson Memorial Church, the home of the Judson Poet's Theatre since 1961. The founder and director of that theatre is the Reverend Al Carmines, who also served as minister of the church. Carmines is a composer, playwright, director, and performer whose productions include Gertrude Stein's *In Circles*, Maria Irene Fornes's *Promenade*, Aristophanes's *Peace*, and his own *Christmas Rappings*. In a recent interview Carmines discussed his theatre and its relationship to the church.[2]

Interviewer: What is the relationship between the Judson Poet's Theatre and the Judson Memorial Church?

Al Carmines: When we began the theatre in 1961, there wasn't much of a relationship, really. We began the theatre as a service to the artists, because we felt the artists needed space and a congregation to see what they had done. Gradually, through the years, as suspicions had been allayed on both sides, there has come to be a very close relationship between the church and the artists. Today, I think that relationship is as close as ever.

Interviewer: Could you talk about that relationship a bit?

Carmines: I think one of the things the artist does for the church members is to humanize them. It used to be people were divided into saints and sinners by church members. And what the artist does is to humanize the sinner and humanize the saint, show the foibles, the joys, the unhappiness, the sadness, the tragedy of everyone's life. And in humanizing them I think the church is immensely enriched. On the other hand, I think the church provides for the artist the kind of support that a lot of artists are looking for—a group of people who say we are going to stand by you and be with you, whatever you do. I think that is a very supportive and mutual relationship.

Interviewer: Would you say that the church is a natural environment for drama and theatre?

Carmines: Yes, it certainly is, because drama and theatre occur in every worship service. As soon as you decide to have a hymn after a prayer, you are making an aesthetic decision, as well as a religious decision. As soon as you decide to have your church in one form of architecture or another, you've made an aesthetic decision. So I think that drama is a natural place for the church, and the church for drama.

Interviewer: What kind of plays have you been developing over the years?

Carmines: We began by doing one-act plays, most by poets like Molinaro, George Dennison, Bob Nichols. That's why we called ourselves the Judson Poet's Theatre. Then we moved into what we call the musical state in Judson history where we did one-act musicals for about four or five years. By that time, in 1968 and 1969, so many Off-Off Broadway theatres had developed. When we began there were only three: the Cafe

Cino, The Cafe LaMama, and ourselves. I decided that we needed to do something different from the other Off-Off Broadway theatres, so I developed the concept of the oratorio and invited anyone to sing with us in a production. We had 103 people in our first oratorio; in others: 80, 60, 90. That has been a very successful contribution.

Interviewer: What about the content of your plays over the years? Do they deal with ethical and religious themes?

Carmines: I don't think the plays have dealt mostly with religious themes, because in the very beginning when we started the theatre, we decided that we would not be a religious theatre, in the sense that some churches do religious drama. We did drama by people who were writing as much against God as for God. I think our themes, however, in the past five or six years have been, more than anything, political. We've been very concerned about what's happening in the country, what's happening in terms of people, what's happening in the church. We have mostly drawn our themes from political undercurrents in the society.

Interviewer: And how about your music? What kinds of music have you been writing and what are your main influences?

Carmines: I didn't start to compose until I was already a minister and had been at Judson for a year and a half. It was very spontaneous, really. We were doing a play directed by Lawrence Kornfeld, and he said we needed some music. I improvised, and the cast loved the music and said: "Let's keep it in." I decided I was a composer. Since then I have been composing fast and furiously. The influences on me are Mozart, Kurt Weill, and Bessie Smith, if I had to name three. I'm very interested in the blues. I'm terribly interested in what Weill did with minor and major kind of shifts. And I emulate Mozart in terms of melodic strains.

Interviewer: What about church music?

Carmines: I have composed some hymns and some anthems, also using those same kinds of strains. I don't think any one particular kind of music is religious or irreligious. So I might compose a hymn to a very jumpy kind of show tune or compose a hymn to a kind of jazz tune. I believe all music is a gift of God.

Examples of Carmines's music include "Song from the Bonus Army," a spirited piece written about a group of war veterans who, in 1932, marched on Congress to demand an increase in benefits; "Ordinary Things," a love song between Gertrude Stein and Alice B. Toklas from Carmines's play *The Faggot*; and "They Call Me the Virgin Mary," from Carmines's *Joan*, a duet between a latter day Joan of Arc, portrayed as an unhappy hippie, and the Virgin Mary, who visits Joan on the streets of the East Village in Manhattan.

In continuing the interview Carmines discussed the connections between his theatre and the Greenwich Village community:

Interviewer: Who are the actors in your productions? Are they Equity members? Do they come from the Greenwich Village community?

Carmines: They come from all over—Queens, Brooklyn, Westchester, Rockland County, and Greenwich Village. Many of them are members of Equity; some of them have appeared on Broadway or Off-Broadway. And yet something draws them to the church to do a production once or twice a year. So they represent everyone from highly professional people to people who have never been on stage before.

Interviewer: Do you see your work as a community-based theatre, and what does the concept of community theatre mean to you?

Carmines: I don't really see it as a community theatre. I think a community theatre does things that will be popular with the community. They do popular musicals like *The Most Happy Fella*. We are an avant-garde professional theatre; at least that's how we see ourselves. We tend to do works that would not be done in community theatre. We tend to use people who wouldn't be comfortable in community theatre. In some sense we are a community theatre in that our cast, particularly in the oratorios with eighty or one hundred people, form a kind of family that's very close, that has fights and joys and everything else that a family has. But we see ourselves finally as a professional, experimental theatre.

Interviewer: What about your relationship to your immediate community, the West Village?

Carmines: We've always had a close relationship to the West Village. We run our productions for three or four weekends, and we always say that the first weekend is for members of the church and friends; the second weekend is for the West Village; and the third weekend can be anybody. We have a close relationship with that community in that we deal with issues that the West Village is concerned about: homosexuality, poverty, crime, politics.

Interviewer: I'd like to explore with you the function of theatre. Does theatre serve a function similar to that of religion for you?

Carmines: No, not really, although theatre and religion, I think, share many things in common. But I don't think they're the same thing. I remember coming to a symposium led by Peter Brook. A woman said to him: "Peter Brook, don't you think that religion and theatre are the same thing?" And he said: "Madam, you're on the road to fascism." I understood that, because I think theatre and religion are very different. They have different moral guides, different kinds of objectives. What they share is expression, finally. Both are expressions of the human spirit, and in that sense they're close.

Interviewer: Would you say, though, that theatre began from religion?

Carmines: Yes, it probably did begin from religion, until it went beyond the bounds of religion. Then it became anti-religion. So theatre has had a very strange relationship with the church or any organized religion. It has been embraced at times and at other times hated. We're in a period now where it's being embraced for a while, but I expect a time will come when we'll be thrown out again and despised again.

Interviewer: Are you aware of other churches or synagogues doing the same kind of work as you?

Carmines: Some are. St. Peter's Lutheran Church, St. Mark's Episcopal Church, St. Clement's Episcopal Church, and several other churches in New York are engaged in religious drama, or just regular drama, and I'm proud of them.

Interviewer: I'm sure some people think of the relationship between drama and religion as religious education, the acting out of Bible stories. Do you see validity in using more improvisational drama to teach religion?

Carmines: Yes, I do. I think improvisational drama is great for church committees, to get out their hostilities, and to get out what they want to say. I think for children, also, it's enormously helpful to act out the stories from the Old Testament that are so dramatic and so filled with tragedy and joy. When the stories are told, somehow something is missing, but when they're acted out, I think it's enormously helpful. So I think there is that part of drama that is good for the church.

Interviewer: What about the traditional Christmas play, performed in so many churches? Each year you do a production of *Christmas Rappings.* Could you talk about how that developed.

Carmines: Christmas Rappings began about ten years ago when I wanted to take the Christmas story literally from the Bible. I took the language of the story, itself, totally from the scripture. But I set it to many, many different styles of music. I set it to a tango, to jazz pieces, to country-western. A friend of mine bet me that I couldn't set the geneology to music, which is so-and-so begot so-and-so, who begot so-and-so. . . . I decided that I could do that, and I used the history of music from Bach all the way up to John Cage. So *Christmas Rappings* is that kind of a piece. It's straight in terms of its words, and it goes all over the place in terms of its music.

Interviewer: What about other groups who are working with the traditional Christmas material?

Carmines: I think working with the Christmas story is a very delicate thing. On the other hand, it can become terribly smug. You can simply tell it and sing it in the kind of self-righteous way that turns everyone off. It doesn't illuminate anything by imagination. On the other hand, you can become a little bit sacreligious in telling the story. I think *Christmas Rappings* walks the middle path. It tells the story with great joy and delicacy, but it finally doesn't ever make fun of the story. And I think that's very important. I think other groups have also been interested in the Christmas story, but I have really never seen anything they have done that is quite like *Christmas Rappings*.

Interviewer: Did you see the recent performance of a reading of St. Mark's Gospel?

Carmines: That was Alec McCowen. I think that was very good. Part of it was because Alec McCowen is such a great actor. Part of it is because the Gospel of Mark is the tersest and most dramatic, in some ways, of all the gospels. Reading that story in one evening to an audience was terribly moving.

Interviewer: Could you talk about your current production, *Dr. Faustus Lights the Lights.*[3]

Carmines: We're engaged in our seventh Gertrude Stein opera. We began with *What Happened?* then *In Circles*, then five more. *Dr. Faustus Lights the Lights* takes the Faust legend by Goethe, Marlowe, Gounod, and turns it on its head. Stein sees Faust as a different kind of hero than the others did. She sees the woman as representing something different too. She sees Faust as a kind of Promethean figure who invents light. The stage is going to be lit up like no other stage in New York. Gertrude Stein is a kind of patron saint of Judson Poet's Theatre. We continue to do her plays.

Interviewer: Why is Gertrude Stein so important to you?

Carmines: I think because, strange as it may seem, from people who've read her, she says things more clearly than any modern playwright I know of. When she speaks and describes an apple or a pear or a painting or a person, she is so careful to describe it exactly to a "T." For a composer, like myself, that's terribly important, because I can work with her words and the repetition of her words in a very musical way.

Interviewer: How can other clergymen and women, who do not share your gifts for drama, use drama and theatre in their congregations?

Carmines: One of the ways I have been advocating for years is that congregations adopt playwrights and give them full sway to write a drama about anything that's occurring in the church at the time or in the world at the time. I don't think that "professional" means you have to have been on Broadway or Off-Broadway. "Professional" means that you do your job well. I think that churches can do drama, dance, painting, all of those things, with professional standards, without having a talented minister.

The relationship between the church and the theatre is extremely complex. The Judson Memorial Church and several others mentioned above have produced or encouraged many diverse forms of theatre for years. Also, religious or church-related dramas have been a mainstay of professional theatres for centuries. Recent commercial productions have included Elizabeth Swados's dramatization of the Passover story, *The Haggadah*, as well as Bill C. Davis's *Mass Appeal* and Alec McCowen's performance of St. Mark's Gospel. Both the church's presentation of sometimes secular theatre and the theatre's presentation of sometimes religious drama relate directly to audiences in a community who need to establish or redefine their relationship to religion through theatre.

A unique example of a theatre that fully exemplifies both the sacred and the secular is the Bread and Puppet Theatre, directed by Peter Schumann. This group performs in churches, streets, schools, theatres. Its concerns are political, aesthetic, and transcendental. Its puppet plays are often based upon Bible stories, as well as folk and fairy tale material, current political events, and classical dramatic texts. After each performance actors engage in a kind of theatrical sacrament, distributing bread to the audience.

The Bread and Puppet Theatre is in part a self-contained community of puppeteers, based in Vermont, who live and work together, creating a lifestyle that is mirrored in their art. They have played to audiences in New York churches, Vermont farms, Iranian streets, Parisian theatres, and offered people in a wide variety of communities the highest ideal of both theatre and religion—"An insight into the (value-laden) nature of things."[4]

Shifting to educational drama, we find frequent applications to religious education. Pam Woody, for one, has written about ways to apply informal and creative drama to the teaching of Bible stories.[5] In a recent article she documented an approach to teaching the story of the Prodigal Son through the educational drama methods of Dorothy Heathcote.[6]

Given a confluence of indigenous church drama, relevant theatrical productions in several settings, and informal drama applied to religious education, we begin to see the total picture of drama and theatre in the church. The values in any of these forms for any individual are significant: the development of a sense of shared community, of insight, of joy.

NOTES

1. Courtney, *Play, Drama, and Thought*, pp. 178.
2. WCBS-TV, *Sunrise Semester*, "Drama in Education: The Church as a Source of Community Drama" (November 14, 1979).
3. Gertrude Stein's *Dr. Faustus Lights the Lights* was directed by Al Carmines at the Judson Memorial Church in November 1979.
4. Stefan Brecht, "Sacral Theatre," *The Drama Review* 14, no. 3 (1970): 81.
5. Pam Woody, "A Comparison of Dorothy Heathcote's Informal Drama Methodology and a Formal Drama Approach in Influencing Self-esteem of Preadolescents in a Christian Education Program" (Ph.D. diss., Florida State University, 1974).
6. Pam Woody, "Informal Drama in Religious Education: An Innovative Approach," *Children's Theatre Review* 25, no. 3 (1976): 13-17.

BIBLIOGRAPHY

Bruce, Violet R., and Joan D. Tooke. *Lord of the Dance: An Approach to Religious Education.* Oxford: Pergamon, 1966.

Burger, Isabel B. *Creative Drama and Religious Education.* Wilton, Conn.: Morehouse-Barlow Co., 1977.

Burton, E. J. "The Communication of Religious Experience: Myth, Symbol, and Allegory." *Discussions in Developmental Drama 8,* Department of Drama, University of Calgary (August 1973): 3-31.

Ehrensperger, Harold A. *A Conscience on Stage.* New York: Abingdon-Cokesbury Press, 1947.

Fedder, Norman J., ed. *Wrestling with God: An Anthology of Contemporary Religious Drama.* New Orleans: Anchorage Press, 1982.

Miller, Donald; Grayton Snyder; and Robert Neff. *Using Biblical Simulations.* Vol. 2. Valley Forge, Pa.: Judson Press, 1975.

Rott, Dale, ed. *Religion and Theatre.* Vol. 1, no. 4. Children's Drama Issue. St. Paul, Minn.: Religious Drama Project, University and College Theatre Association, 1977.

Woody, Pam. "A Comparison of Dorothy Heathcote's Informal Drama Methodology and a Formal Drama Approach in Influencing Self-esteem of Preadolescents in a Christian Education Program. Ph.D. dissertation, Florida State University, 1974.

_____. *Creative Dramatics as a Subject or Method in Religious Education: A Bibliography.* Los Angeles: Religious Drama Committee of the Children's Theatre Association of America, 1976.

_____. "Informal Drama in Religious Education." *Religious Education* 71, no. 6 (1976): 629-42.

_____. "Informal Drama in Religious Education: An Innovative Approach." *Children's Theatre Review* 25, no. 3 (1976): 13-17.

_____. *Religious Plays for Children, Youth, and Family Audiences: A Bibliography.* Los Angeles: Religious Drama Committee of the Children's Theatre Association, 1976.

6
DRAMA AND CONFLICT
IN THE COMMUNITY

TRAINING COUNSELORS THROUGH IMPROVISATION

Turning our attention to the streets and families of a community, we find two other settings where drama can be applied. In focusing on crisis situations, such as assault and child abuse, the community personnel involved—police officers, social workers, and medical personnel—are not often sensitized to the needs of the victims. Given the rapid increase in so many communities of violent crimes such as rape, and given continued tensions within traditional family units that have resulted in child abuse and other violent crimes, it becomes evident that human service personnel must develop skills to counsel the victims of such crimes successfully.

Traditional counselor education has not generally addressed itself to crisis situations, but rather to more controlled, ongoing group or individual sessions. Newer forms of crisis intervention training have been successful, but the trainees tend to be higher level mental health professionals, rather than the paraprofessional, police, and medical workers who most often initially encounter individuals in crisis.[1] For the most part, police and hospital emergency departments are staffed by people with limited training in crisis intervention techniques.

To meet the needs of training personnel in hospitals, police departments and many social service agencies that deal with community crisis situations, several organizations have adopted drama techniques. For example, the New York City Police Department now routinely uses simulations and role-playing to train detectives and officers in coping with holdups. In a recent article Leonard Buder described one dramatic training program set in a simulated tavern.[2] There, officers in the roles of holdup men confront a group of trainees in the roles of off-duty officers. The holdup scenes are acted out and then critiqued.

A second outstanding example of drama applied to training is in the work of the Criminal Justice Repertory Group (CJs) of John Jay College of Criminal Justice in New York City. The CJs, founded in 1970, are a group of theatre artists and criminal justice and social service professionals, who have extended improvisational techniques to the training of those individuals who must deal with people in crisis. In a recent workshop and interview with the associate directors of the CJs, Joyce St. George and Frank Canavan, their dramatic methods of training counselors were demonstrated and discussed:[3]

Interviewer: How did you discover that improvisation was useful in training counselors to deal with crisis situations?

Joyce St. George: Counselors have to deal with people in crisis, which means the clients are going to be in a state of emotional upheaval. Training them through improvisation allows us to take the situations that they might face in real life and bring them into the classroom. They can see the situation they may confront one day, and they can participate in it. It helps them gain experience and knowledge before they actually go out there.

Interviewer: How do you find your material for improvisation?

Frank Canavan: We rely very heavily on actual case histories. If someone has a particular problem, he'll come to us and say, for example: "I have a problem with a runaway." He"ll give us a case history, and we'll turn that into an improvisation.

Canavan explained that the CJs usually work in a classroom setting. In demonstrating their case study approach, he chose an example of training a counselor to work in a social service office with a family crisis situation. Joyce St. George played the role of a teenage runaway. Canavan played the role of her father. A volunteer trainee, Boyd Masten, played the role of the counselor in a social service office. Canavan set up the scene:

Frank Canavan (to the trainee): The police department has brought to you a young girl, fifteen years old. She was found in the company of a twenty-three-year-old man in a stolen car. Because of her age she was brought to the social service office. The father has been notified. He's on his way to pick his daughter up. It is your role as a counselor to help these two people in their time of crisis.

(Enter Joyce St. George, as the teenage girl.)

Counselor Trainee: Hello, Joyce. My name's Boyd. I need to speak to you for a few minutes.

Joyce: I already talked to the cops.

Counselor: Well, your father is on his way to pick you up. Before you go home, we'll need to know. . . .

Joyce: I gotta go home?

Counselor: Yes, you have to go home. You're in a court situation now. You've been involved in a stolen car.

Joyce: I'm not arrested. Nobody said I was arrested.

Counselor: No, but you now are involved. . . .

Joyce: But I didn't do anything.

Counselor: Well, I don't know about that. All I know is that your father's going to come and pick you up, and we don't want to have any complicated problems later. Is there any particular reason why you couldn't get along with your father? Was there an argument, or was there some reason you left home?

Joyce: Yeah.

(Enter Frank, as the father.)

Father: In trouble again, hah?

Counselor: Mr. Canavan, hello. My name is Boyd Masten. Won't you sit down. We need to try to. . . .

Father: Listen, I'm really embarrassed here, and I'm sorry she's gotten into trouble. Is she under arrest here or what?

Joyce: Why couldn't Mom pick me up?

Father: Shut up!

Joyce: Why couldn't Mom pick me up?

Father: I said shut up!

Counselor: Now let's discuss this quietly.

Joyce: You see what I mean? That's all he ever does to me.

Counselor: Is your wife at home?

Father: Listen, my wife can't handle these kinds of problems. I have to make all the decisions at home.

Joyce: See, he always does that to Mom. You do that all the time to her.

Counselor: Let's discuss what's going on here. Joyce, you're going to be leaving to go back home, and we don't want to have any complicated problems when that happens.

Father: There's no problems. She'll listen to what I say, and there's no problems.

Joyce: And then I'll run away again. Doesn't make a difference. So send me home.

Counselor: That's the problem. We can't have you do that again, so we want to try to prevent that.

Joyce: Tell him not to report me.

Father: Tell her not to run away.

Counselor: Could you speak to your mother? I think what we should do is sit down. . . .

Joyce: He won't let my mother talk.

Counselor: Perhaps we should get together and have a family talk. If you can't concentrate and you can't discuss anything with each other, then you would have a tendency to run away again.

Father: Can you promise to get her not to run away again if I bring in my wife?

Counselor: We cannot make any promises.

Father: Look at the way she's sitting there. She's not interested in any of this. She's a punk kid.

Joyce: He's gonna do the same thing all over again. Right? Embarrass me in front of my friends again, right?

Counselor: We don't want the same thing to happen again, and that's the point.

Joyce: He's always talking about my friends.

Father: Well, you have some bad friends.

Joyce: What about your friends?

Father: What would you do?

Counselor: It's probably a good idea if we could get everyone together and sit down and calmly, after this crisis is over. . . .

Joyce: You're not going to get him to calm down.

Father: Shut up!

Counselor: Would it be possible to get together with your wife some time and. . . .

Joyce: He's not going to let my mother do anything. Every time my mother tries to help. . . .

Father: If it takes her mother to be here, then I'll bring her in.

Following the dramatization St. George and Canavan asked the classroom group to pose questions to them. Questions can be of two kinds: technical questions asked of the actors out of role and exploratory questions asked of the actors in their roles of father, daughter, and counselor. Examples follow:

Question: Joyce, do you in these training sessions expect the trainee to resolve the situation right there?

Joyce: Not usually. It's a practice session, and conflict or crisis resolution usually takes a long time. We try to have the counselor learn to listen to the two disputants, learn to take in as much of the story as he can, and try to have the people return.

Q: Boyd, as the counselor, who did you feel was manipulating you?

Boyd Masten: It's a difficult situation, not knowing all of the background history. I was feeling manipulated by both people at the same time, trying to decide what was the basic conflict. At the same time, I was arranging for having everybody come back for counseling in the future.

Q: Frank, do you think the father is willing to come back for counseling?

Frank: I believe so. At this point in his life he feels inadequate. He needs desperately to feel that the daughter, who is an extension of himself, will be able to be a winner in the world. I think it's important for him to realize that he can accomplish something, and if it takes thorough sit-down sessions with the counselor, he'll do it.

Q: Who would be in the class where you would do this improvisation?

Frank: In this case it would be social service workers, who must cope with runaways. We would come in and do a whole training package for them. This would be just one improvisation.

Joyce: It can also be related to police work. There are several juvenile diversion programs where police are asked to intervene in some sort of family crisis where a child is arrested.

Canavan then set up another improvisation dealing with a crisis confronting women—rape. He instructed a second counselor, Flora Colao:

Canavan: You are now in an emergency room of a large metropolitan hospital. A woman has been brought in who was raped in her home. You have been with her for the last hour and a half. She has received medical attention and has been interviewed by the police department. It is your job to wait with her until her husband comes and to counsel both people if the need arises.

(Enter Joyce, as the rape victim.)

Counselor: Hi, Joyce. I just spoke to the head nurse. She called your husband, and he's on his way now.

Joyce: He's on his way?

Counselor: Yes.

Joyce: Do I have to go through any more tests?

Counselor: No. As far as tonight is concerned, you're all finished. You have an appointment to come back in a week and another appointment to come back in six weeks. The police officer said before he left that a detective will be calling you at home in a couple of days.

Joyce: So I just go home now?

Counselor: Yes. Have you thought about what you want to tell Frank? The nurse only told him that you were assaulted, and that you're here.

Joyce: I thought a lot, and I just don't know what to do. We've never had anything like this in our family. The kids have never even been in a hospital. I don't know how he's going to take it. I'm just so scared of hurting him.

Counselor: Sometimes it helps to think about what his best reaction would be and what his worst reaction would be.

Joyce: He's gonna tell me I can't have the business any more. I know that. I know he's not gonna let me have any more people in.

Counselor: It's hard to make a decision in the middle of a crisis. Do you think he might consider coming in for counseling? We have some male counselors involved in the program.

(Enter Frank, as the husband.)

Husband: Joyce, are you OK? What happened?

Joyce: Frank, this is Flora. She's been helping me out.

Husband: I got a call she was assaulted. Is she all right?

Counselor: Yes.

Husband: She see a doctor?

Counselor: Yes. She's been through the whole process. She has an appointment to come back in a week and then in six weeks. Joyce, do you want to tell him what happened?

Joyce: I gotta tell you something.

Husband: What?

Counselor: Do you want me to tell him?

Joyce: I don't know how.

Counselor: Mr. Canavan, as the nurse told you, your wife was assaulted. What she didn't tell you was that your wife was sexually assaulted. And she's been through the whole process now.

Husband: You mean raped?

Counselor: Yes.

Husband: Oh, God!

Counselor: She's OK physically now.

Husband: Where did it happen?

Joyce: In the house.

Husband: How could it happen in the house? I have locks on the windows. And I have two locks on the doors.

Joyce: I didn't mean to. He said he was a salesman.

Frank: It's my fault. That stupid business. I should have. . . .

Joyce: I'm sorry.

Counselor: Mr. Canavan. . . .

Husband: No, I shouldn't have let her have that business.

Counselor: It's not anybody's fault.

Husband: It is. I should have laid the law down.

Joyce: He's the first one I didn't check. I'm sorry.

Husband: There'll be no more business. That's the first thing. I'll put more locks on the door. I'll. . . .

Counselor: Mr. Canavan, something that might help you to understand what Joyce is going through right now is that she's very frightened. . .

Husband: I'm frightened, too!

Counselor: . . . and feeling very vulnerable. One of the things she will need from you now, more than ever before, is a sense of calm, but also a sense of control. She lost control of her life in that situation. Unfortunately, the hospital setting is not the best place to be. What she needs now is a sense of things getting back together. To try to make a decision like that in the middle of a crisis. . . .

Husband: Lady, don't tell me what I'm gonna do here. I know my wife and I know my family. I wanna protect my family, and I know how to protect my family. It was my fault. . . .

Joyce: Frank, don't take it away from me. I'll sit around all day thinking of this.

Husband: Fine, but you'll be sitting around safe. I cannot have people walk into my house like this. I should have said no at the beginning, and you never would have been raped.

Joyce: But Flora said it could've happened anywhere.

Counselor: It could've been anywhere. It could've been anyone in any number of situations. It just happened to be this particular situation. We've seen women of all ages and all different backgrounds in every kind of situation—at home, on the street, in a supermarket. . . .

Husband: OK. If you're gonna guarantee me that my wife will never get raped again, I will let her. . . .

Counselor: I wish I could make that guarantee, Mr. Canavan.

Husband: What am I supposed to do now? I'm supposed to go home and have the same thing happen all over again?

Joyce: Maybe we can move.

Husband: How can I afford to move?

Joyce: We'll find a way.

Counselor: Mr. Canavan, the problem is trying to make a decision in the middle of a crisis. I think it would be better if things calm down a little bit. You're both in a state of shock. When the shock wears off, it'll be easier to think more clearly and to come up with a decision that you both can feel comfortable with. Right now, in the middle of a crisis, you're both trying to make everything better immediately, and that's not going to happen. It's going to take time.

Husband: How much time?

Counselor: It varies with each individual situation. We can offer you a number of services here. We have a counseling program that both of you can be part of.

Joyce: Can we try it? I gotta know when. I don't know. I don't know how I'm gonna feel. I know it's ugly at home. I don't wanna be there.

Husband: OK, fine. But no more business.

Joyce: Don't do that to me, please.

Husband: Joyce, I made up my mind on that. No more business. I gotta live with myself.

Joyce: I gotta live with myself. I don't wanna sit home all day. Please.

Counselor: OK. Speaking from other situations, I think it's very difficult trying to make this kind of a decision now in a hospital waiting room. It's really not the time.

Husband: You're repeating yourself here, and you're not telling me what I want to know. I want things to be the way they were, and you're not helping me here.

Counselor: I don't know how long it's going to take. From experience, I can tell you you're both in a state of shock. You're both feeling very frightened, angry, and upset, and it is going to take time. We can offer you services throughout that time to help you get things back to the way they were.

Husband: You don't understand. We have our own problems. I've never talked to anybody about them. . . .

Following the dramatization, questions were again asked by the classroom group, as follows:

Q (to the counselor): What can be done for Frank, the husband, in this situation?

Flora Colao: As I was trying to explain to him, we do have a number of support services for Frank and Joyce, separately and together. At this particular time it would be very hard for him. But maybe with a follow-up call or when she comes in for a follow-up visit, we could make an appointment for him.

Q: Joyce, is it important for you to keep your business?

Joyce: Yes. It's about the only thing I can do for myself. The kids are at school. How long can you clean a house? It's been keeping me busy and motivated. It's very important for me to keep that kind of control in my own life.

Q: Flora, is that a good idea for somebody who has just been raped because she had her own business?

Flora: It's been our experience that the quicker she can get back to the routine she is used to, the more quickly she'll be able to resolve the conflict. She may, in time, decide that she doesn't want the business. But at this point, having somebody else take that away from her would be devastating.

Q: Frank, do you think you could be persuaded to have Joyce keep the business?

Frank: At this point in time it would be really difficult for me. Perhaps eventually I could. But now, I feel that somehow I let my family down. I let the defenses down. I cannot imagine anyone convincing me to let her have that business again.

Following the dramatizations and question and answer period, St. George and Canavan discussed their work with improvisation:

Interviewer: What do you see as the main differences between improvisation and other counselor training techniques?

Joyce St. George: Primarily, what others are using now to train counselors are group discussion, role-playing, and general lecture/discussion. The problem is that none of these gives the trainees or students the pre-experience they need before they go out. This training, using improvisation, allows someone to experiment with what he has learned through his other methods and to develop a style. Improvisation removes a lot of the risk of going into the real world unprepared to deal with real victims.

Interviewer: Was the improvisation we just saw based upon a case history?

Frank Canavan: That was based on an actual case history where the wife had been raped and the husband decided there was nothing that could be done other than building a fort around her. He was brought into counseling with his wife, and over an extended period of time came to realize that life does go on, and that his wife needed to know that she could continue to live as she had lived. There were many other problems.

Interviewer: Did they go into counseling together or separately?

Canavan: The woman was in counseling for six months before the husband came in. He had a whole bunch of problems at home with her. He came in by himself for two visits, and then they sat down for three visits with the rape counselor together.

Interviewer: How did you translate the case history into the improvisation?

Canavan: In this case there were two characters plus a counselor. We break the case history down into its component parts. Joyce will assume the role of the rape victim, and I will assume the role of the husband. We each are given our own objectives, justifications, and actions. We are actors and yet we are trainers. When we bring the counselor into the situation, we give him the concepts and the theories he's already learned, then get him to use those skills.

Interviewer: We've already looked at the concept of the actor-teacher or teacher-actor; now the actor-trainer. Have you had a formal background in theatre, as well as in counseling? Is that how you would define an actor-trainer?

St. George: By actor-trainer we mean that we are not just up there to perform. We're up there to teach. We have both had actor training. But we are primarily interested in using the acting in conjunction with teaching, so that if a counselor is going off on a wrong route—say, instead of calming us down, he incites us more, we'll try and work around that to show the person where he's going wrong.

Interviewer: Could you tell us a bit about your group, the Criminal Justice Repertory Group.

Canavan: The group was founded at John Jay College on a concept originally developed at the New York Police Academy in 1968, where police recruits were trained in family crisis intervention.

St. George: They found that 85 percent of the police at that time were getting hurt just from family disputes.

Canavan: The group was founded at John Jay and used primarily to train in the college. They expanded to train other police departments, community service organizations, and other college classes in history, sociology, etcetera.

Interviewer: How do you train your actor-trainers?

Canavan: With strict acting techniques of having objectives, justifications, and actions, as well as short characterizations.

Interviewer: Must they have a counseling or education background?

St. George: No. The group originally had quite a few people from policing, social work, educational, and psychological fields. Really, the background in working with the CJs includes not only acting but exhibiting sensitivity so that counselors can respond to you. It's not just standing up and doing a scene, but doing it for the sake of teaching somebody.

Interviewer: Who in the community benefits from this kind of work?

Canavan: Everyone: the social worker, for example. If he's dealing with a victim in trauma, he loses his fear of further traumatizing that victim. The community is affected by this, because they know that the people properly trained can deal with the problems they face.

Interviewer: Where are you going with this work?

Canavan: Our eventual goal is to start a crisis intervention center. . . .

St. George: . . . where we can be used by different social service and police agencies around the country.

In recent months Joyce St. George and Frank Canavan have developed a new organization, Performing Arts for Crisis Training, based upon their principles of training social service and police personnel through improvisation. Their present work extends to other sectors of the community, as well, including issues concerning the elderly, the medical student, and the alcoholic.

DRAMA AND FAMILY LIFE

There are other examples of social service organizations that dramatize real life situations to explore issues of vital importance in the life of a community. Staying within the area of family conflict, we find a further example of applied drama, this time within a hospital setting in New York City. The work of the Family Life Theatre, located within the Family Life Division of the New York Medical College, complements that of the CJs. Yet as the CJs' concern is primarily social service personnel and counselor education, the Family Life Theatre works in the area of health education.

Described as a teenage improvisational theatre company and educational outreach program, the group has defined its goals as follows:

1. To create a personal and group statement about teen issues that could be shared with a large audience of parents, professionals and other young people;
2. To give young people an opportunity to develop personal skills of communication and leadership qualities which will enable them to share information and make informed, responsible choices;
3. To present and explore in an open forum the emotions and feelings that young people have about issues affecting their lives;
4. To give young people an opportunity to better understand personal relationships and commitments through working together in a group.[4]

In a recent interview and demonstration Edward Welch, co-founder and director of the Family Life Theatre, discussed his community drama work:[5]

Interviewer: How did the Family Life Theatre begin?
Edward Welch: The Family Life Theatre began about ten years ago. Dr. Maria Boria, who heads the Family Life Division, was looking for a way to reach out to young people and involve them actively. I was contacted and came on to develop the program. We thought that theatre as an active, creative experience would be one way of involving young people in concerns about themselves. We also began to realize the need for a public forum for young people to speak out about the issues that concern them most intimately and deeply. So often there just isn't an opportunity for a young person to talk out about the issues that many adults pontificate about. This is one way we have now of putting people together, of

dialoguing, putting a scene on that really is about life, then letting an audience react to that.

Interviewer: Is the purpose the same for the actor and the audience member?

Welch: For the actor, it's going through a process to choose, first of all, the subject matter that he wants to deal with and then to create a character and a situation around that subject matter. For the audience, I think it's a kind of release. Finally, in a public forum we're able to deal with really tough issues openly. The audience can talk objectively about the third character up there. It's not me; it's not you; it's that other person up there who has the problem. In the meantime we can open up and exchange our ideas.

Interviewer: What kind of issues do you deal with?

Welch: We deal with the communication block between young people and their parents or adults in general. We deal with problems of growing up, identity, sexuality, the use and abuse of drugs, alcohol, emotional problems, problems of joy and creativity; also, how to discover that we can resolve problems together.

In a demonstration of their work two teenage members of the Family Life Theatre assume the roles of a mother and father, waiting for their seventeen-year-old daughter, played by a third actor, to return home from a party. It is two A.M., and she was to have returned by twelve.

Within the dramatization the mother and father improvise their concern and anger while waiting and then confront their daughter upon her return. The daughter also presents her point of view and feelings of being misunderstood and overprotected. At the end of the dramatization each actor delivers a soliloquy, summarizing his or her point of view.

The next step in the process, like that of the CJs, is for the audience to ask questions of the actors who respond in role and, in fact, continue the dramatization. An example follows:

Q: Father, I noticed that you were pretty upset. You said that you weren't communicating with your daughter anymore. Why is that? Why don't you sit and talk with her?

Father: It's impossible to talk to her. We used to be very close. We used to talk to each other. But as she got older we started to talk less.

Q: Do you talk to your wife about your daughter? Do you care about her anymore? You just seem to have abandoned her altogether.

Father: I don't think I have a daughter anymore.

Q: Mother, how do you feel about that?

Mother: It's my responsibility. I know it. He leaves it to me. I know he is busy, and he can't always take time to spend with her.

Q: Is it always the mother's responsibility? Doesn't he have any responsibility?

Mother: Yes, he has responsibilities, but I think for the most part, it's my responsibility, because she is a girl, and I think a mother and a girl have a lot more in common than a father and a daughter.

Q: Rita, how do you feel about communicating with your Mom? Do you really let her know what's going on in your life?

Daughter: I can't, because let's say I really tell her what's going on in my life; she'll yell at me. You know. She won't accept me for what I really am. She just wants to hear everything that's going on good, but not my problems.

Q: What kinds of problems are going on that you don't want to share with them?

Daughter: Are you kidding? They'll kill me.

Q: They can't hear you. So what's happening?

Daughter: Well, I'm having problems with my boyfriend. I want to get some birth control, and I don't really know if I should do this.

Q: Do your parents know you're going out with this boy and dating?

Daughter: They expect that I'm dating, but. . . .

Q: They don't know your boyfriend?

Daughter: No.

Q: You wouldn't bring him home?

Daughter: No.

Q: Why?

Daughter: Because he's older. They want me to go out with someone my own age.

Q: Do you think they know you're sexually involved with your boyfriend?

Daughter: Are you kidding?

Q: Father, if you were to know that your daughter was sexually involved with her boyfriend, what would be your reaction?

Father: I'm surprised. She never told me she had a boyfriend. I don't know.

Q: Mother, how do you feel about that?

Mother: I figured she was doing something of the sort. She keeps coming home two hours late. I had no idea it went this far.

Q: Now that you know, do you think you have some responsibility toward your daughter about helping her?

Daughter: She can't deal with it. She has nothing to say, because she can't deal with it.

Q: Do you want to be able to talk to your parents about this?

Daughter: Yeah. I wish I could. But I can't.

Q: Is there anybody you could talk to?

Daughter: My friends, but what do they know? They just tell me to do it. They don't care.

Q: So there's nobody right now you're close to and you feel you can share with and talk about your problems?

Daughter: My boyfriend, but what does he care? He just wants to go to bed.

Q: Anybody in school? Teachers?

Daughter: No.

Q: Father, now that you know that your daughter has nobody to talk to, what do you think you could give her in the way of communication?

Father: That I don't know either. She doesn't talk to me. She doesn't tell me her problems—school, friends, anything.

Daughter: That's because you never ask me. You never say: "Hey, how was school today?" You're too busy doing your. . . .

Mother: That's not true.

Daughter: Yes, it is. You're always covering up for him, you know.

Father: You could come to me.

Daughter: Oh, I'm going to come to you when you're busy?

Father: You could tell me if you have a problem.

Daughter: Yeah, I'm gonna go up to you and say: "Daddy, I have a problem." It's so easy, isn't it?

Father: You could try it.

Daughter: No. I tried it once and you told me: "Go talk to your mother." I talked to her and she tells me: "Ask your father." You know, I'm going back and forth. I feel like a ball.

Q: Can any of you see a way to break through this inability to communicate? You seem locked into your roles. What can you do?

Daughter: I feel if the two of them would get along better, it'd be a happier family and we could talk together. But when your mother and father can't communicate, how am I going to communicate with them?

Mother: That's not the problem. She's making excuses. I think she's wrong in what she's doing, and she knows it. It's something that we didn't bring her up to do. It's something she's gonna have to stop doing, because I'm just not gonna accept it while she's living here.

Q: Do you have a problem communicating with your husband?

Mother: No. I think it's fine.

Q: Father, how about you?

Father: Our marriage is OK.

Q: It sounds to me that you're all putting the blame on the other person. Mother and Father, it sounds to me like you're putting the blame on Rita. And Rita, it sounds to me like you're putting the blame on your parents. Is there any way that you, yourself, might have something to do with this?

Daughter: I don't have anything to do with it. I feel like I'm a normal teenager, that it's not my problem. It's their problem.

Q: Mom?

Mother: I think that's a terrible thing to say. I think she's just putting up excuses. I feel we've done our job well as parents.

Q: Did you do it perfectly?

Mother: No. I know we're not perfect.

Q: How are you not perfect?

Mother: I know there are certain things I was not always ready to talk about.

Q: For example?

Mother: Well, about birth control and actual sex. It's just not something you can sit down with your daughter and tell her about, because. . . .

Daughter: Why not?

Mother: Well, because we were afraid you might go out and do these things. I just thought that by not informing her so much, she may wait longer.

Q: But you didn't talk to her about that. You're just presuming that if you don't talk to her she won't be involved. She's living out in the real world.

Mother: Well, look, they learn about these things in school. They have health education, and they teach them the basics. I think the rest is something you have to experience.

Q: And that's what she's doing.

Mother: Yes, but she's kind of young for that.

Q: But the fact is she is experiencing, and she's had no help from you. We really don't know what she's learned in school.

Q: Father, how do you think your daughter should get her sex education?

Father: It's hard for me to talk with her about that. I feel it's the mother's job. And she could learn that in school.

Mother: Her boyfriend wants to do nothing else. She knows this, and she still goes on. I think it's her fault.

Q: Rita, where do you think your sex education should come from?

Daughter: From your parents, especially your mother. My friends always tell me what they talk about with their mother. It seems so easy and so natural. I have to go out there and ask other people. It feels really uncomfortable.

Father: You should know what's wrong and what's right by now.

Daughter: You don't just go out in the world and know everything. You gotta live through things. Maybe if she told me, I wouldn't be doing some of the things I'm doing today.

Mother: Or maybe you would have done them a year before.

At the end of this improvised question and answer period, Welch made a concluding statement that focused on the main issues of the argument and provided a closure to the drama:

Edward Welch: It seems right now you are beginning to listen to one another, even though you're disagreeing. You're at least sharing your real feelings. Before, you hadn't done any of that. You've been out, Rita, away from them, wanting to be with them and not finding an opening. The mother presumes you're going to learn everything at school. Father says you should know what's right and wrong without any kind of teaching. And the parents are sharing some of their fears and worries. They're not perfect, and I think Rita can accept that. Part of the process is just sharing where we are and how we think and feel.

In training his teenage actors to dramatize issues of concern to themselves and their peers, Welch uses many game techniques, role-playing, and movement exercises. He teaches listening and interaction skills, as well as improvisational skills. Keeping within the tradition of improvisational drama, he does not work with scripted material. The material to be presented generally evolves from the actors' own experiences with their parents, teachers, and peers.

Further training involves health education seminars concerning topics such as sexuality, abortion, and drugs. Before public performance, actors generally train for ten weeks, twelve hours a week in improvisational techniques and three hours a week in health education.

The Family Life Theatre has made a contribution to community life in many cities throughout the United States. They have presented their work at professional conferences, schools, senior citizens groups, family planning groups, and other recreational, social, and health-related organizations. In discussing the values of the Family Life Theatre, Edward Welch noted that although his work is not therapy, it is therapeutic. It often provides a release or catharsis for both actor and viewer. The work always allows the actors and viewers the chance to discuss relevant problems and explore many complex and ambiguous issues of growing up in a particular community at a particular time.

NOTES

1. See, for example, Donna C. Aguilera and Janice M. Messick, *Crisis Intervention* (New York: Mosby Publishers, 1978).

2. Leonard Buder, "Police Learning How to Cope with a Holdup in a Bar," *New York Times*, May 13, 1981, pp. B1, B13.

3. WCBS-TV, *Sunrise Semester*, "Drama in Education: Training Counselors through Improvisation" (November 16, 1979).

4. Anthony Vargas, assistant director for program development, Family Life Division, New York Medical College, from a brochure describing the Family Life Theatre.

5. WCBS-TV, *Sunrise Semester*, "Drama in Education: Exploring Concerns of Teenagers through Drama" (November 19, 1979).

BIBLIOGRAPHY

Boria, Maria C.; Edward J. Welch; and Anthony M. Vargas. "Family Life Theatre and Youth Health Services." *American Journal of Public Health* 17, no. 2 (February 1981): 150-54.

Fink, Albert H., and Keith Brownsmith. "Training Teachers in Behavior Management through Simulations and Role-Playing." *Improving Human Performance Quarterly* 4 (April 1975): 157-64.

Horesji, Charles R. "'Home-made' Simulations: Two Examples from the Social Work Classroom." *Journal of Education for Social Work* 13 (Winter 1977): 76-82.

St. George, Joyce. "The Use of Theatre Techniques in Crisis Intervention Training." (M.A. thesis, New York University, 1980).

Teevan, Katherine Grady, and Harris Gabel. "Evaluation of Modeling-Roleplaying and Lecture-Discussion Training Techniques for Training College Student Mental Health Paraprofessionals." *Journal of Counseling Psychology* 25 (March 1978): 169-71.

7
DRAMA THERAPY IN
THE COMMUNITY

Drama often plays a therapeutic function in the life of a community. Through the efforts of groups such as the CJs and the Family Life Theatre, and through the play of children and the ritual and cultural participation in the drama of the church and the museum, individuals are allowed to release pent-up emotions, act out their fears and hopes, and move toward an understanding of themselves and the communities they live in.

But drama can also become a form of therapy. Eleanor Irwin, a prominent drama therapist, made a distinction between a therapeutic experience and the act of therapy. According to Irwin: "Any experience which helps an individual to feel a greater sense of competence and well-being may be thought of as being therapeutic."[1] She counted among therapeutic experiences the creation of a work of art and the performing of a play on stage, accompanied by applause from the audience.

Many dramatic experiences in everyday life, such as children playing with dolls, adolescents imitating their favorite movie stars, and adults "rehearsing" their behavior before job interviews, can be seen as therapeutic. They allow us to feel more competent and more calm.

Irwin sees therapy, on the other hand, as the planned application of drama/theatre techniques "to aid in remediation, rehabilitation, or personal or social adjustment," and "to bring about intrapsychic, interpersonal, or behavioral changes."[2]

Drama therapy implies an environment removed from the everyday, where everyday experiences can be re-presented, explored, and integrated. This environment can be a classroom, a theatre, a dayroom of a hospital or clinic, or an all-purpose room in any community institution.

Also, drama therapy generally implies work with a group that is in some way disabled. Typical drama therapy groups include the emotionally disturbed, physically disabled, deaf, blind, developmentally disabled, sociopathic, or elderly. Drama therapy is also practiced with individuals who are not clinically disabled, but who are in crisis or in need of more fully realizing their human potential.

The leader of a drama therapy group can be either a trained psychotherapist with substantial background in drama/theatre or an expert in drama/theatre with substantial training in psychotherapy or counseling.

Some would claim that a drama therapist must be medically trained, that is, he or she must be a psychiatrist. Others would insist that drama and therapy are incompatible concepts and that the primary aim of drama/theatre for disabled groups must be aesthetic rather than therapeutic. Because drama therapy is interdisciplinary, combining the art of drama with the science of psychology, integrating an aesthetic process and a therapeutic one, and because both *drama* and *therapy* are conceptually complex terms, confusions are inevitable. But for the field to exist intact, one must be able to transcend a compartmentalized vision and understand that the dramatic experience is inherently interdisciplinary and is rooted in several related modalities.

At present, there is no official certification for drama therapists, since this is a relatively new discipline, and there are few training programs available. One exception is the SESAME program in London, England, founded by Marion Lindkvist, where individuals are trained in movement and drama therapy. Using Peter Slade's child drama techniques and Rudolf Laban's movement techniques, among others, the SESAME method prepares individuals to work with mentally, physically, and emotionally disabled populations.

There is also a professional organization in England, the British Association for Dramatherapists, that has adopted the following definition of drama therapy:

> Dramatherapy is a means of helping to understand and alleviate social and psychological problems, mental illness and handicap; and of facilitating symbolic expression, through which man may get in touch with himself both as *individual* and *group*, through creativity structures involving vocal and physical communication.[3]

In the United States there are several courses and workshops in drama therapy, including those at the University of Pittsburgh, California State University in Los Angeles, Avila College in Kansas City, Antioch College in San Francisco, and Loyola University in New Orleans. Furthermore, there is a professional organization, National Association for Drama Therapy, that sponsors various workshops and conferences and is working toward developing standards and accreditation procedures. Also, a program at the University of Connecticut in Storrs, Media and the Arts for Social Sciences (MASS), combines sociodrama, video, and film to explore significant social issues.

One of the most comprehensive academic programs in progress is at New York University within the Program in Educational Theatre. There, one can study for a master's or doctoral degree in educational theatre with a specialization in drama therapy. The program includes study and training in the related fields of drama/theatre and psychology, as well as practical field-work and internship at various psychiatric hospitals, special schools, nursing homes, and other community institutions serving disabled populations in the New York metropolitan area.

THE ROOTS OF DRAMA THERAPY

At the roots of drama therapy are the elements of play, theatre, ritual, magic and shamanism, catharsis, role-taking and role-playing, and action-oriented psychotherapies such as psychodrama and sociodrama.

The literature on play is vast. Theories of play range from the psycho-analytical through anthropological, behaviorist, and cognitive perspectives. For our purposes the most relevant ones are those of Freud and Piaget. For Freud, play is a symbolic expression of the unconscious.[4] For Piaget, play is a means of assimilating new experience, of taking in new information about the world and transforming it into knowledge.[5] Freud's theory is affective; Piaget's, cognitive. Taking both together, we can see play as an inherent process that reflects the emotional and intellectual growth of all human beings.

Peter Slade, as we have seen, viewed play as the beginning of all dramatic activity. For Slade, play is the method by which the infant tests out and masters reality, and the child begins to discover rhythm and movement, social awareness, and a sense of self. According to Slade: "Lack of play may mean a permanent loss of ourselves."[6]

Many practicing child psychotherapists would agree with Slade and often use play as a form of therapy to foster healthy affective and cognitive development.[7] In effect, these therapists are employing a dramatic modality to treat their clients, for, as we have seen above: "Wherever there is Play, there is Drama."[8]

Performance theory, as relating to modes and purposes of theatre performance, also provides a source for drama therapy. During the twentieth century several prominent theatre artists and theorists have viewed theatre as an instrument for intrapsychic and/or interpersonal change. The theatre artist and theorist, Bertolt Brecht, wrote:

Sink down in the filth
Embrace the butcher
But change the world: it needs it![9]

For Brecht, the theatre was a forum where man's inhumanity to man, his filthiness and butchery, could be displayed and debated, and where strategies for change could be considered.

For Antonin Artaud, the theatre was like the plague, an extreme form of revelation and purgation of the "latent cruelty" within the mind of man and the streets of his communities. Yet in this dark vision of the theatre Artaud also saw the hope for a new world. He wrote:

> The theatre . . . releases conflicts, disengages powers, liberates possibilities. . . . The action of the theatre, like that of plague, is beneficial, for, impelling men to see themselves as they are, it causes the mask to fall, reveals the lie, the slackness, baseness, and hypocrisy of our world . . . and in revealing to collectivities of men their dark power, their hidden force, it invites them to take, in the face of destiny, a superior and heroic attitude they would never have assumed without it.[10]

For Constantin Stanislavski, the theatre was a kind of laboratory for changing the individual actor and ensemble of actors into keen observers of life, artists who had access to their creative imagination, movements, feelings, past experiences, and future projections. Speaking in a language of images often borrowed from psychoanalysis, Stanislavski wrote:

> . . . periods of subconsciousness are scattered all through our lives. Our problem is to remove whatever interferes with them and to strengthen any elements that facilitate their functioning.[11]

In the radical theatre of the 1960s and 1970s groups such as the Living Theatre, the Open Theatre, and the Bread and Puppet Theatre commited themselves to the principles of Brecht, Artaud, and Stanislavski in their search to represent a vision of man's cruelty and a re-vision of a sane society inhabited by sane individuals. In speaking of his apocalyptic production, *Paradise Now*, influenced, in part, by the work of the existential psychologist R. D. Laing, Julian Beck of the Living Theatre wrote:

> Anger and violence. Passion, rather. The ravings and raging often carry the performer to a level of poetry and creativity, the unleashing of forces that know the passwords that open sealed passages, the creation of psychic changes that penetrate the armor of the mind.[12]

It is not only in the twentieth century with the new theatre aesthetics of Brecht, Artaud, and Stanislavski but rather throughout the history of theatre that various theorists have looked upon the theatrical experience as healing, both for the individual and the society. As early as Aristotle we find the notion of catharsis, or emotional release, on the part of the spectator. In many early forms of Western theatre, as well as continuous forms of non-Western theatre—for example, that of the Kathakali dance dramas in India and the dance dramas of the Zarma of the Republic of Niger—we find theatrical presentations clearly performed for healing and religious purposes.[13]

Throughout the centuries dance dramas and ritual dramas have been practiced in diverse cultures that incorporate other elements at the roots of drama therapy: ritual, magic, and shamanism. In these dramas actors, usually village priests or shamans, impersonate mythological or religious characters and dramatize a story often reflecting aspects of tension and anxiety within the community. Through the dramatic enactment the audience becomes a kind of congregation that participates emotionally in the enactment and releases its anxieties through tears and/or laughter. An example is the comic ritual dramas of Sri Lanka. As described by Ranjini and Gananath Obeyesekere, these dramas help the male members of the community deal with their fears of castration.[14] The enactment of a myth where the god Sakra is represented as an old, impotent man is exaggerated, allowing members of the audience to ridicule the old man and thus, through laughter, release their own fears of impotence.

Richard Courtney in his research referred to the dramatic dances of the shamans of Siberia and Mongolia, of the witch doctors of African tribes, and the Alfurus of the Celebes, who practice their dramas for magical, therapeutic purposes, that is, to ward off evil spirits and promote a sense of well-being within their communities.[15]

In his book comparing the essence of the theatrical event to shamanism and possession, David Cole referred to many healing-oriented rituals of cultural groups in Haiti, Bali, and India.[16] A Haitian possession ritual, for example, is similar in tone to that of the comic ritual dramas of Sri Lanka. A description by Alfred Métraux follows:

> Whenever a depressing atmosphere develops as a result of the violence of possessions, then Guédé appears, puckish and obscene. He sits on girls' knees and pretends to be about to rape them. The congregation revels in this sort of fun and laughs heartily.[17]

Voodoo and related rituals of projecting feelings and wishes onto inanimate dolls and statues are also examples of a kind of primitive drama therapy.

At the heart of much of the ritual dramas and magical practices is the notion of healing through catharsis, adapted from Aristotle by Freud to explain a psychotherapeutic process of purgation or release. Human beings carry around an enormous emotional burden of unexpressed and unresolved feelings. Through the process of catharsis one releases these feelings by identifying with a dramatic situation that mirrors the experience of the viewer who, fearing for his or her well-being, releases tension in tears or laughter or symbolic action, for example, the manipulation of voodoo dolls.

As catharsis, exemplified in ritual dramas and margical practices, is at the roots of drama therapy, so are the related processes of role-taking, the internalization of a role-model, and role-playing, the imitation, in action, of the role model. Like ritual and dance dramas, role-taking is a social process that fosters a continuity between the individual and the community. Significant role models in one's immediate environment, such as mother, father, sister, brother, become a kind of looking glass through which one sees a reflection of oneself.[18] As we have seen above, as one takes on the roles of others, one develops a fuller sense of self.

The process of role-taking occurs naturally. There are no shamans or priests to guide one through it. Yet when the process breaks down, that is, when one becomes unable or unwilling to take on roles of others, thus limiting one's own repertory of roles, help is needed.

The contemporary Western shaman can be seen as the therapist. The classical psychoanalyst, though, who primarily relies on verbal, narrative means to help a client achieve a greater sense of equilibrium, is not an appropriate choice, given the model of role-taking. One who works through action and drama techniques is more appropriate, because he or she can help the client learn how to assimilate the role models and role behaviors needed to be more fully functional in a society that demands not only a diversity of roles but flexible behaviors within a single role. One primary intervention of the drama therapist, then, is through role-playing, which is the active component of role-taking.

PSYCHODRAMA

The exemplary model for this kind of dramatic therapy is psychodrama, which is both a root and a technique of drama therapy. Psychodrama is one of several action-oriented therapies that lie at the roots of drama therapy. Others include play therapy, Gestalt therapy, and transactional analysis.

Developed in the early 1900s by the Austrian psychiatrist J. L. Moreno, psychodrama is a form of group psychotherapy where the clients act out events of significance in their lives. Through an elaborate process of role-playing and role reversal, the clients are led, by a director, into experiencing and then understanding the dimensions of a conflict. For the client limited in the ability to take on or play a single role, such as mother, father, son, daughter, psychodrama helps that person assume appropriate behaviors and feelings in role. For the client limited in the ability to play several roles, psychodrama helps to increase that person's repertory so that he or she can successfully play diverse roles, all with a degree of competence and with an understanding of the differences between roles.

Sociodrama, an extension of psychodrama, functions in a similar way, but instead of working to help an individual achieve competence and understanding of his or her roles, the director works toward elucidating a social issue, such as sexism, racism, and authoritarianism.

The following dialogue is an example of a psychodrama concerning a man's exploration of his role as son. As mentioned previously, psychodrama and role-playing techniques, in general, usually consist of three stages: a warm-up, the actual body of the drama, and a closure. In a recent demonstration Dr. James Sacks, clinical psychologist and director of the New York Center for Psychodrama Training, began with a verbal warm-up.[19] The setting was in a television studio, and the participants were clients of Dr. Sacks. Sacks asked all of the participants to take hands and then began:

Sacks: How do you feel at the moment?

Mr. A: Sadness and panic. I don't know why I chose to do this.

Ms. B: Nervous and out of control. But I feel it's kinda special to be here, so I guess I'm also excited.

Mr. C: I feel good in general. Expectant. But I do feel tension in my arms here.

Ms. D: I feel nervous. I feel it mostly in my throat. I feel like this is gonna work out well also.

Sacks: Sometimes the act of describing your feelings has an effect on them in itself. Can we do the same thing again, and tell us if there's any difference. Tell us how you feel right at this moment when it's your turn.

Mr. A: More paranoid. More aware of what's going on. Sort of scared of what people are gonna think. Will somebody see this? Will they think less of me? That sort of crazy kind of feeling.

Ms. B: I'm still scared. But it seems that everybody's kind of scared, so I don't feel so lonely about it.

Mr. C: I still feel expectant. A little impatient, wanting to get into something deep.

Ms. D: I feel a little better. I think I feel more nervous holding your hand, because I feel the tension in your hand, and it reminds me that my hand must feel the same way.

Sacks: For this part, it would be a good idea for the person speaking to look down at the floor. That might help block out extraneous stimuli a bit. Think of something that happened in your life, maybe when you were a kid, something that you haven't thought of before. In the first sentence tell us the thing that happened. In the second sentence tell us how you felt at the time the event occurred. If for any reason at all you feel like passing, just pass and we'll go on to the next person.

Ms. B: I'm surprised at what came to my mind. I was at graduation from junior high, and I was in the front row, because I was short, and I wanted to be very serious about it. But my brothers took seats right opposite me, and they kept laughing. I just laughed through the whole thing. It wasn't what I wanted to do, but I appreciated having some humor in what could have been a solemn occasion. It left me with a better memory.

Mr. A: The whole setting brings up theatrical stuff. I remember a show I did when I was involved with scouting. It was a big thing. I invited my family to be there, especially my mother, because I wanted her to approve. She came, and she never acknowledged it. To this day she's never acknowledged how proud she was, and I needed so much for her to say that.

After hearing the experiences of all four participants, Sacks chose Mr. A as a focus, as the protagonist of the psychodrama.

Sacks: In psychodrama we can have people take the part of the auxiliary ego, which means somebody takes the part of somebody else. Since there were feelings about your mother from that time and maybe something still unresolved, would you pick a person to take her part.

Sacks also asked Mr. A to choose a double, a kind of alter-ego who would assume his role and speak for him during moments when he became blocked or avoided the expression of his innermost feelings. Sacks asked the auxiliary ego as mother to face away from the protagonist and for the protagonist to place his hands on her shoulders. The double at all times stood beside the protagonist, mirroring his gestures. Sacks asked Mr. A to compose a letter to his mother.

Mr. A: Dear Mother, I remember where you sat that Sunday. In spite of the fact everybody else was there, how much I just needed your approval, how much I needed you to tell me that you were proud. You never did that. I did so many things just to get you to say that it was good. So many times I still need you to say that.

Double: I was too young sometimes to get that for myself. I need that from you. I especially needed that then, but I still need it now.

Mr. A: Especially since you are the only parent, and I needed you to validate it. . . .

Sacks: Could you now have your mother face you. I'd like to ask you to reverse roles with your mother and to pretend to be your mother. Assume that your mother has actually received that letter. What is it you might have liked her to say to you?

Mr. A, as mother: I do appreciate you. I can't express it the way you probably needed it. But I was very proud of you. And I've been very proud of you many, many times. I wish I could tell you how, but I can't do that. I love you.

Sacks: Reverse back again. In similar words, maybe you can give him the experience he would have liked by taking the role of his ideal mother.

Ideal Mother, played by auxiliary ego: You know, son, it was so moving. You did such a beautiful job. I acknowledged it to everyone else, you know, how good I felt about it. I'm sorry I wasn't able to acknowledge it to you also. It's just communication was so difficult, and I hope you forgive me for not being able to put that in words. I had to lead my own life the only way I could at that time. I hope you continue to do well, even though I haven't always been there for you.

Mr. A: A lot of the things I do now I do because I need you to approve.

Ideal Mother: You're free to do the things you want to do. Whatever you want to do, even if you don't do it well, is fine. It's good and it's enough. I don't mind.

Sacks (to Mr. A): I'm not sure of the feeling inside of you or the extent of the capacity for forgiveness at this point. I wonder if in some non-verbal way you could express what feeling would be in you after hearing your mother speak in this way.

Mr. A (to mother): I'd just like you to hold me and tell me I'm good enough. (They embrace.)

Mother: You're good enough. Whatever you do, it's wonderful for you. Everything that you do is really the best. No one can judge you harshly.

Following this enactment Sacks moved into the closure phase of the psychodrama:

Sacks: Can we sit down for a minute. I feel very cruel breaking that. I'm sure these were meaningful things for others too. I wonder if you could describe anything from your own lives or feelings you had from Mr. A, who gave us a bit of his heart here, that may have touched off something meaningful to you.

Ms. B: It did in me. There's a part of me that always wanted a lot of approval. I always seemed to want more than I could have. Sometimes there didn't seem to be any. And sometimes when there was some, I needed more. Even when I think I don't need so much now, it keeps surprising me how much I still need approval.

Mr. C: I identified very closely with your need. The only difference was the women in my early life did give me a lot of approval, maybe too much, and I didn't get enough from the men. And I always kind of wondered why the men didn't, and I wanted more approval from them. I kind of blamed some of the men in my life for not giving me that kind of approval. It's only now that I've begun to learn that the men did give me the approval. They just weren't demonstrative about it. They did it in other ways. The lesson I have learned is in working it out with my own children, making sure they are aware when I do approve.

During the closure the aim is to verbalize a personal experience based upon an identification with the protagonist. If the protagonists have enacted an authentic drama of themselves, then, in theory, they should have exposed a universal human experience that, like the work of a great playwright, all people can identify with. In that Mr. A's drama concerned a universal issue, a child's need for approval from a parent, all members of the psychodrama group were able to participate in the dramatic experience on their own levels. Through reexperiencing psychodramatically a scene with his mother, Mr. A. learned something further about the complexities of playing both the child and the parent role.

Many aspects of role-playing techniques such as psychodrama resemble those of more primitive ritual dramas, for example, the physical aspects of holding hands and embracing, the symbolic aspects of writing a letter and reversing roles, the projective aspects of doubling and speaking to an auxiliary ego, the cathartic aspects of identifying with a universal human experience and releasing emotion, and the communal aspect of sharing stories from one's life with one another.

There appears to be a universal quality of dramatic experience spanning history, culture, and human developmental stages that promotes a kind of individual and group healing. This dramatic, therapeutic quality is to be found in the play of children; in the theoretical writings and practices of theatre artists; in the rituals and rites of Western and non-Western cultures alike; in the dramatic and therapeutic notions of catharsis, role-taking, and role-playing; and in the practice of psychodrama and related action-oriented therapists. Drama therapists draw upon all of these sources and from them fashion specific treatment modalities "to bring about intrapsychic, interpersonal, or behavioral changes."

This discussion of roots of drama therapy is in no way meant to be complete. Many other elements, including diverse psychological theories of personality and human development, as well as further treatment modalities, must also be integrated into the as yet incomplete theoretical canon of drama therapy.

TECHNIQUES OF DRAMA THERAPY

Most all techniques used by drama educators and theatre artists can be adapted by drama therapists to treat various groups. Some drama therapists use story dramatizations and puppetry to treat emotionally disturbed groups. Others use formal theatre to work with the elderly and the incarcerated. Improvisational work is practiced in most all drama therapy groups to a certain extent.

The group most associated with drama therapy is the emotionally disturbed, since drama therapists most often work in psychiatric hospitals and special schools for the emotionally disturbed. One of the outstanding drama therapists, Gertrud Schattner, has been working with the emotionally disturbed for thirty years. Schattner's work at Bellevue Psychiatric Hospital in New York City is primarily with short-term patients, which poses a particular challenge. Since she meets with the same groups for no more than one or two fifty-minute sessions, she must limit her goals and modify her techniques in order to maximize expressivity without opening up large issues that would take many weeks, months, or years to treat in depth.

In demonstrating her approach to working with short-term psychiatric patients, Schattner led a simulated workshop with four of her students.[20] Before proceeding she explained her particular situation at Bellevue:

> *Gertrud Schattner:* We might start a very structured session which we might have to change on the spur of the moment, because we have to work according to the needs of the special populations. There are patients who want to perform; there are patients who want to do nothing. There are patients who want to just sit there and listen. In starting a session I usually tell them what we will do, but I try to avoid the word therapy, because when I say it is a therapy session, they walk out. If I say it is not a therapy session they also walk out. So I really have to have my eyes on the patients from the moment I come in to let them set the mood for the session.

Then she began a simulated drama therapy session:

> *Schattner:* I'm Gertrud Schattner, and I'm going to work with you today. I'd like to know who you are. I want you to tell me your name. Then I want you not to tell me how you feel, but show me how you feel. I want action, doing.

The students stood in a circle. Each one in turn spoke his or her name and then the words "I feel," followed by a gesture and/or sound.

Schattner: Some of you are very tired or have had medication, so if you feel like sitting, sit; or if you want to get up, get up. What I want to do is simple movements. Put your arms up for a minute. Stretch them forward and then down. Now do it again, but this time, put an idea or image into it. Tell me something you are really reaching for. It can also be more than one thing. Then when you put your arms down, tell me something you want to get rid of. I will start: "I'm reaching for the strength of continuing to work. I'm reaching for all my students and all my patients. I want to get rid of cigarettes, and I want to get rid of pressure." Now reach up for someone and push away what you don't want with all your strength.

As the exercise proceeded around the circle the following examples were offered:

I'm reaching for more energy. I'm reaching for more of my son. I want to get rid of tiredness.
I'm reaching for more time to do what I have to do. I want to get rid of negativity.
I'm reaching out for my family whom I don't see enough of. I want to get rid of disorganization.
I'm reaching for my husband. I want to get rid of cockroaches.

Schattner then shared these anecdotes:

Schattner: Let me give you two examples of actual patients who did this exercise with me. I once had a catatonic patient brought into my session in a wheelchair who was sitting there staring at me for fifty minutes, doing nothing. After the session, as I was leaving the room, he went: "M-m-ma-maaa!" I know if I had time to work with this patient, I might have achieved a little more. The second example was a girl who, when I asked her what she wanted to push away, reacted violently and screamed: "I want to get the hell out of this nuthouse! I want to kill my mother! I want to shoot the cop that brought me here! I want to get out! I WANT TO GET OUT!" She had to be restrained and taken out of the session. But after the session, she came to me and said: "Gert, I thank you so much. It was such a help for me to yell this out. It was such a relief, and I feel so much better."

In demonstrating a second exercise in mirror imagery, used often in educational drama, Schattner began:

Schattner: Look around the group and choose a partner, someone you would like to get to know better. Once you have made your choice, go to the person and stand opposite one another. Try to let your whole body relax. Sense where you feel tense. Try to relax the part of your body that feels tense. When you feel sufficiently relaxed, look at one another and maintain eye contact. Try to look at one another's eyes. Out of the communication between you, one of you will begin to move your hand and later your whole body, if you want to. The other one will try to mirror your movement. Don't watch each other's hand, but look into each other's eyes. Try to continue the movement without breaking eye contact. As the communication between you grows, the one following may begin to lead. Try to let what you receive from your partner affect the movement. If you feel angry or sad or happy, let's see it. Whatever your feelings are, allow yourself to express them in sound or movement or both. Try to let what you see from your partner affect you and your feelings. Go with what is going on. Don't impose any feelings. Allow them to happen and express them in any way you feel.

After the demonstration of these techniques Schattner offered the following thoughts about drama therapy:

Schattner: In drama therapy we use all aspects of drama, from the simplest movements, up to polished performances, for the purpose of helping people of all ages, with all kinds of disabilities, at any time. Improvisations are very important, because usually the patients, themselves, bring up situations which they want to act out. For instance, at Bellevue it's very important for patients about to be released to get ready for their work in the community. There are dozens of improvs we can do to help them get adjusted. I'm thinking of one improvisation we did where a girl was supposed to go to a job interview. She was scared. We set up a scene and acted it out.

Another exercise used often by Schattner is building a thematic machine, for example, a love machine, anger machine, city machine. One participant begins a movement and sound, related to the theme. Others join in, one at a time, becoming interrelated parts of the machine, until everyone is participating. Furthermore, Schattner might ask a verbal group to tell her three lies about themselves. Both exercises are generally enjoyable, as well as revealing. At the conclusion of her sessions Schattner usually asks all participants to stand in a circle, arms around one another, eyes closed, and share one wish for the future.

In applying educational drama and theatre techniques to the demands of a drama therapy group, an important principle is to understand the needs of the individuals in that group and choose the appropriate techniques accordingly. Gert Schattner works on a level appropriate to a short-term psychiatric population. The kinds of extended dramatizations used by Dorothy Heathcote and Gavin Bolton, on the other hand, also have great potential as therapeutic drama when applied to the therapy of a much longer term group that must be able to sustain attention and commitment to the dramatic tasks at hand.

Psychodrama, as we have seen, proceeds rapidly from a more superficial level of exercise to a deeper level of reexperiencing a significant event through role-playing, role reversal, and doubling. As a technique, it has been used with a wide variety of psychiatric and normal populations. Yet again, there are many situations, given the nature of a group and the experience of the director, when this form of treatment is not indicated.

In a recent interview Richard Courtney also discussed several principles and techniques of drama therapy:[21]

Interviewer: How do mental health personnel use drama to work with emotionally disturbed individuals within a hospital setting?
Richard Courtney: Brian Way always used to say about all forms of drama: "Start from where you are." Everybody is different. If you are dealing with individuals who are emotionally disturbed or any other way different from normal, you should attempt to identify who they are and where they are in that moment in time. Accept them as who they are first. You can really do nothing until they can trust. If trust involves hitting, for example, then they've got to hit. As an example, Judith Koltai worked in Victoria, British Columbia, several years ago with two emotionally disturbed, brain-damaged children, a boy and a girl. They had a small room. The boy wanted to hit everything, including himself. The girl was aggressive too. It took some time for Judith to discover that the only way for them all to cope with this aggression in the initial instance was to provide these two children with large sheets of foam rubber. Then they could roll themselves in the foam rubber and bang themselves together without getting hurt. They found ways in which they could hit in safety. Then Judith could start the drama. The problem is that although you start from where they are, you never quite know where they are when you first walk in. Every individual is radically different, and you must really get to know them.
Interviewer: Let's take a radical example of a severely withdrawn, autistic child. This child has few ways of relating to the outside world. If you make an attempt to relate to the child he does not respond in any way. Where do we start in drama with that child?
Courtney: Let me give you an example of particular graduate student who worked with this kind of child. I think her opening was beautifully

done. The child was sitting in an isolated position, rocking and banging her head on the floor. In the hospital other people not trained in drama would come along and try to stop the child from rocking and banging. The child would stop, then do it again a little later on. The student went over to the girl and put the soles of her bare feet against the bare feet of the autistic girl, which surprised her. She stopped banging her head for a moment. Then she went on banging her head. The student started banging her own head. And then they started to bang their heads together, in time. Not too heavily, of course. And then one of them started to push the other's foot, and some communication was taking place. The student was trying to be the autistic child, to dramatize the situation by empathizing with the child—acting as she would act if she were the child. The child started to respond. The first step is trust. Once trust is established they start sharing.

Another technique of broad relevance to drama therapy is puppetry. Puppetry, along with mask work, has been used effectively with emotionally disturbed groups, language-impaired groups, mentally retarded groups, and deaf groups. This technique is most effective in that the client is able to project his or her role onto the puppet and thus achieve a kind of safe distance. It is in exploring that distance between the puppeteer and the puppet where the therapy occurs.

In a sense puppetry and psychodrama are the two sides of the coin in terms of therapeutic role-playing techniques; the former requiring the enactment of a projected role, the latter requiring the enactment of the role of self.

Other techniques used by drama therapists include a wide range of creative dramatic exercises, story dramatization, pantomime and movement work, interrelated work in music and visual art, and formal theatre production. In fact, the entire spectrum of dramatic activities from play through performance to an audience can be applied to a drama therapy session, given the reality that the drama therapist makes his or her choice of technique based upon a knowledge of the group, a knowledge of the technique, and the ability to translate that knowledge into effective therapeutic practice.

NOTES

1. Eleanor Irwin, "Drama Therapy with the Handicapped," in Ann M. Shaw and Cj Stevens, eds., *Drama, Theatre, and the Handicapped* (Washington, D.C.: American Theatre Association, 1979), p. 23.

2. Ibid., p. 24.

3. The British Association of Dramatherapy's definition of *dramatherapy*, as reprinted in *Dramatherapy* 2, no. 4 (Summer 1979): 19.

4. See Sigmund Freud, "The Relation of the Poet to Daydreaming," *Collected Papers*, vol. 4 (London: Hogarth, 1953).

5. Piaget, *Language and Thought of the Child*.

6. Slade, *Child Drama*, p. 35.

7. See, for example, Virginia Axline, *Play Therapy* (Boston: Houghton-Mifflin, 1947); and Rudolf Ekstein and Seymour W. Friedman, "The Function of Acting Out, Play Action, and Play Acting in the Psychotherapeutic Process," *Journal of the American Psychoanalytical Association* 5 (1977): 581-629.

8. Slade, *Child Drama*, p. 23.

9. Bertolt Brecht, "Change the World, It Needs It," from "The Measures Taken" in *The Jewish Wife and Other Short Plays* (New York: Grove Press, 1965), pp. 96-97.

10. Antonin Artaud, *The Theatre and Its Double*, pp. 31-32.

11. Constantin Stanislavski, *An Actor Prepares* (New York: Theatre Arts Books, 1936), p. 293.

12. Julian Beck, *The Life of the Theatre* (San Francisco: City Lights Books, 1972), p. 35.

13. Judith Gleason, "Out of the Water, onto the Ground, and into the Cosmos," unpublished paper, 1981.

14. Ranjini and Gananath Obeyesekere, "Comic Dramas in Sri Lanka," *The Drama Review* 20, no. 1 (March 1976): 5-19.

15. Courtney, *Play, Drama, and Thought*, p. 160.

16. David Cole, *The Theatrical Event* (Middletown, Conn.: Wesleyan University Press, 1975).

17. Alfred Métraux, cited in Cole, *The Theatrical Event*, p. 38.

18. See Cooley, *Human Nature*.

19. WCBS-TV, *Sunrise Semester*, "Drama in Education: Sociodrama and Psychodrama in the Community" (November 21, 1979).

20. WCBS-TV, *Sunrise Semester*, "Drama in Education: Drama for/with Emotionally Disturbed Individuals" (November 30, 1979).

21. WCBS-TV, *Sunrise Semester*, "Drama in Education: Drama and Therapy" (November 28, 1979).

BIBLIOGRAPHY AND RESOURCES

Books and Articles

Artaud, Antonin. *The Theatre and Its Double*. New York: Grove Press, 1958.
Axline, Virginia. *Play Therapy*. Boston: Houghton-Mifflin, 1947.
Bentley, Eric. "Theatre and Therapy." In Walt Anderson, ed. *Therapy and the Arts: Tools of Consciousness*. New York: Harper and Row, 1977.
Blatner, Howard. *Acting-In*. New York: Springer, 1973.
Bobula, James. "The Theatre of Spontaneous Man." *Group Psychotherapy* 22 (March 1969): 47-64.
Bolton, Gavin. "Some Issues Involved in the Use of Role-Play with Psychiatric Patients." *Dramatherapy* 2, no. 4 (Summer 1979): 11-13.

Cole, David. *The Theatrical Event*. Middletown, Conn.: Wesleyan University Press, 1975.

Cooley, Charles H. *Human Nature and the Social Order*. New York: Scribner's, 1902.

Corsini, Raymond J. *Roleplaying in Psychotherapy*. Chicago: Aldine, 1966.

Ekstein, Rudolf, and Seymour W. Friedman, "The Function of Acting Out, Play Action, and Play Acting in the Psychotherapeutic Process." *Journal of the American Psychoanalytical Association* 5 (1977): 581-629.

Eliade, Mircea. *Shamanism: Archaic Techniques of Ecstasy*. Princeton, N.J.: Princeton University Press, 1972.

Fanchette, Jean. *Psychodrama et Théatre Moderne*. Paris: Editions Buchet Chastel, 1971.

Fleshman, Bob, and Jerry L. Fryrear. *The Arts in Therapy*. Chicago: Nelson-Hall, 1981.

Goffman, Erving. *Asylums*. Garden City, N.Y.: Anchor, 1961.

———. *Interaction Ritual*. Garden City, N.Y.: Anchor, 1967.

———. *The Presentation of Self in Everyday Life*. Garden City, N.Y.: Anchor, 1959.

———. *Stigma*. Englewood Cliffs, N.J.: Prentice-Hall, 1963.

Goodman, Judith, and Mario Prosperi. "Drama Therapies in Hospitals." *The Drama Review* 20, no. 1 (March 1976): 20-30.

Hindman, James. "Developmental Theatre." *The Drama Review* 20, no. 1 (March 1976): 75-78.

Irwin, Eleanor C. "Drama Therapy with the Handicapped." In Ann M. Shaw and Cj Stevens, eds. *Drama, Theatre, and the Handicapped*. Washington, D.C.: American Theatre Association, 1979, pp. 21-30.

———. "Play, Fantasy, and Symbol: Drama with Emotionally Disturbed Children," *American Journal of Psychotherapy* 31, no. 3 (July 1977): 426-36.

———, and M. I. Shapiro. "Puppetry as a Diagnostic and Therapeutic Technique." In Irene Jakab, ed. *Psychiatry and Art*. Basel: Karger, 1975, pp. 86-94.

———, and Judith Rubin. "Art and Drama: Partners in Therapy." *American Journal of Psychotherapy* 29, no. 1 (January 1975): 107-66.

Jean, Norma, and Frantisek Deak. "Anna Halprin's Theatre and Therapy Workshop." *The Drama Review* 20, no. 1 (March 1976): 50-54.

Jennings, Sue, ed. *Creative Therapy*. London: Pitman, 1975.

———. *Handbook of Dramatherapy*. London: Pergamon, 1982.

———. *Remedial Drama*. New York: Theatre Arts Books, 1974.

Johnson, David, and Richard L. Munich. "Increasing Hospital-Community Contact through a Theatre Program in a Psychiatric Hospital." *Hospital and Community Psychiatry* 26, no. 7 (July 1975): 435-38.

Karpilow, Babette. "Drama Therapy." *Therapeutic Recreation Journal* 4, no. 1 (1970): 15-16, 44.

Laing, R. D. *The Divided Self*. Chicago: Quadrangle Books, 1960.

———. *The Politics of Experience*. New York: Pantheon, 1967.

Malatesta, Daniel I. "The Potential Role of Theatre Games in a Therapeutic Recreation Program for Psychiatric Patients." *Therapeutic Recreation Journal* 6, no. 4 (1972): 164-66, 190.

Mead, George Herbert. *Mind, Self, and Society*. Chicago: University of Chicago Press, 1962.

Moreno, Jacob L. *Psychodrama*. 3 vols. Beacon, N.Y.: Beacon House, 1946, 1959 1977.

———. *The Theatre of Spontaneity, An Introduction to Psychodrama*. Beacon, N.Y.: Beacon House, 1947.

Perls, Frederick S. *Gestalt Therapy Verbatim*. Moab, Utah: Real People Press, 1969.

Ryan, Paul Ryder. "Theatre as Prison Therapy." *The Drama Review* 20, no. 1 (March 1976): 31-42.

Schattner, Gertrud, and Richard Courtney, eds. *Drama in Therapy*. 2 vols. New York: Drama Book Specialists, 1981.

Schechner, Richard, and Mady Schuman, eds. *Ritual, Play, and Performance: Readings in the Social Sciences/Theatre*. New York: Seabury Press, 1976.

Shaftel, Fannie, and George Shaftel. *Role-Playing for Social Values*. Englewood Cliffs, N.J.: Prentice-Hall, 1967.

Slade, Peter. *Dramatherapy as an Aid to Becoming a Person*. London: Guild of Pastoral Psychology, 1959.

Strauss, Anselm L. *Mirrors and Masks: The Search for Identity*. Glencoe, Ill.: Free Press, 1959.

Turner, Victor. *From Ritual to Theatre: The Human Seriousness of Play*. New York: Performing Arts Journal Publications, 1981.

Winnicott, D. W. *Playing and Reality*. London: Tavistock, 1971.

Woltman, Adolf G. "Concepts of Play Therapy Techniques." *American Journal of Orthopsychiatry* 25 (1955): 771-83.

Yablonsky, Lewis. *Psychodrama: Resolving Emotional Problems through Role-Playing*. New York: Basic Books, 1976.

Organizations and Programs in Drama Therapy and Psychodrama

American Society of Group Psychotherapy and Psychodrama
39 East 20 Street
New York, New York 10003

British Association for Dramatherapists
College of Ripon and St. John
University of York
York Y03 7EX England

California State University, Los Angeles
Roger Alternberg
Department of Theatre Arts
Los Angeles, California 90032

Institute for Therapy through the Arts
Marilyn Richman
Music Center of the North Shore
300 Green Bay Road
Winnetka, Illinois 60093

Lesley College
Shaun McNiff

Expressive Therapies Program
35 Mellon Street
Cambridge, Massachusetts 02138
Loyola University
Bob Fleshman
Drama Therapy Program
P.O. Box 155
New Orleans, Louisiana 70118
Media and the Arts for Social Services (MASS)
Michael and Linda Gregoric
University of Connecticut, U-Box 127
Storrs, Connecticut 06268
Moreno Institute
259 Wolcott Avenue
Beacon, New York 12508
National Association for Drama Therapy
Barbara Sandberg
Theatre Department
William Patterson College
Wayne, New Jersey 07470
New York Center for Psychodrama Training
James Sacks
71 Washington Place
New York, New York 10011
New York University
Robert Landy
Program in Educational Theatre
829 Shimkin Hall
New York, New York 10003
SESAME
Christchurch
27 Blackfriars Road
London SE1 8NY
England

Journals and Periodicals

The Arts in Psychotherapy. P.O. Box 426, Fayetteville, New York 13066.

Dramatherapy. British Association for Dramatherapists, College of Ripon and St. John, University of York, York, England.

Group Psychotherapy, Psychodrama, and Sociometry. 4000 Albemarle Street, N.W., Washington, D.C. 20016.

Sociodrama Quarterly MASS, University of Connecticut, U-Box 127, Storrs, Connecticut 06268.

Films and Videotapes

Available through the Concord Film Council, 201 Felixstowe Road, Ipswich IP3 9BJ, England:

Dorothy Heathcote: *Three Looms Waiting* (BBC Omnibus Film)
  Seeds of a New Life
  Albert (Mental Health Film Council)
Veronica Sherbourne: *In Touch*
  A Sense of Movement
Sue Jennings: *Role Play with Maladjusted Adolescent Boys* (Open
  University Film Library)
Available through SESAME, Christchurch, 27 Blackfriars Road, London SE1 8NY,
England:
  Drama with Autistic Children
  Drama with Schizophrenics
  Drama with Subnormal Young Men
Available through MASS Resource Library, University of Connecticut, Storrs,
Connecticut 06268:
  Drama Therapy (One-half inch video-tape) with Zerka Moreno and David
  Johnson
  Drama Therapy (One-half inch video-tape) with Bob Fleshman and
  Richard L. Klepac
Available from Renee Emunah, 6547 Whitney Street, Oakland, California 94609:
  Introduction to Drama Therapy (video-tape)
  Episodes (video-tape)—an improvisational theatre performance
  Reflections and *Breaking Through* (video-tapes)—drama therapy in a
  residential treatment program

8

DRAMA AND THEATRE
WITH THE DISABLED
AND THE ELDERLY

Although drama therapy applies to work with various disabled populations, many professionals who use dramatic and theatrical activities with the developmentally and physically disabled, as well as with the elderly, tend to see their work as drama or theatre, rather than drama therapy or theatre therapy. Many would well affirm the therapeutic values of their work, but would also point to the aesthetic values as equally or more essentially valid. Within this group we find a strong emphasis upon a process of rehearsal that often leads toward a product—performance to an audience.

There is a fine line between drama therapy and drama/theatre with the disabled. The difference often seems to be one of degree rather than kind, attributable to the intentions and training of the group leader. In that so much of the work with the disabled is performance-oriented, a major variable comes into play that may well obscure the purer therapeutic aspects of the dramatic experience—that is, the temptation to measure the work against critical standards applied to professional theatre productions. That is not to say that many special theatre productions are not excellent by any critical standards. The work of the National Theatre of the Deaf, for example, has merited recognition by major theatre organizations around the world. Yet if a special group's emphasis becomes more commercial and more competitive for popular acclaim, there are implications that could well obscure the original vision and intentions of its founders.

DRAMA/THEATRE WITH THE DEVELOPMENTALLY DISABLED

In a recent discussion and demonstration Lea Wallace, puppeteer and educator, spoke of her work with mentally retarded, also known as developmentally disabled, adolescents:[1]

Interviewer: When did you become interested in working with disabled people through puppetry?

Lea Wallace: I performed for cerebral palsied and other disabled groups, but only for Christmas shows and entertainment. Through the Bureau for Speech Improvement at the New York City Board of Education, one of the directors suggested I could be more useful to the special education population through puppetry.

Interviewer: Why is puppetry so effective in working in special education?

Wallace: All children respond to a puppet, because, first of all, it's smaller than they are. Immediately, they feel at home. Adults are all giants to children. For the older students, it gives them a chance to explore theatre. They all want to be actors. They all want to prove themselves before the public, and here's an instrument for them to do it. The onus isn't on them. They can be any character. It doesn't require much acting technique. The puppet is already concentrated in his role.

Wallace then introduced three students from the Manhattan Occupational Training Center who demonstrated two plays they had performed at the Very Special Arts Festival at Columbia University in the spring 1979. She noted that the students had constructed the puppets according to themes they had selected and developed. Although their plays followed a consistent story-line, the actual dialogue was improvised.

The first brief puppet play, "The New Girl," involved a realistic social situation. A teenage girl who recently moved to the United States from Puerto Rico enters an American school for the first time. She feels frightened and alone. In the lunchroom she meets a girl friend who takes her out dancing later in the day. At the dance the new girl is introduced to a boy. While they dance she becomes homesick and begins to cry. Her new friends comfort her by singing a popular Puerto Rican folk song. The play ends as the new girl joins them in the chorus.

The second play is structurally more complex and involves a fantasy situation. The play "Meeting at the Park," inspired by recent science fiction movies, concerns the space voyage of Johnny, the protagonist of the sketch. While in the park Johnny meets Evelyn. As they talk he realizes Evelyn is a neighbor and invites her out that night. Suddenly, a space ship appears in the park. The two are afraid, but fascinated. Jack the Alien exits from the ship and invites Johnny to go for a ride. He accepts, after first asking Evelyn's permission and informing her: "I'll be back for the date."

After the ship takes off Evelyn decides to inform Johnny's mother of the mysterious events. The mother's reaction is to call the police, but Evelyn convinces her to wait until tomorrow.

During the next scene a day has passed, and Jack the Alien returns Johnny to the park. He is concerned both that Johnny enjoyed the ride and that he will be able to find his girl friend. As he leaves the following is spoken:

Johnny: I hope to see you again.
Jack: Me, too. Well, I must go now. They need me back on the base.

Johnny then searches for Evelyn. When they meet, he apologizes:

Johnny: I'm sorry it took so long. I promised you the date last night, and I didn't keep my promise.
Evelyn: Your mother worried about you.
Johnny: Oh, my God! We'd better go.

The play ends with Johnny and Evelyn returning home. Johnny apologizes to his mother who admits that she was frightened and tells him never to go away again without first informing her.

Both plays are social and moral tales. In the first the students explore their feelings of being an outsider to a culture and act out ways to help the outsider feel more socially acceptable. Their solution is a particularly sophisticated one—rather than imposing their culture upon the new girl, they show her that they understand something of her culture. That is, they demonstrate that her cultural experience is not alien, but a part of their consciousness.

In the second play the puppeteers again draw upon the image of the alien who is not at all a negative force, but rather a source of joy for the protagonist. Although the idea of space people as enlightened or positive forces is probably borrowed from the film Close Encounters of the Third Kind, the students clearly relate this notion to their own experience. Further issues in "Meeting in the Park" concern responsibility, making choices, and relationships between boyfriend and girl friend, child and parent.

The values of this kind of work in puppetry with developmentally disabled adolescents include physical coordination and the development of speech skills, as well as the exploration of social and moral issues. During the improvised puppet shows, the speech of the students became noticeably more articulated, conversational, and expressive. Furthermore, one student with apparent physical coordination problems demonstrated remarkable skill in hand-eye coordination, laterality, concentration, and creative speech as he simultaneously manipulated two puppets, Johnny and Jack the Alien.

In further discussing the use of puppets for enhancing speech skills, Wallace introduced a hand puppet, Rover, who "spoke" with the interviewer:

Interviewer: Rover, I understand you can teach special skills to people, is that true?

Rover: That's very true. You see, I assist Miss Wallace when she teaches speech, because sometimes with my big mouth, you can see things a little more clearly. And if I can learn to talk, anyone can. It's not talking—anybody can talk—it's the way you make the sound. For instance, to say a "t," my tongue goes up behind the teeth and I blow my tongue down. If I put my tongue out like that, I can make "th," like "think." Also, we do tongue exercises. We go around and around, side to side.

Then, out of role, Wallace shared these thoughts:

Interviewer: In teaching speech we have a great flexibility with Rover, the hand puppet, in opening the mouth and manipulating the tongue. Do the students imitate the tongue movements?
Wallace: Oh, yes. Even when they won't with me, they will with the puppet.
Interviewer: Why is that?
Wallace: I think they feel more comfortable with the puppet. They want to come over and caress it immediately. It breaks down a certain barrier reserve between teacher and student. A teacher can immediately begin to work. Once she brings the puppets in the children will love her too.
Interviewer: Is there any advantage in using marionettes in special education?
Wallace: Aside from making them, they're more like people. They're easily made and cost nothing. Students prefer hand puppets to rod puppets. You get more movement, and because students are closer to the puppet, they put more into it.
Interviewer: I noticed some extraordinary changes from the pre-play discussion to the actual puppet play. How do puppets affect language usage?
Wallace: The language will come because of the situation. They want to be more precise in their feelings and more expressive. When your language is limited, you need to develop a richer vocabulary and more descriptive, imaginative speech. We use all kinds of characters which would require different uses of language. Expressing feelings is one of the most difficult things, and puppets help us in this way.

In his book *Puppets and Therapy* A. R. Philpott documented many examples of puppetry used to treat several disabled groups, such as the emotionally disturbed, deaf, orthopedically disabled, and developmentally disabled.[2]

There have been some outstanding examples of treating the developmentally disabled through drama and theatre. Sue Jennings, for one, specified several techniques that she has found useful, including controlled sword fighting and improvisation based upon television serials and themes selected by the group.[3] Dorothy Heathcote also worked extensively with mentally handicapped groups, using her unique methods, again based upon the interests of the group. As an example, she once worked with a group of fifteen year olds in a special school. Her goal was to help them discover that they could succeed at accomplishing a difficult task. After a preliminary discussion Heathcote presented the task: they were in China and had to bring back an important message to the queen of England. She added a warning: "If you are caught, nobody must know what the message is."

During the session Heathcote led the group through a symbolic journey from China to England. To remember the message and avoid detection, each person was given one word, to be concealed in his or her clothing. When the group finally reached the queen, they reassembled the message intact and experienced a great sense of accomplishment.[4]

In the United States several theatre-oriented groups have been working with the developmentally disabled. In San Francisco, for example, David Morgan directs Theatre Unlimited, described as "an ensemble company consisting of equal members of able and disabled."[5] Through the work of this group, originally modeled after the National Theatre of the Deaf, Morgan aims:

1. To explore new theatre forms appropriate to its unique ensemble makeup
2. To put emphasis on the developmental theatre process
3. To present pieces that represent an extension of the actor's resources and abilities rather than a director's superimposed structure[6]

Morgan noted, also, that his company aims to change attitudes of audiences toward disabled persons by presenting developmentally disabled adults as positive role models for "normal" children.

Other examples of theatre for the developmentally disabled include the Process Theatre with the Handicapped of the Alan Short Center in Stockton, California, and the San Diego Theatre for the Disabled, also in California. Both groups produce theatre pieces reflecting the concerns of the disabled and aiming toward raising the consciousness of audiences.

DRAMA/THEATRE WITH THE PHYSICALLY DISABLED

Drama/theatre with the physically disabled includes work with the orthopedically disabled, blind, and deaf. Although improvisational, creative dramatic, and other nonperformance techniques are used in school or workshop situations, directors and community leaders have most often used theatre and performance in working with the physically disabled. In fact, groups such as the National Theatre of the Deaf and the National Theatre

Workshop of the Handicapped would argue that although their work may be therapeutic for participants and audiences, it is certainly not therapy. Their aims are primarily aesthetic, and their work involves creating the art of theatre.

The National Theatre Workshop of the Handicapped, designed as an integrated group of orthopedically disabled, visual and hearing impaired, and able-bodied individuals, was founded by Rick Curry in 1977. Recently, three disabled student members of that organization discussed their experiences with drama and theatre.[7]

Interviewer: When did you first become involved in drama?

Jane Zirinsky: I always enjoyed theatre. I took some theatre classes when I was a teenager outside of the school setting. But I never had any real opportunity to perform outside of these classes, because the high school I attended was not ready to see me on stage and wouldn't allow me to read for a part.

Elliot Schloss: This past summer some friends told me about Rick Curry's workshop, and I went with extreme apprehension. The first couple of sessions were really terrifying. I didn't want him to call on me.

Interviewer: What kind of things were you doing?

Schloss: Improvisation. Breathing exercises. Concentration exercises. It wasn't until the third or fourth session that I started getting accustomed to it. For my own peace of mind I would obliterate everything around me and focus in on what I had to do. Now I enjoy it immensely.

Karen Luxton: I think I've been involved in drama since I was two years old. Both my parents were actors. When your parents read you stories as a kid or when you play house, there is drama. In elementary school we did these fantastically advanced plays about Snow White and the Seven Dwarfs.

Interviewer: Were you in a special school?

Luxton: No. Not until high school. I have to say to the credit of the New York City schools and the schools in Connecticut where I was, they were game enough or fool enough to let me be in the plays that the classes were doing. So I've always had little bits of experience in drama. But this theatre workshop (National Theatre Workshop of the Handicapped) is the first time I've had a chance to really confront the realities of trying to do acting incorporating the disability and allowing something to happen that's real and true.

Interviewer: Has there been a point when you couldn't participate in drama?

Zirinsky: I was taking a theatre class on Saturdays. We were doing some improvisation and scene study. I was having a really good time. We would put on things for parents once a year. I decided I would like to read for the school play. I went to the audition. The theatre coach got everybody up and let everybody read. Then she said: "Is there anybody else who wants to read?" I said: "Yeah." She said: "We don't have a part for you." It was not as if she let me read and said that these are the people we've picked. She wouldn't even let me read, because she didn't want me on stage.

Interviewer: What grade was that?

Zirinsky: Junior high school. As a college student I did a lot of backstage work. I stage-managed; I did makeup and wardrobe. I was not onstage in a single production there either.

Interviewer: It seems to be typical of humanistically dealing with disabled students in high school to have them work backstage. Elliot, did you have any difficulties in wanting to do drama or theatre but not being allowed to?

Schloss: As a youngster, no. I was terribly inhibited. I tried to put my disability in the background. Unfortunately, I don't share Karen's enthusiasm for the New York City educational system, because my experience was horrendous. I was put into a health class, because the local school in my neighborhood didn't want the responsibility of some-one with crutches. They wondered what would happen if I walked down the steps and tripped another student? There would be two disabled students in the class. But the health class at the time was really abomina-ble. So I never wanted to do anything where I would be publically on display. I always felt a desire to do it, and now with Rick's workshop the inhibitions are diminishing fairly rapidly.

Luxton: About the New York City schools, it seems to vary so much from teacher to teacher or from class to class. If you do get to participate in something, it's luck. It's one teacher who happens to have the intelli-gence to know that it's all right or that it's possible.

Interviewer: You're all in Rick Curry's workshop. You mentioned before that you are doing improvisational work. What's the nature of the improvisations?

Schloss: In a typical class we would start by doing breathing exercises, relaxation, and concentration exercises to get us prepared for improvs. We're just beginning to do scene work. We take a scene and read it. We have assignments to memorize the lines, then come back the following week to rehearse and then perform in front of our classmates.

Luxton: Before we got into improvs Rick started with mime, trying to get at the essence of your own experience. I think the first assignment we had to do was to physicalize, pantomime some action that we do all the time.

Interviewer: Had you ever experienced pantomime before?

Luxton: No.

Interviewer: What effect does pantomime have on your lives?

Luxton: I found it absolutely terrifying, because I felt totally out of control. Everybody else could watch each other doing all these things, but I couldn't watch them. Also, I thought that I don't know how everybody else does those gestures. How am I going to make my gestures clear to somebody? Gradually, you learn that it isn't one of those impassable blocks. It was wonderful to find out that you could learn and you could begin to communicate.

Schloss: At the beginning my mind would freeze up. I couldn't think of something to do. Almost at the last moment something would occur, and I'd go ahead and do it. I'd work from my personal experiences or situations I've discussed with friends. One time I did a mime which involved a police officer who was dating a girl friend. They came home and the next morning, as he strapped on his gun belt, the gun discharged, killing his girl friend. I worked with the effect and impact that tragedy had on him.

Interviewer: Where did that story come from?

Schloss: It was an actual incident that occurred when I was out in the Midwest in 1975. Someone told me of the event.

Zirinsky: I'm a teacher. I'm constantly improvising. I get up with a group of students, and I have to improvise. I have to think what I can teach them and how I can make it relevant to where they are at this particular moment. It could be that I'll come in with something already prepared and something's happening that morning to somebody in the class. I have to be ready to change that lesson and teach it from a whole different perspective.

Interviewer: You are bringing up an important point, that the experience of drama is not specific to one workshop in one place, but rather has to do with your whole existence. It occurs in a work situation, as a teacher, or growing up and having stories told to you. How can you further incorporate drama within the setting where you work?

Zirinsky: I work with students who are physically and intellectually limited. I'm in special education. But I can have students tell me stories. To some degree I can have them act them out, depending upon the limitations of the classroom and the individual. I might have them draw the stories if they can't verbalize them. I've also worked with senior citizens. They love to tell stories and they're really good at it. It's a good way to draw them out. I teach sexuality. If I go in and ask a senior citizen: "Tell me about your sex life," forget it. But if I say: "What was it like growing up in 1901 when your parents wouldn't talk to you about sex," they would tell me a fifteen-minute story about how they first learned about the birds and bees. I don't have to prod them. So there are all kinds of ways to use storytelling and improvisational techniques with students on all levels.

Luxton: I work with handicapped college students and I'm very aware of the problem of job placement, of packaging themselves so that they will project something an employer will buy. If you can try out a role that might have scared you to death before, like going on a job interview, and you're trying it out in a no-risk situation, then when you walk into an interview, it's possible for you to feel prepared. I think drama makes me more aware of people's differences.

Interviewer: What community resources are available to allow disabled people to participate in drama and theatre?

Luxton: The National Theatre Workshop of the Handicapped is somewhat revolutionary. There has always been the feeling in the blind-ness system that we should teach the nice little blind kid or blind adult to act. But there's been one catch, and that is that the whole idea is to see if we can make this individual be sighted. Let's see if we can teach him to pass. The whole premise is confining. It says: "Here, you be something you're not. Don't look blind to those people." But Rick is saying: "Look, what you are, what you bring to this is legitimate." This distinction has been freeing for a lot of people in that class.

Interviewer: What about other community resources?

Zirinsky: I don't know of any. I think it would be great if more commu-nity organizations realized that there are disabled people who can act and who have been through Rick's classes or other classes. I know a professional actor who's disabled and has a terrible time, because the immediate fantasy of the director or teacher is: "Well, I don't have a blind person in this play and therefore I can't use you"; or "there isn't anybody in this play who's on crutches." Why the next door neighbor couldn't be in a wheelchair or on crutches or be blind is beyond me.

Interviewer: What do we do to raise consciousness within a given com-munity?

Schloss: Of primary importance is to go to the educational system, into the schools and hospitals, and let people know there are programs and there are people who are willing to start acting programs for the dis-abled. I'm also a wheelchair athlete. If a friend hadn't introduced me to wheelchair athletics, I wouldn't have known about it.

Rick Curry has been letting people know of his theatre work with the disabled for several years. In two recent demonstrations and discussions of workshop techniques focusing on training blind and orthopedically disabled actors, he offered the following:[8]

Interviewer: When working with the blind through drama or theatre, what are your aims?

Rick Curry: My aims are no more specific than working with any other groups. I try to get into the interior of the actor and break down, step by step, the component parts of what it takes to learn acting and just be very aware of the excitement the actor brings. At the beginning of every class, we work to get the actor attuned to his body.

After several warm-ups in breathing and body relaxation, Curry led his group of one blind and three orthopedically disabled actors through a series of basic exercises in pantomime. In a follow-up discussion the actors offered the following:

Interviewer: How does pantomime relate to your education through drama?

Diane Kobilca: Pantomime always seemed like something that would be easy, but I learned that it wasn't. If you pick something up, you have to remember to put it down. If you pick up a can or a cup, you have to make sure you keep holding a can or a cup. It makes you more aware of where your body is.

Interviewer: Is it different for you, a sighted person, than you would imagine it to be for a blind person?

Kobilca: I would imagine it would be different.

Interviewer: How?

Kobilca: Because I can see what I'm picking up. But I suppose even without sight, you have a sense of how it feels.

Alice Watson: Pantomime is such a visual thing, so there's no means of comparison. The blind person doesn't see what she should be doing in pantomime. She just has to feel. It takes a great deal more concentration.

Luxton: The real difference is that if you're doing it visually, you've got a vocabulary to work with. With me, when I'm washing dishes, I never think about how it looks to other people. But I know there are stereotypical ways that people wash dishes.

Interviewer: Are you concerned with an audience at all, and what is your relationship to that audience?

Luxton: You have to make them know what you're doing. I don't know if the audience knows what I mean when I perform a gesture for happy or sad.

Interviewer: Are you concerned about that?

Luxton: Of course.

Interviewer: Are you concerned about that as an actor in everyday life as well? Does being blind change your whole perception of how other people see you?

Luxton: No. What ends up happening is that you've got enough of a mix of experiences. You have a bunch of strengths and weaknesses to bring and it works in the real world. But when you isolate a specific gesture, it's tricky. You don't know how well it's working.

Interviewer: Elliot, as you become more relaxed in the workshop, what are you learning from the experience of pantomime?

Schloss: How I feel in different moments. The pantomime I did was of a man entering his office early, a very punctual person who is a bookkeeper, bored to tears with his life and his job. He reads his newspaper and the first thing he sees is a war article. I was rehearsing this on the bus coming down. All of a sudden I realized other passengers were watching me and it broke my concentration. Then it occurred to me that it's good to watch other people watching me do this, in spite of what they may think. The mime is also important for self-concentration, so that when I go on to more advanced work, I won't be distracted.

Interviewer: Karen, does the experience of watching others watch you make sense to you?

Luxton: Observation makes sense to me and paying attention and listening and being aware.

In a second demonstration and discussion Curry worked with three orthopedically disabled students, two of whom were in wheelchairs. The introductory discussion follows:

Interviewer: Do you find that the orthopedically disabled people you work with have backgrounds in drama?

Curry: Precisely the opposite. I think most of us are in theatre today, because as children we went to the theatre. Most of the theatres are totally inaccessible to orthopedically disabled persons. When a child goes with his parents to see a show, he says: "I can do that." But if a child is in a wheelchair and the theatre has been barred to him, he doesn't have the opportunity to say: "I can do that," because he's never seen it.

Interviewer: What about more informal, improvisational drama? Do your students have backgrounds in that area?

Curry: Very little. Most of the students I work with come with a tremendous background in watching television.

Interviewer: What brings them to the National Theatre Workshop of the Handicapped? Why do the people you work with have a need to do drama or theatre?

Curry: Because I think they realize this is an opportunity to explore parts of themselves that they never had before. When they see that the theatre is accessible to them, they get excited about it and want to explore it. They come with a wide range of hopes. Some come for the sheer recreational aspects of it. Others come with an eye for really looking at this as a possible career.

Interviewer: Where do you begin with someone in a wheelchair who has had no background in drama or theatre?

Curry: We begin with relaxation exercises, in trying to get the students in touch with their own bodies.

Following his demonstration of physical warm-ups, Curry proceeded into situational improvisations and finally worked with a script, Dorothy

Parker's *Here We Are*. Following the scenework, Curry spoke further of his intentions:

Interviewer: Why was the Dorothy Parker play chosen?
Curry: I wanted to try to find a scene that would be suitable for my students Lois Benjamin and Richard Rosenbaum. They have a strong sense of the period the 1930s. And since the scene takes place on a train, I was excited about the fact that Lois and Richard are in chairs.
Interviewer: What about the fact that Lois and Richard are in wheelchairs? Does that say anything to you about the choice of script? Are there scripts for orthopedically disabled actors, or is there no necessity for special scripts?
Curry: I don't think there's any necessity for special scripts. I think after a while it's like watching a foreign film. When you initially introduce a new audience to this, they're going to be distracted, possibly in the first few minutes. But after a while, it's going to become so natural to them if, in fact, the actors are natural.
Interviewer: So it's an acting problem.
Curry: Exactly.
Interviewer: One of your aims is to train actors.
Curry: Exactly.
Interviewer: Are there opportunities for these actors in the professional world?
Curry: I think the future of our actors is now. I think that the industry is getting very tired of having hearing actors play deaf roles and sighted actors play blind roles and the orthopedically disabled being portrayed by the able-bodied. I think that the authenticity of the role is really going to demand authentic actors. What we'll be demonstrating at that time is the fact that we have orthopedically disabled, blind, and deaf students who are trained to be able to portray those roles with authenticity and pizazz.
Interviewer: What can we do to raise the consciousness of community organizations in encouraging disabled people to participate in drama and theatre?
Curry: There are two things: one is that it is terribly important that their facilities be made accessible to the disabled; and secondly, it is tremendously important that their minds and hearts are accessible. I think we all believe that the disabled have a place in our lives, but I don't know if we are willing to let them give us something in return.
Interviewer: How do we open up the hearts and minds of people in positions of power?
Curry: I think we provide opportunities by demonstrating that much of our disabled community is very talented.

Other groups have begun to offer training in drama and theatre for the physically disabled. In the mid-1970s, for example, the Center for Independent Living in Berkeley, California, developed theatre workshops for the severely disabled. At Wright State University in Dayton, Ohio, William Richert worked to build a company of able-bodied and physically disabled actors, The Rolling Stock Company, that tours local community organizations. In Las Vegas the Rainbow Company has achieved acclaim in developing and performing *Special Class*, an original play acted by an integrated group of disabled and able-bodied young people, intimately concerned with their personal experiences with disability.

DRAMA/THEATRE WITH THE DEAF

Certainly, the most acclaimed group working in the area of drama/ theatre with the disabled is the National Theatre of the Deaf, which began in 1967 as a professional theatre company of deaf and hearing performers presenting their work to integrated audiences. Many members of that organization would emphatically deny that they are engaged in drama therapy. However, the therapeutic benefits of their work would include developing a sense of dignity within the deaf performers and deaf viewers, an awareness within hearing performers and audiences of a whole new culture, and an interrelationship of mutual respect between the two groups.

In a recent discussion and demonstration two members of the National Theatre of the Deaf (NTD), Mary Beth Miller and Ray Parks, were joined by three others with extensive experience in drama/theatre with the deaf, Shelly Raffle, Alan Barwiolek, and Sally Jones. They shared the following:[9]

Interviewer: What is the importance of drama and theatre in the education of deaf individuals?

Ray Parks: It's very interesting to look at the attitudes of many schools for the deaf toward theatre arts as part of their curriculum. Many often view theatre arts as a frill and never consider it an important part of the curriculum. I've encouraged schools to accept theatre arts as part of their curriculum, because it's a real help for the children to develop their skills in reading and writing.

Interviewer: What about performance by the deaf? Would you recommend that a deaf elementary school student should be encouraged to perform in a formal production?

Shelly Raffle: No. I think it would be the same for hearing children. My personal feeling is that you wouldn't want to put a hearing child of elementary school age on the stage performing for an audience either. I'd like to add to Ray's statement. Not only is the experience of participating in dramatic activities important, but also attending theatre as children. That is one way future audiences will grow and develop.

The major portion of the group's demonstration concerned performing a scene from Dorothy Miles's script *A Play of Our Own*. Before that, though, they demonstrated part of their rehearsal process in which they used improvisation to explore the central idea of the script, misperceptions deaf and hearing people have of one another.

For example, in exploring notions of waking up in the morning, the hearing actors stretched their fingers, shook out their hands, then in a parody of sign language, began to gesticulate wildly. The deaf actors yawned, stretched out their mouths, exercised their jaws, gargled, and then, in a parody of oral language, began to "talk" in an exaggerated fashion.

In a second example, exploring misconceptions deaf and hearing people have of each other's behavior at a disco, the hearing actors entered the disco, got down on the floor to feel the rhythm, and then got up, snapped their fingers, and danced awkwardly. The deaf actors, in turn, entered the disco with totally blank expressions on their faces, began to dance wildly as the music started, and then cut off all expression when the music stopped.

The full group prepared to perform the scene from *A Play of Our Own*, which was written with the Hartford Thespians in 1973 and is modeled somewhat after the film *Guess Who's Coming to Dinner*. The playwright, Dorothy Miles, is a deaf actress, writer, and educator who lives in England and has worked in America with the NTD and various educational institutions. The play is characterized as deaf theatre, as opposed to sign language theatre. The actors spoke of the distinctions:

> *Ray Parks:* Deaf theatre includes deaf culture and deaf actors, and we present our work to a deaf audience. Sign language theatre incorporates hearing actors and deaf actors. Hearing actors can use signs at the same time as they speak. When a deaf actor signs, a hearing actor will speak his lines to convey the idea to the hearing audience.
>
> *Shelly Raffle:* The basic distinction is that sign language theatre can be any material translated into sign language, Shakespeare or whatever. Deaf theatre is based upon deaf culture, deaf ideas, and experiences.

The scene from the play concerns a deaf man and a hearing woman who plan to be married. Neither has informed his or her parents of the marriage plans. The occasion of the scene is the meeting between the couple and their respective parents. The cast included Alan Barwiolek playing David Daniels, a deaf man, with Mary Beth Miller and Ray Parks playing his parents, who are also deaf; Shelly Raffle playing Ruth, David's hearing fiance, and Sally Jones playing Ruth's mother, Mildred:[10]

> David and Ruth have just entered the Daniels's household.
> *David* (to his parents): Let me introduce my girl friend, Ruth.
> *Ruth:* I am very happy to meet you. (She shakes hands with Mr. and

Mrs. Daniels.)

Mrs. Daniels: I'm happy to meet you too.

Mr. Daniels: Where are you from?

Ruth: New York.

Mr. D: What school?

Ruth (signing): "Whiskey."

David (to his parents): I forgot to tell you. She's hearing.

Mrs. D. exits, followed by Mr. D.

Ruth: You didn't tell your mother?

David: I tried, but Mother was busy.

Ruth: Oh, that's wonderful.

David: Is your mother coming?

Ruth: Yes.

David: What time?

Ruth: I told her to come early. (She looks at her watch.) She should be here any time now.

David: I better tell Mom. . . . What did your mother say? When you told her I'm deaf. She accept me?

(Ruth doesn't answer. David persits.)

Ruth: Well, I didn't tell her that. . . .

David: You mean you didn't tell your mother that I'm deaf? You stupid!

Ruth: Who is stupid? You didn't tell your parents that I was hearing.

David: But that's different. . . .

Ruth: It's not different. . . .

David: I tried to tell my mother this afternoon but she wouldn't listen to me.

Ruth: Well, my mother wouldn't listen to me either. She was upset because we were getting married so soon.

David: But why did you give up and leave?

Ruth: Give up and leave? It was hard enough to persuade her to come here and meet you. What more do you want?

David: Fine way for us to start our wedding plans. I feel like you pushed me in the water over my head.

Ruth: You want to call the whole thing off? (She moves away. David runs after her and takes her arm.)

David: No, Ruth. It's just that it's much harder for your parents to accept me than for my parents to accept you. They are all right now, but how will I face your parents? I won't know what to do. I will feel so awkward.

(David uses the sign for clumsy. Ruth does not know the sign. She repeats it, incorrectly, and taps David impatiently for a translation. David repeats the word, then shouts it.)

David: Awkward, awkward, nervous, upset!

(Ruth now understands the word but still gets the sign wrong.)

Ruth: Awkward! You think hearing people don't feel awkward too? How do you think I felt when you all left the room. I felt awkward.

(Ruth walks away. David is shocked into silence. The idea that hearing people can really feel as helpless as deaf people in situations like this is new to him, and he realizes he has been unfair. This is their first serious quarrel. They stand apart for a while; then Ruth moves back toward David and touches him. They embrace.)

David: Sorry.

Ruth: I'm sorry too. (They embrace again and kiss.)

David: It will be all right. We knew we would have problems. (The doorbell flashes.)

David: Doorbell. It must be your mother.

(Ruth gestures for David to go to the door. The doorbell flashes again. Mr. Daniels enters from the kitchen, points to the lamp and the door, and gestures: "What's going on?")

David: I think her mother.

(David encourages Ruth again, and this time Mr. Daniels gestures encouragement too. Ruth braces herself and goes to the door. David asks his father, urgently:)

David: How's Mom now?

Mr. D: Your mother's all right. Now she's blaming me!

David: Sorry. Fetch Mom, meet. . . .

(Mr. Daniels exits. David checks his appearance. Mildred enters with Ruth, talking when she enters, and continues while Ruth helps her out of her coat.)

Mildred: I hope I haven't kept anyone waiting. I stopped for gas and I was worried about the oil filter. . . .

Ruth: No, you made good time. . . .

Mildred: This is really nice. Oh, that must be David. (She crosses to meet David, holding out her hand. To Ruth:) You didn't tell me he was so handsome. (Mildred takes David's hand and holds it while she talks.) Hello, David. I must say that when Ruth told me she was getting married, I really. . . . (Ruth has put her mother's coat on the chair and now runs to place herself between David and Mildred.)

Ruth: He can't hear you, Mom.

(She uses a sign only for the word, hear, using the hand on David's side.

Mildred doesn't notice it.)

Mildred: Can't you hear me? I'm sorry. I'll talk louder. When Ruth told me she. . . .

Ruth: No, Mom, you don't understand. He's deaf.

(She signs only the word deaf.)

Mildred: Deaf? Oh, oh. . . . (She shrinks back a little, smiling nervously at David, as if he had changed into a strange animal. Enter Mr. and Mrs. Daniels, reluctantly, with some encouragement from David.)

Ruth: Mom, these are David's parents.

(Mildred, who has been frozen in shock until this moment, now rushes forward, smiling frantically.)

Mildred: Please forgive me. It's so nice to meet you, but I can't quite get used to the idea. . . . I wasn't told that your son was . . . ah . . . ah . . .

Ruth: Mom, they are deaf, too.

(There is a frozen moment. Then Mildred turns to Ruth.)

Mildred: O-o-oh, Ruth. They're all deaf!

(She bursts into tears and clings to Ruth, who persuades her to sit on the sofa.)

Mildred (to Ruth): Why didn't you tell me this before?

Ruth: I tried to tell you this afternoon, but you were so upset.

(Mr. and Mrs. Daniels whisper in signs: "She cry, upset, what-to-do?" etc.)

Mildred: What are we going to do? They're all deaf. What kind of a husband will he make for you, Ruth? He'll be utterly dependent on you. How can he work? Why he won't even be able to get up in the morning if he can't hear the alarm clock. And of course he can't help with the driving. You'll be killed by a truck because he can't hear it coming.

(David turns from Mildred to see what his family is doing. Focus shifts to Mr. and Mrs. Daniels.)

Mr. D: See, they won't accept deaf.

Mrs. D: "Normal." "Face-to-face," shock. Will "fade-vanish" later.

(David turns back to the other group. Mildred raises her voice again.)

Mildred: But what about children? You can't have children . . . my grandchildren. . . .

David (tapping Ruth's shoulder): What she say?

Ruth: Later. (to Mildred): It so happens, Mom, that only 10 percent of deaf people have deaf children.

(David turns back to his parents again.)

David: Come on, help!

Mr. D: I "know-that" "those-two" think deaf stupid, can't do anything.

Mrs. D: Seems she will oppose your marriage.

Ruth: Mom! Deaf people live like everyone else. You don't have to worry about us.

(Mildred is shocked into silence.)

Mrs. D (crossing to Ruth): Would she like something to drink?

Ruth: Would you like a drink?

(Mildred hasn't answered.)

Ruth: Want a drink, Mom?

Mildred: No, no, I don't want anything. I think I'm starting a headache.

Ruth: Have some coffee, Mom. (to Mrs. Daniels) Do you have any coffee?

Mrs. D: Yes, should be ready. Black?

Ruth: Yes, black, thanks.

(Mrs. Daniels exits.)

Mildred (plaintively, but with the beginning of curiosity): Do they cook their own food?

Ruth: Of course they cook their own food, Mom!

(David taps Ruth again.)

David: What she say, "since?"

Ruth: She's worrying about how we will live, if you can work, if you can drive, if we can have children. . . .

(Mr. Daniels makes a sharp movement of exasperation.)

Mildred (to Ruth): Why are you waving your hands about? (She waves her hands in the air to illustrate.) Where did you pick that up?

Ruth (talking to Mildred but signing too) That's how deaf people communicate best. I learned it for my work.

Mildred: Well, I can't wave my hands around like that. Do you expect me to learn. . . .

(David kneels at the side of the sofa, near Mildred, and speaks and signs slowly.)

David: I can read your lips.

Mildred: He can speak!

Ruth: Yes, he can speak.

Mildred: Well, it's all right then. He can speak and she can hear . . . that's fine . . . so together they make one person. (She ends in a wail. Mrs. Daniels enters with the coffee. Ruth takes it and offers it to her mother. She tries to push it away.)

Mildred: No, I don't want any coffee.

Ruth (firmly): Now, Mother. . . .

(Mildred reluctantly cooperates and begins to sip, looking up at Ruth the first two times. Then she looks at the others and sees that they are all watching her.)

Mildred (in a scared voice to Ruth): Why is everyone looking at me? I feel like some kind of freak.

Ruth (soothingly): Oh, Mom. . . .

(Mildred takes a few more sips, then bravely puts down the cup and attempts the sign for coffee. This breaks the tension as they all join in to help her with the sign. She picks up the cup again and drinks. Ruth interprets her last line as she says it.)

Mildred: It's good coffee. . . .

After the scene, the actors shared the following:

Interviewer: Has this play been performed in its entirety?

Raffle: Several times. It was developed by a group in Connecticut called the Hartford Thespians, during the time Dorothy Miles was with NTD. She worked with this community theatre group to develop the script improvisationally during 1970-1972. Since 1972 it has been performed by various community groups all over the country.

Interviewer: Have these groups been specifically oriented toward deaf theatre, or was the play a part of their regular season?

Raffle: I think it has been performed primarily by regular community theatre groups.

Interviewer: How open are community theatre groups, in general, to performing theatre for deaf audiences or theatre about deaf experiences?

Raffle: They're open to it, but many of them have never thought about making their performances accessible. Some become interested after they have seen other companies who use interpreters or produce plays like *Children of a Lesser God.* But even when they make their plays accessible, they often don't know how to reach the deaf community.

Interviewer: What community resources are available to provide the experience of drama or theatre to deaf individuals?

Sally Jones: A year and a half ago my theatre company, the Co-Co-Ri-Ku Theatre, received money from the National Endowment for the Arts, Department of Cultural Affairs, and the New York State Council of the Arts, Special Projects, to do a theatre project for the deaf community. We had both hearing and deaf people in the audience. It was very successful both for the hearing and the deaf audience members.

Interviewer: It seems to me that there are two goals we're talking about in formal theatre: one is the experience of theatre for the deaf actor and for the deaf audience; and two is the education of the general community as to who deaf people are and what their cultural experiences are all about. . . . How do we make theatres or other community organizations more aware of ways to contact the deaf community?

Raffle: They have to involve deaf people in their audience development efforts. There are organizations that should be contacted, such as the New York League for the Hard of Hearing or GLAD in Los Angeles or deafness centers at universities such as NYU and California State University at Northridge. Also, an educational process can occur before the performances, so that the deaf community is motivated to attend the theatre.

There have been several notable theatre groups presenting both deaf theatre and sign language theatre, including the Little Theatre of the Deaf, which has performed for both hearing and deaf audiences of children, and the New York Deaf Theatre, of which Mary Beth Miller and Alan Barwiolek are members. There are also school-related programs in drama/theatre for the deaf, the most notable being at the National Technical Institute for the Deaf in Rochester, New York, with other programs at the New York School of the Deaf in White Plains and the Boston School for the Deaf in Massachusetts. Further information can be found in the pamphlet "Arts Accessibility for the Deaf," by Eugene Bergman, published by the National Access Center (see Bibliography).

With more and more professional theatres employing interpreters to translate spoken dialogue into sign language and installing teletypewriters (TTY) so that deaf people can order theatre tickets by phone, deaf audiences are attending theatre more frequently. A further innovation in audience development is occurring in Georgia where the Atlanta School for the Deaf in conjunction with the Alliance Theatre of Atlanta trains interpreters to perform in sign language on stage. This technique is called *shadowing*, as the interpreters are choreographed into the action and "shadow" the hearing actors' movements as they sign.

With the success of Mark Medoff's *Children of a Lesser God*, concerning the relationship between a deaf woman and a hearing man, and the continued success of NTD, general audiences are able to participate more fully in an understanding of deaf culture.

But much more work needs to be done at the school level as well as the community and professional theatre level. Drama and theatre is still viewed by too many deaf educators as a frill activity, and ironically, the popularity and easy intellectual accessibility of plays such as *Children of a Lesser God* might lead people to view deafness as another popular fad and smugly believe that they now know all they need to know about deaf culture.

To truly affect the consciousness of hearing and deaf people, alike, through drama and theatre, all efforts must be made to mount productions of deaf theatre as well as sign language theatre and to schedule dramatic activities within schools and relevant recreational institutions in the community. Given this kind of commitment, the ends would most certainly be therapeutic and would be justified by means grounded in art or therapy or, better yet, an integration of both.

DRAMA/THEATRE WITH THE ELDERLY

In a recent article on drama with seniors, Susan Pearson informed us that by the year 2000, 20 percent of the population of the United States will be older than sixty-five.[11] Given this situation, she argued for the need to develop quality special programs as a way to "help seniors give form to their rich life experience."[12] Pearson suggested that drama as used in education and therapy is one way to help foster a sense of dignity and positive self-worth within the elderly population. She referred to an Eskimo legend recently dramatized by the Tuma Theatre Company of Alaska, concerning a tribe threatened by famine who leaves their village in search of a new land. Their journey is blocked by a seemingly impassable glacier. While debating how to resolve this life-threatening dilemma, the elderly members of the tribe volunteer to set out within the glacier in search of a passageway. Their reasoning is that they possess the best knowledge of the terrain, and they are risking least as they are the closest to death. Time passes, and as the younger members of the tribe are about to abandon all hope, the elders return, having discovered a passageway. The story ends as they lead the tribe out of danger and toward a new life.

This dramatic vision of the elderly as wise and courageous can serve to inspire many already in the field of drama and theatre for the elderly or those contemplating developing drama experiences for the elderly. With creative drama leaders such as Isabel Burger and organizations such as the American Theatre Association (ATA) focusing attention upon the education and recreation of the elderly through drama, many new opportunities have opened up in community theatres, recreation centers, nursing homes, and other community organizations.[13]

Furthermore, drama therapists, such as Gert Schattner and Claire Michaels, founder of Geriadrama Training Workshops™, have worked in various clinical settings and nursing homes to help achieve therapeutic aims with senior citizens.

As in the areas of deafness and physical disability, the argument of drama as therapy versus drama as an art form is still debated. Many leaders of drama workshops for the elderly arguing against the drama therapy position, often refer to their work as recreational drama. One example is in the drama program at the Jewish Home and Hospital for Aged in Manhattan, directed by Dr. Paula Gray. In a recent discussion and demonstration Dr. Gray worked with two residents of the Jewish Home and Hospital for Aged, Rose Berger and Frank Zimmerman.[14]

The demonstration began as Berger, eighty-three years old, led a series of physical warm-ups including stretching various parts of the body, neck-rolls, breathing exercises, and a series of swimming movements. Then Gray introduced several imagination and pantomime exercises. For the first exercise, difficulty with a small object, Gray gave the following instructions:

Paula Gray: Without telling us what you are going to do, show us that you are having difficulty with some object.

Zimmerman pantomimed putting on his shoes, and Berger chose to mime a struggle with a zipper as she got dressed in the morning.

In a further exercise, also on the theme of pantomiming objects, Zimmerman began by threading a needle, and Berger followed by sewing buttons on her dress. After the pantomime, Gray set up a brief mirror image exercise that was followed by an improvisation involving an outing:

Mrs. Berger: How about a walk in Central Park?

Mr. Zimmerman: Oh, that'd suit me fine.

Mrs. B: Do we need a coat or is it warm enough to go without?

Mr. Z: It's 45 degrees.

Mrs. B: I didn't realize it was that cold. I'll tell you what. We'd better go to a movie.

Mr. Z: To a movie?

Mrs. B: Yes.

Mr. Z: I'd like going to a movie. What kind of movie? Drama or a musical?

Mrs. B: I am not exactly sure whether the picture is a musical, but I understand the acting is very good in that picture. Let's try it.

Mr. Z: I don't know. I like a musical. For instance, Fred Astaire is playing in *The Bell of Avenue A.* These old days come back to me. Why I want the old days, I don't know.

Mrs. B: I don't know either.

Mr. Z: These are good days for me now, better than they were in the old days. But I want it just the same. I think we'll go. If not, you can suggest something else. I don't like a deep drama, and I don't like tragedy. The other day I saw *La Traviata.* Everybody was stabbing someone else. I don't like that.

Mrs. B: That's right. You don't like to see trouble.

Mr. Z: I've become a critic now.

In a second improvisation Gray, in the role of a daughter, visits her parents, played by Zimmerman and Berger:

Mr. Z: Fine. We're set in here now.

Gray: I think we'll be sitting. Let's say I've already come in.

Mr. Z: I want a baby in this.

Gray: I've got the baby.

Mr. Z: Oh, how is little Michael getting along? Let me see him, will you?

Look at the little guy.

Gray: I think I'd better give him to Mama first. Mama, now don't let Dad drop Michael.

Mrs. B: No, darling.

Mr. Z: Oh, will you look at the guy. He's looking at me.

Mrs. B: Give me a chance to look at my grandchild.

Mr. Z: Baby, baby. He wants my glasses. You can't have Grandpa's glasses. Grandpa can't see the beautiful baby. Now you take him over, Rose.

Mrs. B: I had him for a minute, then you grabbed him. Look at him smile so beautifully. I love him.

Gray: Mama, be careful with the baby.

Mrs. B: What did I do?

Mr. Z: You had your hand underneath his leg.

Mrs. B: He's perfectly all right. He's fine.

Mr. Z: Let's not have an argument again. I've argued in the morning and that's all.

Gray: Mama, he's crying. Give me the baby.

Mrs. B: OK, here you are.

Gray: Michael, poor Michael.

Mrs. B: I haven't seen him in about two months and he's certainly changed.

Gray: Have you changed, Michael?

Mrs. B: Too young to answer you.

Mr. Z: Let me have him a minute.

Gray: Now, Dad, you be careful.

Mr. Z: I want to see if this guy knows how to walk yet. Eleven months old, he should be able to walk. I'll just put his little feet on the ground. Don't start crying, my little Michael, my little darling. That's it.

Zimmerman ended the improvisation abruptly, and the group moved into a final improvised situation, where Zimmerman played the role of a door-to-door salesman whose objective is to sell clothing to the women. The women are resistant, since Zimmerman's merchandise is priced cheaply and doesn't fully meet their specifications. But through his dialogue Zimmerman displays a wide knowledge of the merchandise and of salesmanship. The improvisation ends as it began—no sale. Following the improvised demonstrations the group discussed their experiences in drama and theatre:

Interviewer: Mr. Zimmerman, could you talk about how you first got interested in drama?

Mr. Z: I started through Dr. Gray. Robert Merrill was at our place. I came in the auditorium, and Dr. Gray said: "Mr. Zimmerman, would you sit over here, please." At that particular minute I said to myself: "Well, here's a woman that has confidence in me. From all the people sitting there, she chooses me in case he said, as most of those singers do say: "Will you sing for me?" And that's how it really started. Whenever there was an opportunity, no matter how small or how large, Dr. Gray would give me that. She chose me. When a person has confidence in you, you sort of build yourself up and say: "Well, this is something." Everybody doesn't have confidence in you.

Interviewer: Mr. Zimmerman, how old are you?

Mr. Z: Eighty-seven.

Interviewer: Is drama important to you?

Mr. Z: It's important to me, because it keeps me busy. I don't want to be idle a half a minute, because I start thinking. And thinking of the old days, that's bad. That's really one of the bad things about being in a home. There's such a thing as lonesomeness. Now how do you overcome lonesomeness? By doing something interesting. I was never able to sing before I came here. And they trusted me with a microphone. And I was singing. I didn't believe myself. And when I heard that applause, I was going to go out and get a size nine hat instead of a seven and a half. So I said: "Geez, I'm something now."

Interviewer: Mrs. Berger, could you tell us how you became interested in drama, and how do you see it as important in your life?

Mrs. B: Well, the same as Mr. Zimmerman said, it keeps me busy. And of course I am very interested in all the activities. We have to thank Dr. Gray for giving us wonderful activities.

The drama program at the Jewish Home and Hospital for Aged is often oriented toward performance. However, the product orientation is rooted in a process of improvisation and discussion.

The first performance experience by the drama group was developed improvisationally by six actors, all at least eighty years old, who reflected back upon their experiences as immigrants living on the Lower Eastside of Manhattan. The director helped them shape each scene and then transcribed the dialogue, as it was improvised. Finally, a full forty-five-minute script evolved, including musical numbers chosen by the actors.

Following the success of that experience Paula Gray began to use drama techniques in the weekly drama group meetings. She adapted the exercises to meet such physical realities of the group members as visual and hearing impairments and limitations in movement and coordination. She further adapted techniques of dance therapy in warming up and articulating body parts.

Gray extended her work to include the more disabled residents on the nursing floors of the hospital. This work required even further modifications of the drama techniques to meet the needs of those who were more seriously disoriented and physically disabled.

Furthermore, Gray has used role-playing techniques to deal with emotional issues such as anger and hurt. As an example, in working with a group of seven elderly women with heart conditions, Gray used role-playing to help explore their feelings toward their doctor. A nurse assumed the role of the doctor, a distracted, godlike figure who never seemed to have time or interest in his patients. Through a series of role-playing situations, where group members assumed the roles of patients in relationship to their doctor, the issues of assertiveness and fear were dramatized and then discussed by the full group. According to Dr. Gray, "members became increasingly assertive as role-play progressed."[15]

In summing up her remarks on drama with the elderly, Gray wrote:

> The elderly as a group are plagued by many physical, sociological and psychological problems. Some of these may limit the scope of their participation in dramatics, but it is because of these problems that dramatics has particular therapeutic value for the elderly. It is particularly exciting for them to find that they can succeed in dramatics with some realistic adaptations. It can open up for them emotions which they have not allowed themselves to experience in real life. It can teach them to work and play with other persons and gives them something to look forward to. Most importantly, it gives them a feeling of self-achievement and shows that an elderly person can learn new things.[16]

In integrating Gray's notion of the dramatic learning of the elderly with the Eskimo dramatization of the teaching or leading by the elderly, the full possibilities of drama and theatre with this special population, whose ranks will be joined by all human beings who live long enough, become apparent.

NOTES

1. WCBS-TV, *Sunrise Semester*, "Drama in Education: Puppetry for/with the Mentally Retarded" (November 26, 1979).

2. A. R. Philpott, *Puppets and Therapy* (Boston: Plays, Inc., 1977).

3. Sue Jennings, *Remedial Drama* (New York: Theatre Arts Books, 1978), pp. 36-40.

4. Betty Jane Wagner, *Dorothy Heathcote*, pp. 211-12.

5. David Morgan, "Overcoming the Tiny Tim Syndrome," in Shaw and Stevens, *Drama, Theatre, and the Handicapped*, p. 44.

6. Ibid.

7. WCBS-TV, *Sunrise Semester*, "Drama in Education: Drama/Theatre for the Handicapped" (November 23, 1979). The disabilities of the three students are blindness (Karen Luxton) and orthopedic disability (Elliot Schloss and Jane Zirinsky).

8. WCBS-TV, *Sunrise Semester*, "Drama in Education: Drama/Theatre for the Blind and Orthopedically Handicapped" (December 3 and 5, 1979).

9. WCBS-TV, *Sunrise Semester*, "Drama in Education: Drama/Theatre in the Deaf Community" (December 10, 1979).

10. Reprinted with permission from Dorothy Miles. In the original production, David was hearing and Ruth was deaf.

11. Susan Pearson, "Drama with Seniors: Breaking the Ice," *Children's Theatre Review* 28, no. 4 (1980): 2-4.

12. Ibid.

13. See Isabel Burger, *Creative Drama for Senior Adults* (Wilton, Conn.: Morehouse-Barlow, 1980). ATA has recently developed a new committee, the Senior Adult Theatre Program.

14. WCBS-TV, *Sunrise Semester*, "Drama in Education: Drama/Theatre for/with the Elderly" (December 7, 1979).

15. Paula Gray, "The Elderly Can Learn through Dramatics," *Sunrise Semester*, "Drama in Education," *Newsletter No. 2*, New York University, Office of Off-Campus Programs, November 1979, p. 9.

16. Ibid., pp. 9-10.

BIBLIOGRAPHY

Aach, Susan. "Drama: A Means of Self-Expression for the Visually Impaired Child." *New Outlook for the Blind* 70, no. 7 (September 1976): 282-85.

Bergman, Eugene. "Arts Accessibility for the Deaf." Washington, D.C.: National Access Center, 1419 27 Street N.W., TTY: 202-333-1712.

Blumberg, Marvin L. "Creative Dramatics: An Outlet for Mental Handicaps." *Journal of Rehabilitation* 42, no. 6 (November-December 1976): 17-20.

Brewster, Jeff. "Drama with Physically Limited Children." In Geraldine Brain Siks. *Drama with Children*. New York: Harper and Row, 1977, pp. 197-202.

Burger, Isabel. *Creative Drama for Senior Adults*. Wilton, Conn.: Morehouse-Barlow, 1980.

Champlin, John, and Connie Champlin. *Books, Puppets, and the Mentally Retarded Student*. Omaha, Neb.: Special Literature Press, 1981.

Clopton, Anna Smulowitz, and Harriet Davis. "Drama and the 'Special Needs' Student." *Secondary School Theatre Journal* 18, no. 3 (Spring 1979): 21-25.

Davis, R. G. "Theatre Arts Training for the Severely Disabled." *Theatre News* 10, no. 9 (May 1977): 21.

Denis, Taras B. "Drama and the Deaf Child." In Geraldine Brain Siks. *Drama with Children*. New York: Harper and Row, 1977, pp. 202-4.

Ginglend, David R. *The Expressive Arts for the Mentally Retarded*. New York: National Association for Retarded Children, 1967.

Gray, Paula. *Dramatics for the Elderly: A Guide for Residential Care Settings and Senior Centers*. New York: Columbia University, Teachers College Press, 1974.

Green, Richard. "Role Playing for Effective Learning." *The Pointer* 20, no. 3 (Spring 1976): 32-34.

Klepac, Richard L. "Through the Looking Glass: Socio-drama and Mentally Retarded Individuals." *Mental Retardation* 16, no. 5 (October 1978): 343-45.

Landy, Robert J. "Drama as an Art Experience for the Handicapped." *Secondary School Theatre Journal* 18, no. 3 (Spring 1979): 19-20.

Loeschke, Maravene. "Mime: A Movement Program for the Visually Handicapped." *Journal of Visual Impairment and Blindness* 7 no. 8 (October 1977): 337-45.

Martin, Sue. "Developmental Drama for Brain-Damaged Children." *Communication Education* 26 (September 1977): 208-13.

Maynard, Marianne. "The Value of Creative Arts for the Developmentally Disabled Child: Implications for Recreation Specialists in Community Day Service Programs." *Therapeutic Recreation Journal* 10, no. 1 (1976): 10-12.

McIntyre, Barbara M. *Informal Dramatics: A Language Arts Activity for the Special Pupil.* Pittsburgh: Stanwix House, 1963.

Miles, Dorothy S. "The Love of Seven Dolls." Unpublished playscript, 1976.

_____. With the Hartford Thespians. "A Play of Our Own." Unpublished playscript, 1973.

_____. *Poems for Sign Language.* Northridge, Calif.: Joyce Media, 1976.

_____, and Louie J. Fant, Jr. *Sign-Language Theatre and Deaf Theatre: New Definitions and Directions.* Publication Series No. 2. Northridge, Calif.: California State University, Center on Deafness, 1976.

Nutial, Mark. "Readers Theatre for the Deaf." *Readers Theatre News* 5, no. 1 (Fall 1977): 10-11.

Parente, Joseph, and Alice Ball. "Fatso: Process Theatre for the Handicapped." *Theatre News* 10, no. 3 (December 1977): 16.

Powers, Helen. *Signs of Silence: Bernard Bragg and the National Theatre of the Deaf.* New York: Dodd, Mead and Company, 1972.

Reich, Rosalyn. "Puppetry: A Language Tool," *Exceptional Children* 34, no. 8 (April 1968): 621-23.

Schattner, Regina. *Creative Dramatics for Handicapped Children.* New York: The John Day Co., 1977.

Shaw, Ann M., and Cj Stevens, eds. *Drama, Theatre, and the Handicapped.* Washington, D.C.: American Theatre Association, 1979.

_____, and Wendy Perks, eds. *Perspectives: A Handbook in Drama and Theatre by, with, and for Handicapped Individuals.* Washington, D.C.: American Theatre Association, 1981.

Sherill, Claudine, ed. *Creative Arts for the Severely Handicapped.* Fort Worth: Perko Printing Co., 1977.

Snyder, Alice B. "Drama and Learning Disorders." *Children's Theatre Review* 25, no. 1 (1976): 10-12.

Sternberg, Pat. *Program Accessibility for the Disabled Theatre-Goer.* New York: Off-Off Broadway Association, 1980.

Strain, Phillip S. "Increasing Social Play of Severely Retarded Preschoolers with Socio-Dramatic Activities." *Mental Retardation* 13, no. 6 (December 1975): 7-9.

Wagener, Elaine Hoffman. "Drama: Key to History for the Visually Impaired Child." *Education of the Visually Handicapped* 9, no. 2 (Summer 1977): 45-47.

Wethered, Audrey G. *Movement and Drama in Therapy.* Boston: Plays, Inc., 1973.

Williams, Lynne D. *From Dream to Reality: The Origins and Development of a One-of-a-Kind Institution: The National Technical Institute for the Deaf.* Rochester, N.Y.: National Technical Institute for the Deaf, 1979.

9
DRAMA AND THEATRE
IN THE INNER CITY
COMMUNITY

We have seen an example in chapter 1 of educational drama applied to an inner city school in the work of Thom Turner, principal of the Street Academy in Bedford-Stuyvesant, Brooklyn. But during the past fifteen years formal theatre has especially been a prevalent force in developing a sense of hopefulness and dignity within many inner city communities and cultural groups. Examples include the National Black Theatre and the Negro Ensemble Company in New York, El Teatro De La Esperanza and El Teatro Campesino in California, and various Nuyorican (New York Puerto Rican) groups in New York, including the Puerto Rican Traveling Company, the Puerto Rican Playwrights' and Actors' Workshop, and The Family.

The Family, which traces its roots to workshops in the prison system led by the group's artistic director Marvin Felix Camillo, established its artistic and sociological reputation with its 1973 production of Miguel Piñero's *Short Eyes*, a play about the emotional and physical brutality of prison life. Since that time The Family has produced more than a dozen plays related particularly to the experiences of inner city populations but more generally to issues of universal relevance.

Several years ago Camillo adapted and directed the Chekhov classic *The Marriage Proposal* by setting the play on a Caribbean island, transforming the Russian characters into Hispanics and blacks, and adding many relevant cultural elements of songs, rituals, games, and foods.

The Family has also run many workshops in prisons, churches, rehabilitation centers, and other community organizations. The group states its goals as follows:

To bring theatre productions to correctional facilities, community arts centers, and other facilities in the inner city, as well as to theatres, colleges, and schools.

To develop training methods and mount productions that relate directly to the disadvantaged, providing positive alternatives to drugs and crime.

To facilitate the re-entry of ex-offenders into society by providing opportunities for involvement in theatre both as actor and instructor, coupled with personal and job counseling. Training and experience in stage management, lighting and set design and theatre company administration and teaching are also offered.

To offer an educational program in all aspects of theatre arts through workshops for people currently participating in therapeutic and rehabilitation programs and in correctional facilities.[1]

In a recent interview with two members of The Family, Camillo and Raymond Ruiz, as well as Rose Colavito, a drama teacher in an inner city junior high school who has been working cooperatively with The Family, the group offered perspectives on the use of drama and theatre in the inner city community:[2]

Interviewer: What is The Family?

Camillo: The Family is a repertory company that tours colleges, theatres, inner cities, all across the country. And it's a workshop program that deals with youth, with people in prisons and other institutions, and it's also a central workshop program in New York City.

Interviewer: Why is it called The Family?

Camillo: Because we have origins in the prisons in New York State. When the workshops started in prisons, they got to a certain point where they became successful and interesting for the men at that time. There was a very unique way of dealing with each other and dealing with the work that's very much like the way families work and develop together. When we just came out into the free world, we met with Colleen Dewhurst, who really said that we should take that name and keep it. We have.

Interviewer: Rose, what is your connection to The Family?

Rose Colavito: We do plays in our junior high school. The kids are age thirteen through fifteen. One of our students knew Pancho (Camillo), and she suggested that he come to see one of our plays. That was a turning point for our drama group. The Family involvement gave them an added impetus, where they felt not only that their self-image was good, but now other people were looking at them and enjoying what they were doing. They learned new techniques from The Family. Some of them became directly involved with The Family. I think it has given them a great sense of confidence. We've taken advantage of The

Family's free acting classes with Raul Julia and singing classes with Gilbert Price.

Interviewer: What kind of community do your students come from?

Colavito: The neighborhood is black and Puerto Rican. The school is an extension of the community base. Even though The Family is based in Manhattan and we're in the Bronx, we still feel like we're part of The Family. I think the relationship has helped the kids grow tremendously.

Interviewer: Raymond, how did you get involved with The Family?

Raymond Ruiz: Back in 1975 I was hanging out in Prospect Park in Brooklyn. The Family was doing a run of a play called *The Shoeshine Parlor.* I came down the first night and I really enjoyed the performance. It really overwhelmed me, because a lot of the things on the stage were reality, things I'd see in the street everyday.

Interviewer: Could you give an example?

Ruiz: One scene was about this young girl who was getting into drugs, and she ODs on drugs. It was not only drugs, but a lot of different scenes of hustling and this and that which you see in the street. The second and third day I came back, a friend of mine introduced me to Pancho. I wanted to get involved in the whole thing, because it was so real to me and so beautiful to see not only talented actors, but a lot of them Puerto Ricans and blacks doing theatre. I came down to The Family to join the acting and singing and mime workshops. I've been doing different productions for five years. I've been to Attica and other prisons, seeing my own friends in the prisons, and they see me grow in the theatre.

Interviewer: What about your friends who stayed on the street? Did they give you a hard time for becoming an actor, for changing and growing?

Ruiz: Not really. A few of them came down and wanted to get involved too, but a lot of them had problems and a lot of them were dealing in the streets. It is a lot of commitment and work. A lot of people couldn't deal with the theatre, because they think it's so unreal. It's a different type of world to them.

Interviewer: Pancho, how do you respond to that? What do you do when you get people who see the theatre as unreal or people whose lives are unstructured and yet see that you are a real hope for them?

Camillo: That's a common occurrence, and everybody's situation is different. If you take the situation of some of Raymond's friends, some of them do come and participate in the workshops from time to time. Also, they have become our audiences. These are the people that come to us and look for support, and we try to support them whenever we can. One of his friends recently, for example, joined The Family and got a scholarship to go to college. The important thing about The Family is that it is an open-door policy, and we try not to have the typical kinds of restrictions. We try to let people know that when you're ready, there is a place for you. The creative experiences that Raymond has or kids in P.S.

118 or a person in Arthur Kill Correction Facility has is really something that should be available to everybody.

Interviewer: There have been so many unsuccessful attempts to deal with people who spend a lot of their time hanging out on the street. Prisons have been unsuccessful; many of the drug rehabilitation programs have been unsuccessful. What is it about theatre, in general, or The Family, in particular, that helps these people?

Camillo: I see theatre, first of all, as a training for life. My personal experience is coming from the city of Newark. At an early age I had a choice to go one way or the other. Fortunately, I was introduced at a very early age to the theatre. Theatre is a discipline, and it teaches discipline. When you really work in the theatre, you don't have time for that other stuff. Sometimes being in this business is very, very difficult. The one thing I have to turn to when the chips are down and everything is going wrong is that I'm an actor, and I can really release myself through a creative means. It doesn't matter whether you're from the inner city or Scarsdale or Greenhaven Prison. I just feel that we're better people when we have a creative outlet. Theatre is the thing that brings us closer together and gives us an opportunity to search and to learn a lot more about ourselves and the world.

Interviewer: Would you agree with that, Rose, in terms of your experience as a teacher?

Colavito: Yes. I see it when the kids are doing improvisations. They open themselves up to many values, including respect for each other. They know that they must listen to the person performing if they want to be listened to. They must give respect to an audience if they want respect from the audience. The improvisational roles they assume are mostly like taking care of the kid sister or arguing with their parents about more freedom. So they're expanding their own experience to be able to deal with these problems realistically. They take to improvisation more than to plays. If they do a play with a script they want to write their own, based upon their own experience or a television program. The goals they set in their improvs are very realistic for them—convincing their parents they should go to a school dance or learning how to play the drums, for example.

Interviewer: Raymond, have you worked through improvisation in training with The Family?

Ruiz: Sure. A lot of our workshops use improvisation. I'd like to comment on the thing you said about the theatre helping people. I've done a lot of workshops with The Family in alternative schools, homes for juveniles, and different kinds of places. I have found for me as a teenager to go into an alternative school or a home and teach them something they never had is really beautiful, because a lot of them can't

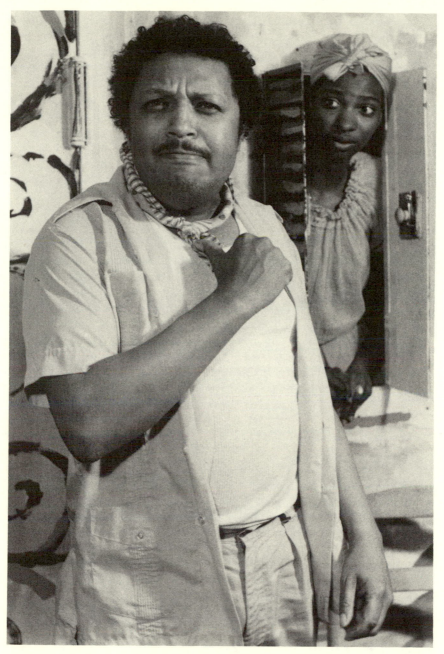

4. Marvin Felix Camillo and Ellen-Leslye Cleghorne in *The Marriage Proposal* by Anton Chekhov, adapted by Marvin Felix Camillo. Photograph by Gerry Goodstein. Courtesy of The Family, Inc.

get into theatre programs. They also look forward to us coming there, because not only do we teach them theatre, but they also learn about themselves.

Interviewer: Let's talk about developing your productions to be accessible to inner city audiences. You chose Chekhov to be performed by black and Hispanic actors to black and Hispanic audiences. Why Chekhov, and what was the process like of making this material accessible to inner city audiences?

Camillo: My introduction to Chekhov was in Spanish with a street theatre company called Teatro de la Calle. I was the understudy to Raul Julia. The inspiration behind *The Marriage Proposal* was really the result of a visit I had in Puerto Rico with a family, the Arufat family, whom I named our characters after. Chekhov is a storyteller. While working in the prisons I met the greatest storytellers in the world. A lot of them were in the joint for telling stories. I wanted to explore the musical aspect of people who existed in the Caribbean, which is Hispanic and West Indian. When I went to Puerto Rico, I also visited the Virgin Islands. And in The Family we are predominantly Hispanic and Black American. But West Indians were beginning to come into The Family. Chekhov's plays are universal. Recently, we did Shakespeare's *Twelfth Night* with a completely mixed cast. In working on *The Marriage Proposal* we stuck to the text. We didn't change any words. In Russia they baked bricks. In the Caribbean they cut sugar cane. The girl in Russia was Natalia Stepanovna. In this play she's West Indian, Natalia Olivia Belgrave. The Russian suitor was Ivan Vassilevitch. In this play he is Ivan Francisco Arufat Rivera. We started out in my apartment in Brooklyn. Everybody thought it was pretty silly to do Chekhov. But we began to develop little things. For example, in preparing the first dream sequence we began by improvising. We added rhythms by clapping. Before long the songs began to develop. We took classes with Charles Barney from the American Mime Theatre. We would set up situations around the script that we thought were appropriate. The Family still, after three or four years, continues to develop the play.

Interviewer: I attended a production this summer in the Bronx Museum. It was a very hot and humid day. I felt like I was in the West Indies. The audience was made up of very young black and Hispanic children. They had a tremendous involvement in and appreciation for your work. Some of them were probably seeing theatre for the first time. Others spoke little English and must have had great difficulty following the English dialogue. Why were they so enthused about this play?

Ruiz: I think because a lot of the characters are not only funny, but they also play familiar games. We play Spanish games that they know.

Interviewer: So this was part of their cultural experience.

Ruiz: Yes. And not only was the play in English, but we also spoke a lot of Spanish.

Interviewer: There was also a great deal of audience participation.

Ruiz: Yes.

Colavito: I really didn't question the choice of Chekhov. I feel that the great writers are universal. I think The Family has a classic touch that has to do with their feelings toward each other and their work. This communicates to the audience who feels apart of them.

Interviewer: How do you create this sense of closeness among actors and between actors and audiences? So many other organizations have failed to deal with the basic problems of our society, whereas you've had some real success. What's the magic?

Camillo: It's hard work. When The Family first came out with *Short Eyes*, everybody said: "Well, a lot of them have been in prison and that's what they can do." But even then it was manufacturing the twenty-fifth hour, and encouraging some of the potentially most talented people I know, and giving them the opportunity, and allowing them to bring a lot of themselves into the work. We say: "You should understand what's happening; you should be involved in plays; you should read Chekhov; you should enjoy Chekhov and give this to the audience, no matter where they've come from, whether they're rich or poor, whether they're from the Bronx or Westport." It's daring to really let it happen. It's always work. We have had a lot of successes in The Family. Within The Family we do have a very special thing going on that you can't always have in the commercial theatre, because there you're together for just four or five weeks. I've known Ray since he was a kid and he's a man now. There's a lot of love and a lot of caring. That goes a long way. As a director I might work with a lot of actors and ask certain things of them that they might be a little dubious about, but with this company they know that it's only to make the work better and our productions special and meaningful.

Interviewer: Ray, why is drama and theatre such a significant alternative to drugs and crime?

Ruiz: It gives you something to do, and it takes up a lot of your time. It puts a lot of that time into positive things. Right now, I don't know where I'd be if I wasn't involved with The Family. I was hanging out in the street and doing a lot of negative things. The Family game me a home to come to and keep my thoughts positive. It's hard to keep people together, because we have not had a consistent home. We went from Madison Avenue to Riverside Church. Now we're going to another space. I think if The Family gets its own home, we'll have a place for a lot of people to come to and enjoy that experience as I have.

Interviewer: Rose, why is theatre such an important alternative to drugs and crime for your students?

Colavito: It's a question of self-image. They feel good doing it. Other people feel good about them doing it. They're happy; they're making others happy.

Some of the above statements echo the words of the eighty-seven-year-old Frank Zimmerman who stated that drama is important to him, because "there's such a thing as lonesomeness. How do you overcome lonesomeness? By doing something interesting."

It appears that the sense of waiting, of passing the time in futility and loneliness, has led many young people—inner city, urban, and suburban alike—to drugs and crime and many elderly people to withdrawing more and more into a kind of self-imposed imprisonment. Drama and theatre offer a hope. At the very least they pass the time, a statement that echoes Samuel Beckett's words in *Waiting for Godot*. It is interesting to note that this play, which so baffled and outraged middle-class audiences when it was initially performed in the 1950s, was viewed as clearly reflective of the philosophical realities of the outside world by an audience of prisoners at San Quentin. This special audience attended Herbert Blau's production at their facility in the mid-1950s and later, through a drama group inspired by that experience, produced their own versions of Beckett's *Waiting for Godot* and *Endgame*.

At the very best, drama and theatre "puts a lot of that time into positive things." In his preface to *Short Eyes* Camillo wrote about the early days of The Family:

It was important for members of The Family that they discover that you could get a better high off of your creativity than any of those cold, unnatural, deadly chemicals that they were addicted to, and that they be recognized as serious actors who happened to come from unfortunate circumstances.[3]

Drama and theatre in any community has the potential to transform an unfortunate situation into a fortunate one. Drama and theatre is about struggle. The truly excellent drama and theatre leaders can take the struggles of any group of people locked into any environmentally imposed or self-imposed ghetto and help them pass the time if not in a more positive, more creative way, at least in a less lonely way.

Other organizations, like The Family, have based their work upon providing alternatives to drugs and crime through theatre. Several have committed themselves to working primarily with prison populations. Examples include the New York-based Theatre for the Forgotten, New York Street Theatre Caravan, and the Cell Block Theatre (no longer in operation); the Trenton, New Jersey-based Theatre Without Bars; and the Los Angeles-based L.A. Theatre Works.

In the past the federal government has supported theatre in prisons as exemplified in Project CULTURE, a national program for prisoners in the performing, visual, and literary arts. Furthermore, a national resource center was developed by Steven Hart, a professor of Educational Theatre at New York University. Hart's Theatre in Prison Archives is located at the Graduate School and University Center of the City University of New York.

NOTES

1. From a brochure distributed by The Family, 410 West 42 Street, New York, New York 10036.

2. WCBS-TV, *Sunrise Semester*, "Drama in Education: Drama/Theatre in the Black and Hispanic Community" (December 12 and 14, 1979).

3. Marvin Felix Camillo, Introduction to Miguel Piñero's *Short Eyes* (New York: Hill and Wang, 1975), p. x.

BIBLIOGRAPHY AND RESOURCES

Books, Articles, Scripts, and Dissertations

Alam, Shamsul. "Benpires." Unpublished playscript. New York: Theatre in Prison Archives, Center for Advanced Study in Theatre Arts, The Graduate School and University Center of the City University of New York, 1978.

Arts in Corrections: A Summary of Project CULTURE and a Handbook for Program Implementation. Washington, D.C.: American Correctional Association, 1980.

Blau, Herbert. *The Impossible Theatre, A Manifesto*. New York: Collier Books, 1964.

Brown, Kenneth H. *The Brig: A Concept for Theatre and Film*. New York: Hill and Wang, 1965.

Harris, Neil, et al. "Straight from the Ghetto." Unpublished playscript. New York: Theatre in Prison Archives, CASTA, GSUC, CUNY, 1977.

Hart, Steven. "The Family: A Theatre Company Working with Prison Inmates and Ex-Inmates." Ph.D. dissertation, The City University of New York, 1981.

———, and Stanley A. Waren, "Workshop/Conference: Theatre in Prisons." New York: Theatre in Prison Archives, CASTA, GSUC, CUNY, June 1980.

Herbert, John. *Fortune and Men's Eyes*. New York: Grove Press, 1967.

Huerta, Jorge A. "El Teatro de la Esperanza." *The Drama Review* 21, no. 1 (March 1977): 37-46.

Morton, Carlos. "Nuyorican Theatre." *The Drama Review* 20, no. 1 (March 1976): 43-49.

———. "The Teatro Campesino." *The Drama Review* 18, no. 4 (December 1974): 71-76.

Norman, Marsha. *Getting Out*. New York: Avon Books, 1979.

Piñero, Miguel. *Short Eyes*. New York: Hill and Wang, 1975.

Reyes, Ringo. "Looking for Tomorrow." Unpublished playscript. New York: Theatre in Prison Archives, CASTA, GSUC, CUNY, 1979.

Theatre Companies Working with Inmates and Ex-inmates

The Family
    410 West 42 Street
    New York, New York 10036
L.A. Theatre Works
    P.O. Box 49605
    Los Angeles, California 90049
New York Street Theatre Caravan
    87-05 Chelsea Street
    Jamaica, New York 11432
Pioneer Theatre
    Riksteatern
    Solna S-17130, Sweden
Theatre for the Forgotten
    32 West 82 Street
    New York, New York 10024

Films

Available through MASS, University of Connecticut, U-Box 127, Storrs, Connecticut 06268:
    Once Upon a Man
    Pressure Point
    Time Out

PART III
THE THEATRE AS AN EDUCATIONAL ENVIRONMENT FOR YOUNG AUDIENCES

INTRODUCTION

In the introduction to this book we looked at several definitions in the area of theatre for young audiences, as developed by the Children's Theatre Association of America. That organization, in specifying the term *theatre for young audiences*, rather than children's theatre, emphasizes the point that performance is necessarily presented to an audience of children or youth, but not necessarily performed by them. In fact, as we will see, some of the major theatres for young audiences in this country are staffed by adult actors only.

Throughout this book reference has been made to several of the issues in this area, for example, the child as performer, the relationship of the dramatic process to the performed product, and suitable dramatic literature to perform. We now take a more thorough look at theatre as it relates to the education of young audiences, pre-school through high school.

In a recent interview Nellie McCaslin, professor of Educational Theatre at New York University and one of the foremost experts in theatre for young audiences, spoke of the early history of the field in the United States:[1]

Nellie McCaslin: The year 1903 is given generally as the beginning of children's theatre in this country. There wasn't any distinction made at all between children's theatre and creative dramatics. It was up to Winifred Ward to make that distinction later on. But the first experiment, which was extremely successful, was the Children's Educational Theatre in New York, located at the Educational Alliance, an institution still in existence and still interested in drama. The woman responsible for the first theatre was Alice Minnie Herts. She saw this as a way of bringing wholesome entertainment to children of the slums for whom there was nothing else. We're talking about a period where there was no children's theatre, no television, no radio or movies. Her one major objective was an aesthetic one, an art form to be shared with children in the community. A second objective stated by her was to teach the children the language of the new country. Most of them were children of immigrants, and English was not spoken at home. The third objective, common to all settlement houses, was to provide a place where the people in the neighborhood could come.

Interviewer: Do we have equivalents to settlement houses now? Are there still settlement houses where theatre occurs?

McCaslin: Yes, there are. We tend to call them community centers today. I'm not sure why the name has changed, except that perhaps the lines of communities and the services of the centers have changed. But the old settlement house was always located in a ghetto area, and its aim was to serve the people of that neighborhood. Today, we might find a community center which draws people from a variety of classes and economic backgrounds, not necessarily low income. The play that was chosen for the first production was *The Tempest.* I think that theatre directors today, even with a group of children much older and more accustomed to going to the theatre or watching television, would be reluctant to choose that as an opener. But it was very successful by all accounts. The children not only came, but they brought their families with them. Two thousand copies of the play were said to have been sold within the months of the performance. This theatre lasted for about seven years. It closed for the same reason most children's theatres and many civic theatres in this country have closed— for lack of money. But the idea had caught on. Thereafter, we were to see many children's theatres in large cities under the sponsorship of settlement houses and community centers.

Interviewer: As theatre for young audiences developed through the years, did the content change much? Were people still working with the classics, or was there a body of literature developing specifically for children?

McCaslin: A body of literature was developing, although it was rather slow in coming. For many years the folk and fairy tales, the traditional material, was most popular. I think we'd probably find that true today if we were to take a survey. But within the last ten years, there certainly has been a movement to expand. Some people even want to drop the traditional. Personally, I think that would be a mistake, because that is part of our heritage. But I'm also delighted to see some new material coming in, concerned with social problems, things children are thinking about today. After all, children are exposed to a great deal more than they were before the advent of television.

Interviewer: Do you feel the classics are still appropriate for children?

McCaslin: I certainly do, and I think many people are afraid of the classics. They're afraid they won't hold the child audience, because children see so much entertainment so beautifully produced on television. I think the average producer is afraid of giving children something heavy that would not be done as well as on a television screen.

Interviewer: What are other outstanding events in the early history of theatre for young audiences?

McCaslin: There have been a great many. We were to find other similar ventures in large cities—San Francisco, Boston, Washington, Baltimore, Tulsa. If you look back at the magazines of the period, especially those that had to do with recreation, like *Playground Magazine* and others published between 1910 and 1930, we would find accounts of productions that were given in the community centers, on the playgrounds and camps. They tended to be more in the jurisdiction of the recreational people and social workers than the educators. There was another group we have to remember, the Junior League of America. In those early days they filled a role that was really not being filled by anyone else. They went into the poor neighborhoods, gave classes in creative drama and storyacting. Later on they began trooping plays, but they worked primarily with the social workers. There were a few other troops hardy enough to stand up over the years. One was the Clare Tree Major Traveling Theatre for Children, which went on from the twenties until the mid-fifties. This was a traveling group of professional adult actors doing the classics and the fairy tales from coast to coast. This was not educational theatre, unless we believe, as I do, that everything from which we learn is education. Clare Tree Major was not an educator, but a professional actress who became interested in children's theatre. Her's was entirely formal theatre by professional adults for audiences of children.

As mentioned above, theatre for young audiences is generally performed by adults. There are exceptions, such as the First All Children's Theatre Company in New York City, which is directed and designed by adults, but acted by children for audiences of children. Many precedents for this kind of company can be found throughout history, a most interesting example being Asja Lacis's work during the 1920s in developing a proletarian theatre by and for children in the Soviet Union.[2]

Let us now turn, though, to one of the most renowned companies of adult actors, the Paper Bag Players, to examine the role of the actor in theatre for young audiences. In the following discussion of the roles of the actor, director, designer, and playwright, we will examine the conceptions that each theatre artist has of his work in theatre for young audiences.

NOTES

1. WCBS-TV, *Sunrise Semester*, "Drama in Education: A History of American Drama and Theatre in Education" (September 21, 1979).

2. See Asja Lacis, "A Memoir," *Performance* 1, no. 5 (March/April 1973): 22-27.

10
THEATRE FOR
YOUNG AUDIENCES

THE ACTORS

The Paper Bag Players was founded in 1958 by Judith Martin in collaboration with a group of dancers, visual artists, and actors that included Remy Charlip, Shirley Kaplan, Betty Osgood, Sudie Bond, and Daniel Jahn. Their diverse backgrounds led to the development of a unique, eclectic style of performing for young audiences that includes dance, music, dialogue, and highly imaginative scenic elements constructed from paper and many found objects. Today, the core ensemble group includes Martin, who initiates and directs most of the creative work; Irving Burton, the group's leading actor; Donald Ashwander, the composer; and Judith Liss, the business manager. The Bags describe their work as based upon children's ideas and experiences and speak of their process of creating theatre for young audiences as follows:

> There is no format in the Bags approach to creating new pieces. Usually beginning with a rough idea, Judith Martin starts to work alone in the studio. Often she will work with Irving Burton to crystallize an idea in advance of its presentation to the cast. Donald Ashwander's musical ideas sometimes lead, sometimes follow the course of the action. The company members begin with the suggested dialogue and go about building the scene. Occasionally pieces develop in an orderly fashion. Dialogue-music-movement-props build one element on the other into a whole. More often the development is completely chaotic. The dialogue doesn't develop, but a costume idea shapes the action. A song will be inappropriate, and instead a dance will emerge. Slowly, in a zigzag,

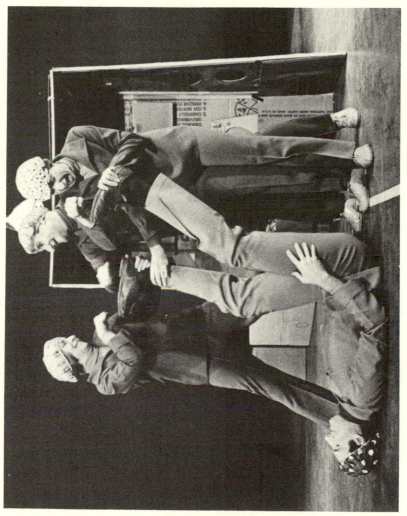

5. The Paper Bag Players in *I Won't Take a Bath*. Photograph by Hugh Grannum. Courtesy of The Paper Bag Players.

backtracking way, the ideas take shape into an organized theatrical piece. Eventually, the various pieces are linked together into the proper pattern for a complete revue that might best be described as a theatrical collage.[1]

In a recent interview with the Bags, Judith Martin and Irving Burton further discussed their work as actors for audiences of young people.[2]

Interviewer: Why did you choose theatre for young audiences, as opposed to going into the commercial theatre?

Judith Martin: I think it's something that really just happened. Many years ago several friends and myself became interested in the idea of working together. One would call our work improvisation, but we were interested in much more. One was a musician, one an actress, another a dancer, and one a painter. We were interested in how we could affect one another, and if we could really do something that was beyond that wonderful moment in the studio. Could we make it a piece of theatre? I'd been teaching children and that was one reason my thoughts went there. But beyond it, it seemed like here was a place where all of us interested in fantasy could work freely, outside those restrictions that one has in conventional theatre. This was what made us so comfortable in doing our first production.

Interviewer: Were you dealing with your own sense of fantasy?

Martin: I guess one always deals with one's own sense of fantasy. There was a princess and there was a witch in our early production, although not the traditional ones. Ours became humorous, and they had an unexpected relationship. But certainly, it was from us, for at that point we still felt ourselves rooted in that kind of imagery. We were immediately successful, and we were propelled into a professional situation where we had to produce so many hour-length plays in such-and-such a time. I think that the struggle over the years has been to keep that sense of excitement, freshness, and inspiration and one person influencing another and not being tied to a formula. It has been hard to keep that along with being professional, being there on time, having the right kind of actor, etcetera.

Interviewer: Let's talk about the actor. Irving, what are the necessary qualities for your actors?

Irving Burton: When we start to look for an actor or an actress, we always look for someone who has a great comic sense. We also look for someone who has to have an imagination. We look for someone who likes to play and have fun; someone who likes to move, to act, to sing, who is not afraid to be absolutely crazy on the stage.

Martin: To me, it's a very interesting and frustrating situation. In the first place, the actor who reads that there's an audition for theatre for children typically comes with the most exaggerated notion of gesture and speech. So we're presented immediately with a cliché. It's not necessarily that the actor is a bad actor, but his idea of what we want is a cliché. This is the first thing to dispell. Then we look for a good actor who's willing to be in a theatre for children. Unfortunately, theatre for children has a very bad name. It is said: "If you're working in theatre for children, it's because you can't get a job anyplace else. If you really were good, you wouldn't be in theatre for children." So you start with a great deal against you. I think the difference that separates our actor from the ordinary actor is not children's theatre but rather musical theatre or theatre of non-illusion; that is, we're always acting or always playing in the theatre. We're related to vaudeville. We have a comic style.

An example of a Paper Bag Players comic vaudeville, involving actors who are playful, versatile, highly comic, and imaginative, is "Apartment," a short piece concerning four people who live together in a very small apartment in a very overcrowded city. The setting is a large cardboard box. One side of the box is painted as a city street, with a row of apartment houses. The box turns to reveal a one-room apartment, equipped with very small cardboard objects that represent clothing, bathing and eating utensils, etcetera. The four roommates sing cheerfully of their arrangement, do their morning exercises, shower, go to work, commute home, and eat dinner, all accompanied by the music of Donald Ashwander on the electric harpsicord. Their sense of cheerful order is temporarily stifled when they receive a phone call from the landlord who threatens to raise the rent. But the undaunted foursome overcome this dilemma by agreeing to find a smaller apartment with a smaller room and a smaller rent.

Judith Martin says of "Apartment":

It examines the notion of living today in a very crowded and unacceptable space. Our point of view is funny. What could be a tragedy for someone else has to be funny for us. It always ends up that way, even when we start with a sad piece.[3]

One aspect seen clearly in "Apartment" is the fact that the actors work so well and so joyfully together. Martin and Burton discussed this aspect of their work:

Interviewer: Could you speak about the sense of ensemble work within your company. In "Apartment," for example, you have four actors, none of whom is a star or has a name as a character. You share and work very well together as a group. Is that typical for your work?
Martin: Yes, the ensemble feeling is very important in our company. "Apartment" is successful, because the people in our company all have

a sense of what Irving calls play. It's like children playing house. Aside from the enormous rehearsal time, there is that willingness of the actors to play, to make believe in a very primitive, obvious way. I think you have to accept that to be happy in our company.

Interviewer: Irving, do you ever feel that you would like to have a character with a name and with long speeches? Or do you play those kinds of roles in other productions?

Burton: I have that occasionally. I play a lot of characters.

Martin: We don't have psychological roles, but the character of a rock or a teacup becomes very important to the children. They say: "I want to meet the Ice-Cream Cone or the Teacup."

Interviewer: What does the actor have to know in terms of performing to an audience of children?

Martin: I think the audience needs to have everything very clear. And my audience is going to be very accepting. I feel I have a tremendous sense of freedom with a children's audience, which I don't think I have anywhere else.

Burton: You have to make it very, very real.

Irving Burton's last statement seems to contradict the fact that the Bags and many actors for young audiences depend so much upon fantasy and non-realistic elements of movement and dialogue in their performances. But in fact, the good actor must be able to portray fantasy, non-realistic characters and situations, in a believable, real way. In his book on children's theatre, Moses Goldberg wrote: "The penalty for failing to achieve a believable human character is quite severe."[4] Thus Burton can portray a teacup by endowing it with human qualities and presenting a character that children perceive as real. The crucial aspect of acting for children is that the actor believes in the truth of his or her actions.[5]

Certainly, what is real in theatre for young audiences is equally real in theatre for all audiences, and that reality rests in the actor's ability to play and to present the essence of his or her fictional character with a sense of commitment and truth.

THE DIRECTOR AND THE DESIGNER

It is difficult to specify significant differences between theatre for young audiences and theatre for adults. Many of the points made by the Paper Bag Players in relation to acting for children are equally true for adult audiences. Many adult directors certainly look for actors who are playful and who can create a sense of truthfulness on the stage.

In looking at the roles of the director and designer in theatre for young audiences, we run into the same problem, because similar aesthetic and philosophical principles hold true regardless of the age of the audience.

Nevertheless, to justify the existence of a theatre for a specific audience, certain relevant differences must be specified.

As mentioned in the introduction to this book, a theatre for young audiences is generally an educational theatre. Audiences are still involved in the process of formal schooling and still very much in process about developing values and conceptual understandings. The fact that this specialized audience is open to various learning experiences implies that the theatre artist is involved in a form of aesthetic education. By choosing a certain moral, political, or intellectual point of view and translating that into a visual concept, the designer and director may in some ways affect the child's consciousness. They may reinforce values familiar to the child or choose to challenge the child through raising questions about the way things are. Even those who would claim that didacticism and teaching have no place in theatre for young audiences must be mindful that no piece of theatre is value-free, and that to audiences very much involved in the everyday process of clarifying values and making sense of the world they live in, all experience in acting or viewing is potential evidence to affirm or challenge their understanding and awareness.

Strictly speaking, educational theatre, as a concept, does not apply to professional adult theatre, where the concerns of producers and viewers are more overtly economics and entertainment. Certainly, the aim of many viewers might be to heighten their awareness, and the aim of producers might be to offer a form of education of the senses; but the term *educational theatre*, as used in this book, is limited to performances to specialized audiences, not ordinarily catered to by the professional adult theatre.

Other differences between theatre for adult and young audiences have been specified by Moses Goldberg. He has written that the designer in theatre for young audiences offers a range of material different from that of colleagues in adult theatre.[6] Goldberg admitted that the designer for adults may be required to create fantasy, magical effects, and non-realistic settings, but that these visual demands are exceptional. Generally, it is the designer for young audiences who most often works in the realm of fantasy and theatricality, which implies that he or she must often create a visual style of production with few precedents.

Furthermore, Goldberg sees the director of theatre for young audiences as needing to respect children and to understand their developmental needs. Like the designer, he or she must have a strong sense of the visual, as a means of focusing attention and stimulating imagination and as a means of underscoring the dramatic narrative. Like the actor, he or she must create a sense of emotional truth and accessibility, so that the audience can identify with the human issues and characters portrayed before them.

For Goldberg, the most crucial artistic relationship in theatre for young audiences is that between the designer and director. He argues that young audiences are more dependent upon visual imagery than are their adult counterparts and that the designer and director as a team must create a clearly focused visual/narrative concept.

This point is debatable. Throughout the 1960s and 1970s adult theatre became so dependent upon visual imagery created by theatre artists such as Julian Beck, Robert Wilson, and Richard Foreman, several of whom played dual roles of director-designer, that critics began wondering whether language in the theatre had become obsolete.

Nonetheless, it is indisputable that theatre for young audiences requires a strong visual concept created through the collaboration of director and designer. When the director and the designer is the same person, there exists the possibility that the visual concept will be most fully realized. Such is the case at the Children's Theatre Company of Minneapolis where the artistic director, John Clark Donahue, internationally recognized as one of the finest artists in the theatre for young and adult audiences alike, often combines his roles as director and designer and, on occasion, playwright.

In an interview with Donahue he offered the following:[7]

Interviewer: How did you begin in theatre for young audiences?
John Clark Donahue: Thinking back on my childhood, I was interested in being a teacher of other children even very early on. I became interested in the arts, because my parents sent me to study the piano at age four. I went to dancing school at age eight. I went to art school by the time I was thirteen. Sooner or later, I would be led towards the theatre, but not until college at the University of Minnesota. I was a jazz musician professionally for many years and thought I was going to become a painter and printmaker. But very surprisingly, one day someone phoned me and said: "I've got an old, abandoned police station. Would you like to come down and design theatre for children?" Trying to be nice, I decided I would go down and take a look at it for a half hour. I'm afraid I stayed a bit longer than that. I decided to cast my lot in trying to make living theatre for young people something viable and important.
Interviewer: What were your early experiments in theatre for young people?
Donahue: They had to do with stories that had been handed down over the centuries, generally referred to by us as the classic tales. We wanted to keep them alive, and I must say we reacted as well to the kind of fractured fairy tale phenomenon that we were seeing not only in theatre, but on Saturday television. We knew that we would devote ourselves to telling the classics and doing it as artistically as possible. Also, we wanted to commit ourselves to at least one contemporary work each year to encourage new plays and playwrights and new ways of storytelling.
Interviewer: Is that how you started writing?
Donahue: Yes it is. That came a few years later after I had a few others on the staff and enough facilities to begin to think about bringing some

of my own visions to life on the stage. Interestingly, the first play I ever wrote had almost no words in it, so I could hardly be called a playwright; perhaps a playmaker. It was mostly in mime. It was about fear and overcoming it, which was indeed what I was immersed in.

Interviewer: When you were writing that script, did you think that you were writing a play for young audiences, or were you just creating a play?

Donahue: I thought about my own child-poet vision. This is an important point I always try to make. I think all of us, artists in particular, but not just artists, scientists like Einstein, too, at a certain point in childhood make a connection with something that is rather mysterious and stays with them. I can't quite put my finger on it. I can only refer to it as the child-poet vision. I guess I intuit that what I felt when I was very young and couldn't quite identify was important enough to trust as I grew and matured. And so, as an artist now, I just trust it in everything I do and trust that it is worth sharing with other young people, because I think it's there, too.

Interviewer: Is this concept the child in you now, or the child that was in you then?

Donahue: The child that was in me then is in me now. But as I mature and grow as a human, as an artist, as a discoverer, the way I can make it manifest is more dense, more complex, more completely realized. I remember as a child looking at the very complex illustrations in lovely books I had seen and remembering how much I responded to them even though they had depths and dimensions that I could not articulate. I trust that. Einstein says that the reason he could do what he did was because he was told fairy tales as a child. He was given the fantastic possibility that lives within these tales. Somehow that stayed with him and provided the opportunity to make the leaps and breakthroughs that he did. And I think Fellini discusses that very clearly in his *8½*, and you often hear people like Cassals, Picasso, Jean Cocteau, talk about this.

Interviewer: Would you tell us about the kind of work you have done and are presently doing at your theatre.

Donahue: In the past, as I mentioned, we worked with the classics. I think we tried to get artists to be around us—designers, writers, musicians—and put the emphasis upon what particular things they could bring. We began on a stage fourteen feet wide and nine feet tall. Now we have a five million dollar theatre, one of the finest theatre plants in the world. Dealing with those classic tales now brings them to life on a spectacular scale, not for the sake of being spectacular, but indeed, many of them, with their transformational qualities and extraordinary visions, require it. And now we can do it. So we tend to do the tales that very few theatres in the world are producing for young people.

Interviewer: Have your plays actually changed, though? Given the scope of your theatre, how has that affected the content of your plays?

Donahue: I think it's not the content so much as the manner of telling. Although over the years we have taken the same tale, such as "Sleeping Beauty," we have told it in at least five different ways, trying to get at the mystery that's within that play somewhere. Bettleheim's book *The Uses of Enchantment*, among other things, reminds us of the mystery inherent in these folk, fairy, and mythic tales.

Interviewer: So given whatever space you found yourself in, you would get into another way of exploring that mystery.

Donahue: Exactly. You know, the exquisite eggs, the tiny Easter eggs, the jewel eggs that were made in Russia, while small, are complicated in their depth and dimension. So it isn't a matter of changing so much, but simply exploring various ways. Now I can have someone swim at a 40 degree angle on a hundred-foot stage. Before, they had to swim perhaps six feet on a dark pedestal. I don't think the audience works any less. I don't think it's any better, just different.

Interviewer: What do you do as a director that's different from what you do as a playwright?

Donahue: I'm in a strange position of being a producer, director, playwright, and designer, sometimes choreographer, all wrapped up in one. If I'm not the playwright and just the director, I suppose I try to discover what it is the playwright has written which the playwright will be quick to admit he or she doesn't know, either. I should point out that all the work we do for young people is original, either new plays or original adaptations. The playwright is almost always in residence with us and we usually create these plays together as a team. So the interaction on the fabric is being woven simultaneously by all of us, rather than me as the director. Trying to make this discovery together, the role of the director is rather intimately interwoven with the playwright's role—much give and take back and forth.

Interviewer: What kinds of problems do you confront when you play both roles at the same time?

Donahue: It has resulted in a way of working that causes me to use a lot of improvisation. Out of the situation of director leading actors improvisationally, Donahue, as playwright, is listening for situation and dialogue, sensitive to whatever comes out of the chemistry of the improvisation which suddenly will allow me to blurt out, without previous preparation, a monologue or dialogue. It is a fascinating process to juggle all of these balls in the air and bring some of them down to look at, and to toss them up again and move forward.

Interviewer: Do you lose anything when you play multiple roles?

Donahue: I'm sure there's a kind of myopia that sets in. I can't really comment very objectively. I should probably go direct elsewhere, doing

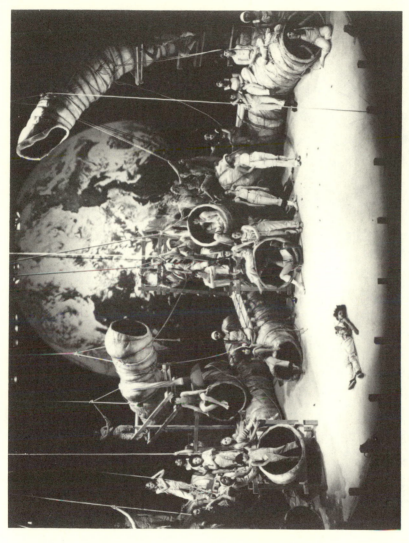

6. The Children's Theatre Company of Minneapolis's production of *A Circle Is the Sun* by Frederick Gaines and John Clark Donahue. Courtesy of John Clark Donahue.

7. The Children's Theatre Company of Minneapolis's production of *The Clown of God* by Tomie de Paola, adapted by Thomas W. Olson. Photograph by George Heinrich. Courtesy of John Clark Donahue.

other people's plays occasionally, in order to be more articulate and objective on the question you're asking.

Interviewer: Do you do a lot of designing as well?

Donahue: I used to do all the designing, many years ago. Now I occasionally design. I like to start out a design in the same way that children will encounter a hillside and without any consultation, merely play on it. And out of the hillside I draw or bring to life the locations and the circumstances. Sometimes I will have a vision for the setting before I will have a vision for any of the words. I'll have a rough idea of the title, and as a designer, I'll create something to play on and to play with.

Interviewer: How do you expect children to react when they see your productions?

Donahue: A sense of wonder, a sense of mystery, a sense of amazement. Also, a sense of a certain amount of fear that goes with mystery and the kinds of shivers that one encounters when seeing the ocean for the first time. Or the sound of the witch in the dark. So that's perhaps what I am looking for first.

Interviewer: Emotional reactions?

Donahue: They're very sensual. Children remember first how something felt, smelled, sounded, what it did to them. And they store that. And I think that's how they begin to build the layers that go into maturing and making decisions about life. So strong sensory things are important, I believe, rather than worrying about what precisely they learned.

Interviewer: Couldn't that be learning, too?

Donahue: I think it is the fundamental learning. You talk about basics. I think finding out how to allow oneself to be open to the bombardment of sensory things that we constantly come in contact with and that a young person is acutely aware of is very fundamental. It's only then that you're seeing, hearing, feeling, taking it in. And it's those things that cause you to celebrate learning and to move forward. And when that isn't happening for children, they lose interest. When it is happening, they don't need to know what it means. They just will take it on.

Interviewer: What about ideas? Are you concerned as a director with presenting the ideas of the playwright and having the child pick up these ideas and relate to them in a certain way?

Donahue: Yes, but only ideas that are never completely understood, I think. Things that are probably worthwhile sharing and taken seriously are never within our grasp completely. René Magritte, the Belgian surrealist, said: "People ask me what my paintings mean. I don't know, but mystery is the supreme thing." I am a person interested in ideas, but I think the most interesting ideas are very difficult to pin down. Why is it that over the centuries we keep returning to tales? What is "Beauty and the Beast" about? What are the ideas inherent there? That something beautiful can be beneath an ugly surface? Look at the interest in *The*

Elephant Man, the juxtaposition between this person and the church model that he's building. But yet it's mysterious. We don't understand it.

Interviewer: Are there ways of knowing or measuring how children experience your theatre? Aside from the fact that your attendance is booming, have there been attempts made to gather feedback from children in your audiences?

Donahue: It's very difficult, isn't it, because children are loath to share with you much that is really happening to them. And I think it's a great mistake to ask them. In fact, often if you ask them what it was about, they'll say: "I don't know." If you ask them whether they like it, they often will say: "No." But I know enough about children to know that it isn't necessarily true. I think you can only feel it. I said to someone who came through the theatre as a sixteen-year-old and a brilliant composer: "Well, where did you come from?" He said: "I have seen all your plays since I was five years old." You don't really know what's happening.

Interviewer: Do you think it's important to know what's happening to your audiences?

Donahue: No, I don't. I'll tell you why. If I bring my children to the forest, I don't need to worry about whether or not they know if anything is happening to them. I only need to know that the forest is a worthy place to take them.

Interviewer: Basically, then, you're trusting your instincts.

Donahue: That's right. And I hope I'm making something that's worth sharing, that is artistically viable and that confronts ideas or thoughts that are worthy of consideration. And then it's all in the telling, I think. Of course, if nothing positive is happening to the children, they don't want to be there.

Interviewer: And what about the adults in the audience?

Donahue: In the early days I used to quip that the audience was essentially eight-year-old females in Brownie suits. But now the audience runs from pre-school all the way through old age. And sometimes in the evening you'll find the audiences to be 80 percent adult.

Interviewer: How do you feel about that?

Donahue: I think that's very exciting. It only goes to show what we said earlier that something vibrates within us throughout our lives that wishes to be returned to again and again, the same way we return to the ocean or the forest. I like the idea of what I call a normal audience, which is a mix of ages and a mix of life experiences. I think it enriches the experience for the young person and gives the event, the gathering, integrity. I do not favor children's audiences only. I think that is an abnormal gathering. I think there's behavior that's the result of peer influence that I find negative to the experience. Children know when they are at important events. All they have to do is look around and see whether the rest of the world is there.

Donahue's notion of the roles of the director, designer, and playwright is consistent with his notion of learning in theatre for young audiences. According to Donahue, one learns through sensory means and through participating in the mysterious "child-poet vision." Donahue sees his inter-related roles of director, designer, and playwright in terms of presenting that vision and making manifest the latent mysteries of life through engaging the senses, feelings, and intuitions of his audience members.

At the core of Donahue's vision of theatre for young audiences is, para-doxically, a theatre for all audiences, a "normal" community of multi-generational viewers that recalls a time when the extended family was intact and envisions a more communal model of social intercourse.

Donahue's theatre is truly a children's theatre, however, in that he, as director-designer-playwright, is on a constant search for articulating his "child-poet vision" in narrative and visual forms. He wrote:

> I make theatre for children because of the significance that the child has for me—as a force, a life force that guides and enlightens. We must con-tinually look to the child for guidance as well as helping to guide the child. If we do so, we will discover a unity among us and a wholeness—a dimension of ourselves that I find missing in the cold, frightened, calculating, and lying worlds that I see around me. If we're not quite sure where we're at, then we should look to the child—but by that I also mean we should look to the child *in us*.[8]

If, as Donahue implies, "The Child is father to the Man,"[9] then the Man, as director or designer, must create a universal vision that resonates within us all.

THE PLAYWRIGHT

Many playwrights for young audiences would agree with John Clark Donahue's assertions. Suzan Zeder, author of *Step on a Crack* and *Ozma of Oz*, wrote: "As a writer, I try to confront the child within myself as simply and honestly as possible."[10] Virginia Glasgow Koste, author of *Alice in Wonder* and *The Adventures of Tom Sawyer*, wrote:

> I recognize a recurring (unplanned) theme in my plays: the fully human being "grows up" only through owning (possessing and acknowledging) that original primal self instead of "putting it away." The child *is* father to the man, just as our wizards—from Plato to Stanislavski—have told us in all of the languages through all of the centuries.[11]

Some playwrights for young audiences, such as Carol Korty, author of *Silly Soup* and *Plays from African Folktales*, see their role as based in a personal sharing of their lives.[12] Some base their work upon spectacle and visual imagery, and others, like Joanna Kraus, author of *The Ice Wolf* and *Mean To Be Free*, see their role as encouraging a depth of thought and feeling.[13]

Jonathan Levy, author of *Marco Polo* and *The Marvelous Adventures of Tyl*, sees the playwright as presenter of the true images of our inner and outer lives.[14] He argued vehemently against a didactic purpose for playwriting. According to Levy: "When art is used to teach, either the teaching or the art must suffer. The didactic imagination and the artistic imagination work in different ways."[15]

On the other hand, in his introduction to an anthology of plays by Grips, a West German theatre company for young audiences, Jack Zipes wrote: "Almost all of their plays are Lehrstücke (learning plays), which are performed in a cabaret style that enhances the estrangement effect and allows for pleasure in learning."[16]

The playwright in theatre for young audiences, like the adult playwright, then, conceptualizes his or her role in a diversity of ways. But although some would claim that writing a play for young audiences is similar to writing a play for adults, most would agree with Jonathan Levy's statement: "For me, at least, writing a play for children is a different experience from writing plays for adults. . . . A writer's sense of audience, like his sense of the occasion he is writing for, must inform and shape what he writes."[17]

Aurand Harris is one of the most widely produced playwrights for young audiences in the world. His many plays, including *Androcles and the Lion*, *Rags to Riches*, and the newly published *The Arkansaw Bear*, exemplify a keen understanding of young audiences. In a recent interview Harris offered the following insights about the role of the playwright:[18]

Interviewer: What is theatre for young audiences?
Aurand Harris: Theatre for young audiences is vast in its implications. I suppose any situation where you have children in the audience and something live going on in front of them that they can enjoy—that's theatre for young audiences. But that's very broad. It would include all ages from the very small up through the teens. Most people think of children's theatre as formal drama for children from about eight or nine years old through the early teens.

I think there is a movement in America now, Youth Theatre, for which I have been writing some plays, that extends theatre for children a little beyond the thirteen and fourteen year olds on to high school.
Interviewer: Is that the age group you're presently involved with?
Harris: No. I still like the children. But I think a good play and certainly my most successful plays have appealed, fortunately for me, to different ages: the young, the middle, the older, and even the adults. Perhaps we could say that a really good children's play will have some elements that

appeal to the younger ones and other elements which will appeal to older children. The play has different levels.

Interviewer: What brought you to write plays for children?

Harris: I didn't start out writing for children. I started writing for adults, and I had a fair success. But the more I discovered children—I worked with them for the past twenty years everyday, or I couldn't write for them—the more I realized that I like in the theatre exactly what children like in the theatre. This was a happy combination for me.

Interviewer: What are those things?

Harris: To begin with, a good, tight story that you can identify with. Something happens; there's a beginning, middle, and end. You feel good when you go out. You're rooting for the right person. Then with this good story, there has to be color, action, music, dance, suspense, lots of fun. This is what I call good theatre. I suppose I deserted adult theatre when it seemed to me that most of the adult plays were getting psychological problems with no endings. They were rather amateurish character sketches. Also, I like to experiment in writing by using different styles. You are limited in adult theatre. Broadway is really very provincial, and as costs go up on Broadway, your chance of getting a play produced, let alone having a hit, becomes less and less. The regional theatre, I feel, is where the future of adult theatre will be, and I think this is healthy. In theatre for children, it has always been regional. There's never been a Little Broadway where you open a play for children. I think that is why theatre for young audiences is now one of the most active and developing areas in American drama. It is not dying; it is growing, because it has grass roots everywhere. But to get back to styles in writing. The dramatic styles in which you can write for children are unlimited. The child comes to the theatre unconditioned. He can relate to anything in any style that's good on the stage by using his imagination. So in many of the plays I've written, I try a different but legitimate style. This is a challenge which I find very exciting.

Interviewer: It's very exciting to observe children who have never seen plays before.

Harris: Theatre for children in America is really a great luxury. There is only a small percentage of children who are ever exposed to theatre. But it should be supported, like the opera. It can never, like the opera, support itself, because the box office will never be big enough. And to have first-class children's productions, which we need, children's theatre will have to have outside support.

Interviewer: Do you remember your reaction when seeing your very first script for children performed?

Harris: I suppose I wrote my first script for children when I was about six or seven years old. We performed it in the back yard with my mother's draperies for curtains. The neighborhood children all came, but they left before the third act, because of a baseball game. That was just as well, because as I remember, we had never rehearsed the third act. Seriously, the first play I really wrote for children was when I was teaching in Gary, Indiana, in the auditorium department.

Interviewer: Could you talk about that experience?

Harris: It was part of the work-study-play program which no longer exists. The auditorium program was started in the public schools of Gary and was the hub of the whole curriculum. Every child went to the auditorium for one hour every day. In that hour, he had something on the stage to watch—a movie or a play or whatever. I was a studio teacher, so thirty students came to my studio every half-hour from the big pool of the auditorium. We rehearsed three weeks, then presented whatever we had for the larger group. Among other things in Gary they had city meets of poetry and one-act plays. I couldn't find the right script for my entry. Incidentally, people are always saying there are so few good children's scripts. There is a shortage, of course. There is a shortage of good scripts on Broadway too. And I'm sure they were telling that to Shakespeare at the Globe. Well, to solve my shortage, I dramatized one scene from *Pinocchio* for the one-act play meet. It proved to be quite a success, and later the play was published.

Interviewer: Could you talk about the process of adapting non-dramatic material for the theatre, like *Pinocchio*. That is something that is often practiced in theatre for young audiences, is it not?

Harris: Yes. Most of my plays have been dramatizations of somebody else's material. I'm not very good at original plots or with titles. But given a good story that excites me, I can't wait to get it on paper and then get it on the stage. First, I begin with a good story, a story I think children also will like. The time element is important. For an adult play you have two or two and one-half hours. For a children's play you have an hour or an hour and a half at the very most. So all exposition has to be minimal, characterization has to be quick, motivations have to be even quicker. It has to be clear who the hero is and what the problem is. Not that you write down to children. Never! They are usually a jump ahead of you. Then you consider the style, the technical problems, size of cast, and so on. When I first started writing children's plays, they kept saying: "There are no good plays." That was very discouraging. Since then I have discovered, however, that there is no *one* good children's play for everyone. But there *are* good plays, good for different groups and different regions whose requirements are different. If you can write a play that's popular in many places, perhaps then you can say that is a good play.

Interviewer: Let's stay with the question, "What makes a good play?" What is it about your play *Rags to Riches*, for example, that's so universally appealing to audiences of young people?

8. The University of Texas at Austin's production of *The Arkansaw Bear* by Aurand Harris. Photograph by Marty Bass. Courtesy of Coleman Jennings.

Harris: The hero is a young boy with whom children can relate. He is very innocent. This is a period piece of the 1890s. If you tried to write that same play in a current setting, it wouldn't work. Right comes out on top. It's an old-fashioned melodrama, and that is what I set out to write. It is also a musical melodrama. The music gives it a great balance and lift. I used the music of the period, which is in the public domain, and I wrote my own lyrics.

Interviewer: Is melodrama a good style for children?

Harris: Yes. I think most good children's plays have some melodrama in them, melodrama in the very best sense, which means there is always a good conflict. Melodrama has fallen into such disrepute for adults. Most plays for children are comedies. There are not very many serious plays for very good reasons. But most of the good comedies have melodramatic elements in them.

Interviewer: What other styles have you worked in that you have found effective?

Harris: My most popular play is *Androcles and the Lion*, which I based on Aesop's fable. I wrote it in the commedia dell'arte style. I must add that I did a year of research on that style before I started. Personally, I think commedia dell'arte is wonderful for children, because it has vitality and spontaneity. There's always the tricking, the slapstick, and other kinds of comedy. The actors break into song and dance; the ending is always happy. But, of course, that is not the only kind of play for children. For instance, I wrote *Steal Away Home*, a drama about two black boys on the underground railroad, which is a serious, realistic play. The styles you can use are endless for children's theatre.

Interviewer: Could you talk about your recent play, *The Arkansaw Bear*.

Harris: I have felt for some time that children's literature has advanced so much more than children's theatre in America. There are many taboos you can write about in a novel for children which you can't put on stage. One subject which has not been dramatized significantly is death. So I thought I would like to try to write a children's play dealing with death. After much research I started to write what might be called a "thesis" play. However, to me, theatre for young audiences must always be entertaining. So first my play must be theatrically effective. It must have an uplift, not in any way be morbid. Although dealing with a serious theme, it must have all the elements of good theatre, which makes for good entertainment. It took me some time to get a plot on which to hang my theme. Once I got that, then I was on my way. It is a fantasy. A modern little girl doesn't understand why her grandfather is dying. She runs away to her secret place on top of the hill, and there in her fantasy she meets the world's greatest dancing bear. He is running away from death. He is old, like her grandfather, and in trying to help him, the girl learns something important about life and death itself.

Hopefully, it is a play that is imaginative and entertaining, that shows, not tells, how one child coped with the problem of death. Hopefully, the audience will leave the theatre with a little more understanding about death. That's all, I think, you can hope for in theatre for children.

Interviewer: Could you talk about your role as a writer, as distinct from a director's role in theatre for children.

Harris: I was trained as a director and actor to begin with. When I started writing, this was a whole new ballgame. I was in control. I could do it all. I became the director and all the actors. And yet I suppose that people can and do write good plays who have no theatre background. But it seems to me, to write a good children's play, I had to know theatre. I had to know what would work in the theatre, all the technical things, what has audience appeal, how long I could carry a joke, exits and entrances, etcetera. Certainly, that knowledge and love of the theatre will help, plus knowledge and love of children. When I write a play, it is all in my mind. I see it all. And for me, it is always in a proscenium arch. There are some plays, I feel, which can be successfully produced on a thrust stage, but I am not in favor of theatre-in-the-round. I resent it when I go to the theatre and half the audience is laughing, and I don't know what they're laughing about. I think every action and movement on the stage must be motivated. In-the-round you are moving actors around just so you can see their faces. I have very little patience with that. And for children not to see everything is poor children's theatre.

Interviewer: It's also a question of focus, since many young children's minds will wander.

Harris: Yes. They must always be able to see and hear so they can understand. In writing I keep thinking I am leading the child by the hand from this to this to this crisis. And it is difficult to do that when staged in-the-round.

Interviewer: When you write, you keep the actor and director roles in mind. What about the designer's role?

Harris: In my mind it's all in color. I know the exact costumes, sets, and lights. It doesn't mean it has to be that way or that I'm even right. Often a good designer can show me something much better than what I thought. But some of my best dialogue will come because I know the actor has to go from here to there, and I know that it's a step up or down or to the window or whatever.

Interviewer: What do young writers need to know about writing plays for young audiences?

Harris: I wish I could tell them and I wish somebody could have told me. But in general, I think they should have a knowledge of the theatre. They must have an urge to write. They must know children. You must be with children every day, laugh with them, cry with them, listen to them.

Otherwise, you'll be writing down to them. Several years ago the Children's Theatre Conference thought of going to Broadway playwrights and asking them to write a children's play. It happened that I saw the late William Inge on the West Coast about then. So I asked him if he would write a children's play. He said: "Write for children? But I have nothing to say to children!" Well, perhaps at this point I have nothing to say to adults. So my advice is if you have something to say to adults, say it. Don't try to "tell" it in a children's play. But if you think you have something to say to children, then do your very best to "show" it in the best theatre terms. When Stanislavski was asked in Russia if there was a difference between children's theatre and adult theatre, he said: "Oh, yes, a great difference. Children's theatre has to be better."

Interviewer: What about the classics for children?

Harris: You mean the great plays of the past? I don't think a child should have a steady diet of only classic plays. But I am all in favor of including classic dramas, the ones suitable for children, in a season of plays. They are part of a child's heritage. But too often, the interest in them has been killed in reading and English classes. Plays are written to be performed and to be enjoyed by a live audience, not read silently or taught by a teacher who doesn't understand theatre. I think children can and should be introduced to the classics, using suitable selections for different age levels. In fact, I am adapting several of the classics for youth theatre in a series, *One-Act Adaptations of Theatre Classics*, for Baker's plays, which includes plays such as *Ralph Roister Doister* and *The Romancers*.

Interviewer: As to the question of whether theatre for young audiences is educational, maybe we have to come up with a new way of talking about education in terms of theatre.

Harris: I don't think theatre should be a teacher or a preacher. There are schools and churches for that. I think theatre for anybody is entertainment. I think every good play for children is great entertainment. Children go away feeling marvelous; they've cried or laughed. But also they have seen a universal truth, and that's the teaching. They have seen somebody go through experiences similar to their own and cope with them. That to me is the education. Any new experience, vicarious or real, educates a child. And certainly in the classics we also educate their imagination and their aesthetic sense.

Although Aurand Harris and Jonathan Levy, among others, are put off by the juxtaposition of the terms *theatre* and *teaching*, they do suggest aesthetic means through which their plays are educational. According to Harris, the teaching/learning experience for young audiences has to do with entertainment values, feelings and identification, and imagination and the many values inherent in the aesthetic experience.

THE CURRENT SCENE:
NEW PLAYS AND NEW PRODUCTIONS OF
OLDER PLAYS

The Arkansaw Bear marks a new direction for Aurand Harris and for American theatre for young audiences in terms of its thematic content, that of a child's conception of death. In surveying the choices of leading American experts about the outstanding American plays for young audiences of the past five years, Lowell Swortzell, director of the Program in Educational Theatre at New York University noted that several chose *The Arkansaw Bear*. Swortzell wrote:

> The theme of death is not new to children's theatre. But Harris does not romanticize the subject. He keeps the focus on this world and the meaning of death to the living. Without sugar-coating, he tells each child, "We all have to die." At the same time he provides comfort, even pleasure, in death's purpose and inevitability: "in every ending there is a new beginning." ... The effective truth of *The Arkansaw Bear*, with its use of the circus as a theatrical metaphor for the circle of life, more than copes: it confronts, reassures and entertains young people and adults alike.[19]

Other choices of outstanding plays include Roger Cornish's *I Remember a Parade*, concerning the relationship of an alienated twelve year old, whose father was killed in Vietnam, with two generations of his family; Wendy Kesselman's *Maggie, Magalita*, again concerning family relationships among generations, in this case, daughter, mother, and grandmother; Suzan Zeder's *Step on a Crack*, concerning the relationship of a young girl to her father and stepmother; John Clark Donahue's production of Timothy Mason's *The 500 Hats of Bartholomew Cubbins*, capturing the fantasy and magic of the original Dr. Seuss story; Kelsey Collie's *Black Images/Black Reflections*, concerning the history, struggles, and contributions of Afro-Americans; Joanna Kraus's *Circus Home* and *The Ice Wolf*, both concerning outcasts from conventional society; and Michael Cowell's *A Memorable Account of Mark Twain in the Sandwich Islands*, a multi-ethnic exploration of life in Hawaii.

These plays represent a change of thematic concerns and style of presentation from the more conventional fare of widely produced plays such as *Hansel and Gretel*, *Pinocchio*, and *Androcles and the Lion*.[20] Many of the new plays deal with social and psychological issues, with history and ethnicity, in styles that often tend to be more realistic than ever before. This trend implies that theatre artists are reconceptualizing the needs of their young audiences and catching up thematically and stylistically with their counterparts in other media.

In a recent interview Lowell Swortzell was asked whether he thought that any play can interest young people. His response was as follows:[21]

> I think most any play can. If the subject matter is well over the head of the child, that's going to pose problems. But if it's a good play there ought to be other dimensions there. We've all gone to plays we didn't fully understand the first time, or even the second and the third time, perhaps. But the reason we go back is that we are challenged and want to find out more. Sometimes we go to a play and don't like it, and yet we know we should like it, or we know other people like it and it haunts us. We try to find out if it's the play or is it me? I think the case has been proven in children's literature. For a long time we were writing books for certain age groups, such as the five-sevens or the seven-nines. Many books come out now that say "all ages" on the jacket. The same is true in the theatre. Years ago, at the children's summer theatre at Rutgers University, we did *The Canterbury Tales*. Three-, four-, and five-year-old children came to see that production. They had never heard of Chaucer or the Middle Ages, but they all loved certain aspects of the tales. They could identify with the story of Chanticleer and Pertelote and the Fox. They could sing the songs. The color and design, movement and action, all led to a gratifying experience. We must not say that a play is just for this age group or that. The Russians, who do marvelous work in theatre for young audiences, are very rigid on this point, but I think it will eventually change. I think we really need to open up the definitions and rethink what we mean by "suitable for children."

Swortzell himself has been at the vanguard of rethinking choices of plays suitable for young audiences. Both as a playwright and as an editor of anthologies of plays for young people, he has created and collected new and older materials. The choice of plays for his anthology *All the World's a Stage: Modern Plays for Young People*, which includes works by Strindberg, Pirandello, O'Casey, Gertrude Stein, and Brecht, among others, and adult themes such as death, nihilism, and sexuality, justifies his notion that theatre for young audiences must include any and all plays that have the potential of expanding the young person's intellectual and emotional experience.[22] In a companion anthology to be published by Delacorte Press in 1984, Swortzell includes newer works of contemporary playwrights of all ages.[23]

In previous chapters we discussed new productions for young audiences of the Chekhov plays *Uncle Vanya* and *The Marriage Proposal* and made reference to the several Albert Cullum collections of classical plays adapted for young performers and viewers. Also, at the Children's Theatre Company of Minneapolis, during their 1981-1982 season, John Clark Donahue and his staff transformed several older pieces of world literature—for example, *The Little Match Girl*, *Phantom of the Opera*, and *Alice in Wonderland*—into their special kind of theatre.

A recent article in the *Children's Theatre Review* makes reference to a production of the Brecht plays *He Who Says Yes* and *He Who Says No*, performed by· eleven- through thirteen-year-old children to audiences of peers and adults.[24] In a 1976 production of Aurand Harris's *Rags to Riches* the director chose a Brechtian epic theatre concept to explore the historical and political implications of the rags to riches ethic.[25]

A strong core of new plays and new productions has also been developing in England, influenced primarily by the work of Brian Way in participatory theatre and many of the TIE teams whose programs deal explicitly with political, psychological, and pedagogical issues.[26]

A final innovation in theatre for young audiences that complements several of the newer American experiments and shares much with British TIE is that of emancipatory children's theatre, practiced throughout Europe but centered most intensely in Germany. The most noted example is Grips, located in West Berlin. *Grips* is a German slang word meaning the use of common sense and wit to overcome obstacles. In fact, the purpose of the Grips Theatre is to help young audiences develop their Grips. As stated by Volker Ludwig, playwright, director, and leader of Grips:

> The purpose of our theatre is emancipatory education. We want to show that our conditions are changeable and to help audiences see this. In this way, we hope to show different possibilities and to foster critical thinking. Primarily this means that we want to encourage children to ask questions, to understand that criticism is their undeniable right, to enjoy creative thinking, and to gain pleasure from seeing alternatives and making changes.[27]

Since the late 1960s Grips has been producing a series of plays dealing with young people's relationships to their own fears, authority, racism, sexism, and juvenile delinquency. Grips' style of presentation is often based upon the musical and satirical elements of a cabaret performance.

Grips offers a model of theatre for young audiences that is explicitly didactic, but that is also highly entertaining and aesthetically pleasing. Jack Zipes noted that "Grips' plays are didactic provocations rather than didactic solutions. None of the plays reached a traditional 'happy end,' though solutions to particular problems were suggested through collective action."[28]

This distinction between ends and means will probably not mollify those who would claim that didacticism has no place whatever in theatre for young audiences. Yet it is nonetheless an important distinction to make. Grips is didactic without being dogmatic. It is a theatre of open-ended ideas that exists to inform, provoke thought, and entertain the senses.

Although many playwrights, directors, designers, and actors approach their work from different philosophical, political, and aesthetic perspectives, it seems that a synthesis can be found by virtue of the fact that all of these theatre artists create their work for a specialized audience, at least in part. Through their efforts, this audience of young people, if they are open, will be educated through their senses, their feelings, their intuitions, their intellects. The commonality shared by Aurand Harris and Volker Ludvig, Alice Minnie Herts, and John Clark Donahue lies in their commitment to create excellent theatre that instructs through entertaining or entertains through instructing. Each would undoubtedly define *instruction* and *entertainment* in a different way, but all would be likely to agree with Jonathan Levy's poetic interpretation of the instructional-entertainment dialectic:

For of course when the theatre is fine it will teach, in the profound ways it always has. It will teach the way *King Lear* teaches, or *The Cherry Orchard* teaches, simply by being; which of course is what our rapt child deserves—the re-presentation of strong human experience, clarified and intensified, like sunlight through a burning glass.[29]

NOTES

1. Judith Liss and Nancy Lloyd, "The Paper Bag Players," in Nellie McCaslin, *Theatre for Young Audiences* (New York: Longman, 1978), p. 106.

2. WCBS-TV, *Sunrise Semester*, "Drama in Education: Theatre for Children #3: The Actors" (December 21, 1979).

3. Ibid.

4. Moses Goldberg, *Children's Theatre, A Philosophy and a Method* (Englewood Cliffs, N.J.: Prentice-Hall, 1974), p. 156.

5. Ibid.

6. Ibid., p. 180.

7. WCBS-TV, *Sunrise Semester*, "Drama in Education: Theatre for Children #2: The Producer/Director" (December 19, 1979).

8. John Clark Donahue, "Tell me Things," in McCaslin, *Theatre for Young Audiences*, pp. 88-89.

9. William Wordsworth, "My Heart Leaps Up," in William Wordsworth, *The Prelude, Selected Poems and Sonnets* (New York: Holt, Rinehart, and Winston, 1965), p. 82.

10. See Virginia Glasgow Koste, "On the Making of Plays for Young Audiences," *ASSITEJ/U.S.A..*, Special Edition, June 1981, p. 10.

11. Ibid., p. 9.

12. Ibid.

13. Ibid., p. 10.

14. Jonathan Levy, "Reflections on Sources of Plays for Children," *Children's Theatre Review* 29, no. 2 (1980): 8.

15. Jonathan Levy, "A Theatre of the Imagination," *Children's Theatre Review* 27, no. 1 (1978): 17.

16. Jack Zipes, ed., *Political Plays for Children* (St. Louis: Telos Press, 1976), p. 16.

17. Virginia Glasgow Koste, "On the Making of Plays," p. 10.

18. WCBS-TV, *Sunrise Semester*, "Drama in Education: Theatre for Children #1: The Playwright" (December 17, 1979).

19. Lowell Swortzell, "The Outstanding American Plays for Young People of the Last Five Years," *ASSITEJ/U.S.A.*, Special Edition, June 1981, p. 15.

20. For a listing of the most regularly produced plays for young audiences in America, see Elizabeth Vickerman, "The Favorite Plays," Ibid., p. 7-8.

21. WCBS-TV, *Sunrise Semester*, "Drama in Education: Definitions and Issues in Drama in Education" (September 19, 1979).

22. Lowell Swortzell, ed., *All the World's a Stage* (New York: Delacorte Press, 1972), p. xviii.

23. Lowell Swortzell, ed., *Playhouse: Uncommon Plays for, by, and about Young People* (New York: Delacorte Press, forthcoming).

24. Linda Suny Myrsiades, "A Project in Brecht and Children's Theatre: Structure through Symmetry," *Children's Theatre Review* 26, no. 2 (1977): 3-5.

25. See Robert Landy, "Measuring Audience Response to Characters and Scenes in Theatre for Children: A Developmental Approach," *Children's Theatre Review* 26, no. 3 (1977): 10-13.

26. See Brian Way, *Audience Participation Theatre for Young People* (Boston: Walter H. Baker Co., 1981).

27. Zipes, *Political Plays for Children*, p. 2.

28. Jack Zipes, "Emancipatory Children's Theatre in the Year of the Child," *Theatre* 11, no. 1 (1979): 90.

29. Jonathan Levy, "A Theatre of the Imagination," p. 17.

BIBLIOGRAPHY

See also Bibliography and Resources in chapter 3, "The School Play."

ASSITEJ/U.S.A. Special Edition, June 1981.

Corey, Orlin. *Theatre for Children: Kid Stuff or Theatre?* New Orleans: Anchorage Press, 1974.

Davis, Jed H., and Mary Jane Evans. *Theatre, Children, and Youth.* New Orleans: Anchorage Press, 1982.

Davis, Jed H., and Mary Jane Watkins. *Children's Theatre: Play Production for the Child Audience.* New York: Harper and Row, 1960.

Donahue, John Clark. *The Cookie Jar and Other Plays.* Minneapolis: University of Minnesota Press, 1976.

_____. *Five Plays from the Children's Theatre Company of Minneapolis.* Minneapolis: University of Minnesota Press, 1976.

Goldberg, Moses. *Children's Theatre, A Philosophy and a Method.* Englewood Cliffs, N.J.: Prentice-Hall, 1974.

Harris, Aurand. *The Arkansaw Bear.* New Orleans: Anchorage Press, 1980.

_____. *Six Plays for Children.* Austin, Tex.: University of Texas Press, 1977.

Healy, Daty. *Dress the Show.* Rowayton, Conn.: New Plays, 1976.

Jennings, Coleman. "The Dramatic Contributions of Aurand Harris to Children's

Theatre in the United States." Ph.D. dissertation, New York University, 1974.

Korty, Carol. *Plays from African Folktales, with Ideas for Acting, Dance, Costumes, and Music*. New York: Scribner's, 1976.

_____. *Silly Soup: Ten Zany Plays*. New York: Scribners, 1977.

Kraus, Joanna Halpert. *Circus Home*. Rowayton, Conn.: New Plays, 1979.

_____. *Ice Wolf*. Rowayton, Conn.: New Plays, 1967.

Landy, Robert. "Measuring Audience Response to Characters and Scenes in Theatre for Children: A Developmental Approach." *Children's Theatre Review* 26, no. 3 (1977): 10-13.

Levy, Jonathan. "Reflections on the Sources of Plays for Children." *Children's Theatre Review* 29, no. 2 (1980): 5-8.

_____. "A Theatre of the Imagination." *Children's Theatre Review* 27, no. 1 (1978): 2-5, 17.

Martin, Judith. *Everybody, Everybody*. New York: Elsevier-Dutton, 1981.

Masters, Simon. *The National Youth Theatre*. London: Longman's Young Books, 1969.

McCaslin, Nellie. *Theatre for Children in the United States: A History*. Norman, Okla.: University of Oklahoma Press, 1971.

_____, ed. *Theatre for Young Audiences*. New York: Longman, 1978.

Morton, Miriam, ed. and trans. *Russian Plays for Young Audiences*. Rowayton, Conn.: New Plays, 1977.

_____. *"Through the Magic Curtain": Theatre for Children, Adolescents, and Young Adults in the USSR*. New Orleans: Anchorage Press, 1979.

Page, Anita. "Some New Aspects of Children's Theatre in West Germany." *Children's Theatre Review* 25, no. 1 (1976): 6-7.

Swortzell, Lowell, ed. *All the World's a Stage*. New York: Delacorte Press, 1972.

_____, ed. *Playhouse: Uncommon Plays for, by, and about Young People*. New York: Delacorte Press, forthcoming.

Ward, Winifred. *Theatre for Children*. Anchorage, Ky.: Anchorage Press, 1958.

Way, Brian. *Audience Participation Theatre for Young People*. Boston: Walter H. Baker Co., 1981.

_____. *Three Plays for the Open Stage*. London: Pitman, 1958.

Wood, Ronald. "The Evaluation of Brian Way's Participational Theatre." Ph.D. dissertation, Florida State University, 1976.

Zipes, Jack. "Emancipatory Children's Theatre in the Year of the Child." *Theatre* 11, no. 1 (1979): 85-97.

_____, ed. *Political Plays for Children*. St. Louis: Telos Press, 1976.

PART **IV**
PUPPETRY IN
EDUCATION

11
APPLICATIONS OF
PUPPETRY IN EDUCATION

Puppetry can be seen as a total dramatic art experience, since it involves design and construction, movement and speech, playwrighting and improvisation, performing and viewing. It is, furthermore, an interdisciplinary art, involving sculpture, painting, dance, drama/theatre, and often music. Like the use of the mask or the technique of the double in psychodrama, a puppet is an extension of the actor, a kind of alter-ego that often liberates the spontaneity of the puppeteer. On a therapeutic level one hides behind a puppet in order to safely reveal oneself through the puppet. On a more theatrical level the puppeteer-actor transcends his or her individualistic and realistic posture to become part of a universal, symbolic means of expression. The educator can work on both levels in applying puppetry to human learning.

Throughout the centuries puppetry has been used within many cultures as both a form of entertainment and a form of education. As we have seen above, puppetry is currently applied to several therapeutic settings. Although classroom use of puppetry has been limited in quantity and quality, many puppeteers, educators, and clerics have used puppets in theatres, churches, and streets to teach moral lessons, to voice political and social criticism, and to promote dialogue with an audience.

To realize fully the values of puppetry in human learning, the educator must be aware of the many technical, aesthetic, and philosophical complexities of this consummate performing and improvisational art. He or she must also recognize the advantages of using puppets in a school or other educational setting. Maurice Stewart, founding member of the Puppet Centre in London, summarized several of these advantages:[1]

1. Puppets have an indefinable power to attract attention and focus concentration.

2. Puppetry combines art/craft/drama in a more complete way than any other art form.

3. Puppetry at any level of intellectual development or technical competence can involve a range of disciplines, aesthetic principles, and craft skills designed to challenge (stimulate) the brightest and least adventurous member of any group.

4. The puppet as intermediary can serve as a safety device, allowing a child to explore ideas in the third person. Social interaction through puppets encourages risk-taking and can often defuse potentially explosive situations.

5. The scale of puppetry enables a teacher to follow most of the processes of an elaborately staged drama project, but eliminates many of the action-space, storage-space, and cast problems.

6. Puppetry generates enthusiasm (when introduced intelligently); with older children it is essential to illustrate that puppetry is not "kid's stuff." It is a challenging/creative/historically mysterious/ technically sophistocated art form that can produce results, a performance that other people can enjoy and admire.

In a recent interview Maurice Stewart discussed several issues relevant to puppetry in education:[2]

Interviewer: What is a puppet?

Maurice Stewart: Anything is a puppet. I think one of the main problems is the name which produces all the prejudices. We tried to find a new word, but this has been impossible. I like to use: "the inanimate object animated," but then I'm really describing the effect I'm trying to get. Human beings are very arrogant. They like to project human sentimentality onto everything. This is why there are cultures that embody spirits in inanimate objects. Your audience animates the puppet; you don't. Wiggling a puppet has nothing to do with puppetry.

Interviewer: Doesn't the word for *doll* in French and German mean puppet?

Stewart: That is part of the problem. I've just come from Holland where the same word, *poppen*, is a doll, a puppet, and a shop window mannequin. To try and identify exactly what a puppet is is quite a big question. At the Puppet Centre in London we tried to say: "Oh, for God's sake, let us have a definition; all the ones in the dictionary fall short." So we came up with: "an inanimate object animated by human agency to a dramatic purpose." That sounds pretty academic, but in fact, that does fill all the crevices. It's not an automaton. It is not a piece of computerized programming.

Interviewer: When a child trips and hits his head against the leg of a table and starts yelling at the table and giving it human attributes, is that child relating to a puppet?

Stewart: No. He's demonstrating the quality that makes puppets a part of our history.

Interviewer: Generally speaking, how have puppets been used throughout history?

Stewart: It's pretty murky in the past, and a lot of it is supposition, because we find dolls with movable limbs in the Egyptian tombs, and we have reference in Greek classic literature to puppets. Even in politics we have the term *puppet governments*, which implies the manipulation of the human figure to one's own ends. Because puppets are so useful in storytelling, which is what we get around to when we talk about education, the church latched onto it very early. Early civilizations often used puppets in teaching, whether it was teaching of law, social order, teaching the young boys to hunt, teaching the young girls the rudiments of housewifery or whatever their position was within that particular society. They would act out these activities with the appropriate dramatic symbols. A good understanding of a puppet is that it is the perfect expressionist actor.

Interviewer: How is acting with puppets different from a live actor performing?

Stewart: We have a system which we call acting in the twentieth century, which becomes losing oneself in the character. I think this distinction in acting terms has to do with whether you should stand behind a character, inside a character, or, as often happens, in front of the character. With the puppet, it is a total projection outside one's self. And this is when the puppet becomes alive. Let's face it, the actor is a combination of puppet and puppeteer. I will stress that I haven't brought any puppets along with me, because I think the moment you get a puppet in view, the externals are what matters—how it is made and how it works. And this suddenly takes over from the intelligence of why we are using it. When we talk about theatre in terms of performance, there is a distinct difference between puppetry and live theatre, because you are stripping away from the actor perhaps two of his main assets—his eyes and facial flexibility. It's like doing sign language for the deaf without a face to back up the literal meaning of the letters. And so the type of performance which one gives with a puppet or a mask is a much more purified or depersonalized performance, which for certain types of drama is excellent, because you don't worry that it's Sir Laurence Olivier playing Oedipus. If he's behind the mask you know that he is Olivier, perhaps, but what comes across to the audience is Oedipus.

Interviewer: The universal comes across; the symbol comes across. The individual disappears.

Stewart: Yes. And much more.

Interviewer: It seems to me that all people in all cultures throughout history have had a fascination for masks and puppets. What is that fascination all about?

Stewart: You're talking about it from the point of view of the performer or the wearer. You give somebody the opportunity to get out of themselves. That is a tremendous experience if you utilize it to the fullest, if you understand the possibilities of it. And as you say, you put a paper bag over somebody's head, and they have to make a lot of reassessments or readjustments. That's very exciting; it's very stimulating and very challenging. But when you present this to someone else, you have this innate human problem of relating to something that is offbeat, out of rhythm with your own existence. The first thing you try to do is relate it to your own existence.

Interviewer: You were a theatre director long before you became involved in puppetry. How did you discover that puppetry was important to your development as a theatre artist?

Stewart: Let's call it a total self-indulgence. As a theatre director I was trying to reassess my own position within an art form, as opposed to a business or a profession. I thought, let's be starry-eyed again after thirty years in the business. I thought first entertainment, then drama; let's go back one stage to popular entertainment. And I made a list of all the things that attracted crowds, that excited people throughout history. Puppets kept cropping up—in the fairgrounds, in the American medicine shows, in advertising, in religion, everywhere. Being British, I really didn't know anything about puppets. Puppets meant Punch and Judy or electronic things that moved on television. I looked in the London and Manhattan phonebooks but could find nothing. I couldn't trace the people who were interested in puppets. Eventually, I finished up in Moscow. I saw puppets like I've never seen puppets—all types, all shapes, all sizes. I became slightly aware of what they could do. I thought I was going after a sort of small theatre backwater. I decided it was a lost continent. And that was even before I got into the educational side of it.

Interviewer: Let's dig into the educational side of it. Can anybody make a puppet?

Stewart: Everybody can make a puppet, because, as I said, a puppet can be anything. If I wrap a handkerchief around my hand and I start implying, not telling you, that this is a rabbit, because I've made a couple of knots for its ears, I cannot only give you a rabbit, I can give up a sad rabbit or a happy rabbit. You're the one that is doing all the work, as audience, because audiences respond to certain signals, a sort of dramatic shorthand, which includes our body language.

Interviewer: How can we train teachers not only to construct puppets, but to apply puppetry to classroom learning?

Stewart: We jumped one stage in this conversation. Puppetry is an attention-getter. That's why it crops up in religion, in the fairgrounds. Children will talk and talk through anything you'd like to give them, but suddenly when the puppets come on, there's a readjustment and a slight coping with the situation. Occasionally, there's a litle fear. They need to establish a relationship with that figure. What a teacher needs most in the classroom is attention, concentration, focus. And I very quickly became aware that in an educational setting or a teaching situation—and I make a distinction between the two, because I think the difference between teaching somebody and giving somebody the opportunity to learn is quite important—you have got a medium that is going to say: "Bang; here I am!" The attention can go very quickly if it's mishandled. So the first question with puppets in education should always be: "Why am I using this medium?" Teachers will not come and ask more about puppets unless they know something about the potential of using animated figures of any kind in a teaching situation. Then when they ask: "If what you say is true about the effect, how do I go about it? I can't sew or paint or sculpt. Can I make a puppet?"—the answer is: "Yes." If I showed you two yoghurt cartons and put eyes in the middle of both and said: "Boy, girl," the audience will automatically say: "All right—boy, girl." And from there on you don't have to do any explaining. If the teacher says: "I'm not a ventriloquist; when I'm working with the puppet, the child is going to know it's me talking for the puppet"— all I can say is make your yoghurt carton, put a glove over your hand or over a styrofoam ball, and start identifying this puppet as somebody, as a character, as a symbol for age or youth or whatever. It's purely Brechtian effect to say: "I am an old man" or whatever. You'll see that the child begins, almost unconsciously, to relate to the puppet and not to you.

Interviewer: Could you bring this down to a specific learning situation?

Stewart: One young teacher brought a problem with her to the Puppet Centre. She had a remedial reading class, and the kids would not read. The problem was solved by using a hand puppet, a piece of fabric stuffed with a single glove. She said to her class: "I have this zany worm." The bookworm read the book with her and asked many dumb questions that the kids would correct. The teacher told us that when she put the bookworm down, glove and all, she would often see a child, perhaps a child who had never read before, pick up the bookworm, put his hand in the glove, and then sit and read the book to the bookworm. Well, that's pure incentive. It's a realm of fantasizing. And that's something else I think we should mention—the ability of a child to relate to something on two different intellectual levels. Sometimes puppetry creates a rather delicious confusion which is very exciting. It's like the children who will know there's a puppeteer behind that booth, yet will shout: "Look out behind you!'' to Little Red Riding Hood with the wolf. They will boo and cheer and do whatever the dramatic circumstances call for. Kids like to know the rules of the game. Then they like to bend the rules or elaborate on the rules.

Interviewer: You're saying that the experience of fantasy and the manipulation of the puppets is motivating enough for the child to want to learn a particular subject content?

Stewart: Yes. But I don't like to think of it as a lollipop. I don't like to think that a teacher who is incapable of interesting the children in a subject should use a puppet to interest them.

Interviewer: But isn't she using the puppet to stimulate interest?

Stewart: It is using a puppet if there's a block, in remedial situations, to ease a child into another situation. It's like using drama in a classroom. We must not think of puppets as something for very young children and for a rainy afternoon. I don't think of using puppets to teach. I see it as learning support. You can use a puppet activity to underpin teaching in a variety of subjects, because the project involves the full spectrum of drama.

Interviewer: Let's expand this a bit. You've been traveling around America and gathering information about puppetry in education. What is happening in America of importance?

Stewart: Quite a few exciting things. It's a big space. Very few countries have focal points for activity. As you've noticed, I haven't been able to explain what puppetry in education is or could be. It's an enormously complex issue that can be happening on so many levels. Already around America there are several universities with departments of puppetry. They are analyzing the potential.

Interviewer: Are there puppetry in educational departments?

Stewart: Yes, indeed. In Connecticut, in Ohio, in California and Georgia, there are already universities with small subsections, usually of the drama department. We need their facilities, but we need to be thought of separately. It should be in the sociology or education department. All media that prove to be valuable must be explored and explored scientifically.

Interviewer: Could you mention some specific resources that are available?

Stewart: In England we have produced a book, by mistake actually. We were trying to make contact with teachers and therapists who used any form of puppetry in their work. We just wrote to everybody and asked: ''Who does it? How do you do it? Where do you do it?'' The ones who weren't frantically busy wrote back. We have a magazine which comes out twice a year which includes these resources. One of the people who latched onto the potential of puppetry in education, A. R. Philpott, in England, was the editor of this. He was also the founder of the Educational Puppetry Association in England, of which I'm now the chairman. He brought together a lot of these essays, three volumes. We lumped them together and Plays, Inc., published them in America as *Puppets in Therapy.* Apart from that, the magazine of the Educational Puppetry Association is published twice a year as is *Animation,* another journal. That sparked off, in California, a newspaper called *Puppetry-in-Education News.* This was launched purely as a personal whim of Bob and Joy Biderman in San Francisco. Now they have a subscription list of about two thousand around the country. People who use puppets or are interested in using puppets can write to the *Puppetry-in-Education News* [see "Bibliography and Resources"] and get published.

Interviewer: Should scripts be used by children when they are working with puppets in education?

Stewart: Many people understand drama as exhibitionism. And many of the therapeutic uses of puppets depend upon the opportunity of the child who will not say to you what he thinks about his parents or his homelife, but will speak through his puppet. Now whether this is behind the screen or not doesn't matter. A teacher must learn how to work with this very powerful medium. And a lot of research has to be done with puppets. You can see a child playing in an improvisational session in drama in frustration, because he is not getting the responses he wants. If you give that child the opportunity to play both sides of the argument with two puppets, no ventriloquism, he might be able to work out his frustration.

Interviewer: So an improvisational script is developing.

Stewart: Yes. It's allowing the child an extention of his means of communicating. We've not discussed what they talk about with their friends while they are making the puppets or the fact that they forget themselves completely when they are discussing in a group what they are going to do. The opportunities in a puppet project are enormous, because it is art, crafts, and drama.

Puppetry in education is inclusive of both improvisation and performance. Like educational drama, it can be applied to the learning of such curricular content as reading. It can also be used in recreational and therapeutic settings as a method to achieve many of the cognitive, affective, and aesthetic aims subscribed to by educational drama leaders. Like theatre for young audiences, puppetry can be performed in theatres by professional puppeteers for audiences of various ages and abilities. Again, a distinction must be made between commercial puppet theatre and the more educationally oriented performances by puppetry in education groups. An excellent example of the latter is the Mermaid Theatre, based in Nova Scotia, Canada.

Mermaid is unique in that it combines puppetry with elements of pantomime and mask work to tell stories and present the mythology of indigenous Canadian cultural groups. In a recent demonstration and interview Tom Miller, director, puppeteer, and co-founder of the Mermaid Theatre, discussed his approach to educational puppet theatre:[3]

Interviewer: How did the Mermaid Theatre get started?

Tom Miller: The Mermaid Theatre was founded in 1972. Before that, another group, called the Acadia Child Drama and Puppet Theatre, was founded by Evelyn Garbary and myself at Acadia University. It was a summer project that came from my interest in puppetry and the interest of Mrs. Garbary's students in putting on plays for young people. In 1972 we decided it would be a good idea to form a permanent theatre to take to children in Nova Scotia.

Interviewer: You've done a lot of traveling in rural areas. I would imagine many of your audience members had never seen live theatre before.

Miller: Yes. We realized the only chance young children in Nova Scotia had to see theatre would be if they lived in a large city, in Halifax. So we decided that our main emphasis would be to take theatre into the rural areas.

Interviewer: Could you talk about the material you brought to them, specifically the Indian myths and folklore.

Miller: When we began working, the idea of doing theatre for young people came first. We began by doing some Brian Way plays and *The Merchant of Venice.* We played to a wide range of audiences, from elementary through university. Then we began to look around for something special, and we realized that nobody was presenting the heritage of Nova Scotia to the children of Nova Scotia. We looked through the folklore and mythology and discovered the Indian Micmac legends. These were stories that had been collected in the mid-1800s by Silas Rand, a Christian missionary. He recorded something like nine hundred different myths and legends. Here was a goldmine that we could draw upon.

Interviewer: Could you speak about the puppet characters you created based upon the Micmac myths.

Miller: We use quite a number of different puppets. One is Kitpoosegunow, a trickster figure, a fat little fellow with a vicious temper, who causes windstorms. This is a puppet that's operated on the stage, Bunraku style; that is the puppeteer is visible to the audience and is dressed in black from head to foot. Curiously enough, the children believe so strongly in the puppet that they see the puppeteer as the puppet's shadow. Another puppet character is Glooscap, the legendary god of the Micmacs. He created man and is a sort of Hercules figure, a super, big, strong man who looks over the Micmac people. He is a giant puppet. The puppeteer is inside the puppet, wearing the mask of Glooscap on top of his head. Glooscap hides his grandmother, who is played

9. Giant puppet of King George of England and mask of the Governor of Fortress Louisbourg in Nova Scotia, from *Louisbourg* by Patrick Walsh. Courtesy of Tom Miller.

10. Giant puppet and mask from *The Wabenaki* by the Mermaid Theatre. Courtesy of Tom Miller.

11. Micmac Indian characters designed by Tom Miller from *The Wabenaki,* as performed by the Mermaid Theatre. Courtesy of Tom Miller.

by an actress, in his robes. Here we have three of the basic elements that make up Mermaid Theatre—the actor, the giant puppet, and the smaller puppet. Another puppet figure is Coolpujot, a large foam statue, a boneless figure who controlled the winds. When Glooscap would turn him around, the winds would change from North to South or South to North, and that helped to control the seasonal change. Here we have the example of the puppet as a static figure, a statue. Another giant puppet, Queen Summer, is even bigger than Glooscap. She does a lot of dancing. Here we have puppetry used to represent something a little more abstract than a person—one of the seasons of the year. Next to Queen Summer is her butterfly made out of two pieces of half-inch foam, and it's carried by a puppeteer dressed in black. She bounces the butterfly from hand to hand, and it flutters around her. Kuh, the earthquake god, is the active principle, and Coolpujot is the passive principle. Glooscap is asked by a man if he can have eternal life. This is one thing that Glooscap could never grant. So he commands Kuh to do something for the man. There's a great rumbling, and the earthquake god opens his arms and his head flies open. This is a device that the Northwest Indians used often, having one mask with hinges that could open up to reveal another mask. The man walks toward the earthquake god who then closes his arms over him. There's tremendous thunder, lightning, and rumbling. When the earthquake god opens up his arms, he reveals a tree. The man has been transformed into the first cedar tree.

We did Indian material for about four or five years. But recently, we've moved into other areas of Nova Scotia folklore. For example, one character, Giant Anna, is based upon the life of Anna Swan, who lived in the mid-1800s and worked for Phineas T. Barnum, touring Europe with her husband, the Kentucky Giant. She is represented by another giant puppet. In this case, she was played by a man.

Miller then demonstrated the construction and movement of various puppets and masks used in Mermaid productions. For example, he presented the Loon, friend of Glooscap, a hand and rod puppet that is operated with the puppeteer's hand in the mouth of the Loon, as the other hand works the rods attached to the Loon's wings. The Loon's voice is created by an onstage flute.

In showing and telling of his masks, Miller remarked:

The use of masks in the theatre is, of course, centuries old. They are used to represent all types of figures. Our masks are made from foam so that they are soft. They stand up quite well to wear and tear. The mask represents the eternal aspect, the true personality of the figure. But, of course, it is immobile. So to create the expression, the performer must use his body.

Interviewer: Here's where your training in pantomime and movement comes in.

Miller: That's right. The performer puts the mask on, and even though I'm a man, I can represent the lightness of a woman. One of the things you must do in a mask is focus.

Interviewer: When you put the mask on, do you become more of the character?

Miller: Yes, and there's a sense of being hidden, a sense of extreme concentration in what you're doing, a sense of being aware how every part of your body is moving in relationship to the mask.

Interviewer: Even though you cannot see yourself, the feeling is present.

Miller: That's right.

Interviewer: You internalize the essence of your character.

Miller: Yes. To put a mask on for the first time, I would look at it very carefully to try to absorb the character of the mask. I might even look at myself in a mirror so I could see a complete image. The bigger the mask is, the more necessary it is to have a complete image of how you look. Naturalistic gestures do not work with a mask. Every gesture has to be bigger than life, because the mask is bigger than life. Masks allow us to play to audiences of over one thousand children, because the mask reads very well from a distance.

Interviewer: Where do you take your models from? Are they actual Indian drawings or are they from your imagination?

Miller: I think them up myself. By and large, the Micmacs have not left us much two-dimensional visual art and not even much of a heritage of mask work. That comes from other cultures.

The work of Tom Miller and the Mermaid Theatre in some ways parallels the work of TIE artist-teachers in that they choose their material from local, often historical sources; they transform nondramatic material into a creative, theatrical form and thereby educate audiences, mostly of students, about areas of their own history and culture often neglected by their teachers.

The aims and values of puppetry and mask work in education very much reflect those stated throughout this book by educational drama and theatre leaders. Puppetry and mask work, though, by virtue of their powerful visual and symbolic qualities, often provide more explicit evidence of the learning of those basic skills implicit in any excellent educational drama experience: attention, concentration, and focus. These and complementary skills, such as spontaneity and risk-taking, often are demonstrated as students actively manipulate puppets and/or work with masks.

NOTES

1. Maurice Stewart, "Puppets in Education: A Developing Science," *Sunrise Semester*, "Drama in Education," *Newsletter No. 1*, New York University, Office of Off-Campus Programs, December 1979, pp. 39-40.

2. WCBS-TV, *Sunrise Semester*, "Drama in Education: Puppetry in Education" (December 24, 1979).

3. WCBS-TV, *Sunrise Semester*, "Drama in Education: Puppetry, Mask, Mime, Myth" (December 26, 1979).

BIBLIOGRAPHY AND RESOURCES

Books

Adachi, Barbara. *The Voices and Hands of Bunraku*. New York: Kodansha International, 1978.

Baird, Bil. *The Art of the Puppet*. New York: Macmillan, 1965.

Batchelder, Marjorie. *The Puppet Theatre Handbook*. New York: Harper and Brothers, 1947.

Beresford, Margaret. *How to Make Puppets and Teach Puppetry*. New York: Taplinger Publishing Co., 1966.

Cole, Nancy H. *Puppet Theatre in Performance*. New York: William Morrow and Co., 1978.

Currell, David. *The Complete Book of Puppetry*. Boston: Plays, Inc., 1975.

_____. *Learning with Puppets*. Boston: Plays, Inc., 1980.

Ehle, Maryann J. "Puppetry Education: Its Role within the Context of the Creative-Expressive Language Arts Curriculum." Ph.D. dissertation, West Virginia University, 1977.

Hanford, Robert Ten Eyck. *The Complete Book of Puppets and Puppeteering*. New York: Drake Publishers, 1975.

Latshaw, George. *Puppetry: The Ultimate Disguise*. New York: Richard Rosen Press, 1978.

Malkin, Michael R. *Traditional and Folk Puppets of the World*. New York: A. S. Barnes, 1977.

Niculescu, Margarita. *The Puppet Theatre of the Modern World*. Boston: Plays, Inc., 1967.

Nobleman, Roberta. *Mime and Masks*. Rowayton, Conn.: New Plays, 1979.

Peters, Joan, and Anna Sutcliffe. *Creative Masks for Stage and School*. Boston: Plays, Inc., 1976.

Philpott, A. R. *Dictionary of Puppetry*. Boston: Plays, Inc., 1977.

Sims, Judy. *Puppets for Dreaming and Scheming: A Puppet Source Book*. Walnut Creek, Calif.: Early Stages, 1978.

Sorell, Walter. *The Other Face: The Mask in the Arts*. London: Thames and Hudson, 1974.

Theatre Crafts 9, no. 2 (March/April 1975).

The Drama Review, The Puppet Issue. New York University/School of the Arts 16, no. 3 (September 1972).

Resources

The National Puppetry Institute
    Box U-127P
    The University of Connecticut
    Storrs, Connecticut 06268
Puppet Centre
    Battersea Arts Centre
    Lavender Hill
    London SWII, England
Puppetry-in-Education News
    Bob Biderman
    164 27 Street
    San Francisco, California 94110
The Puppetry Guild of Australia
    17 Sirius Cove Road
    Mosman
    New South Wales 2088, Australia
Puppeteers of America
    5 Cricklewood Path
    Pasadena, California 91107
    Educational representative: Ms. Nancy Renfro
    1117 West 9 Street
    Austin, Texas 78703
The Puppetry Store
    Jennifer Ukstins
    14316 Sturtevant Road
    Silver Springs, Maryland 20904
UNIMA (Union Internationale des Marionnettes)
    Allelu Kurten, Executive Secretary
    Browning Road
    Hyde Park, New York 10024

PART V

OPPORTUNITIES AND PROSPECTS IN EDUCATIONAL DRAMA AND THEATRE

12
TRAINING AND VOCATIONAL OPPORTUNITIES

In 1976 Wendy Perks, an educational drama specialist, wrote the following: "Although our current national economic environment seems uncertain and perhaps bleak, it is apparent that the fine arts are enjoying a renaissance."[1] As evidence Perks cited the increasing attendance at theatre and related arts performances, as well as the federal and state support of arts-in-education programs.

Today the national economic environment is still uncertain, although the attendance at the commercial Broadway theatre, for one, is booming. But in that the federal government has severely curtailed support of the arts and education, we find a bleaker outlook than in 1976. However, educational drama and theatre programs have expanded beyond the school environment, which has traditionally been a major area of federal funding. Today, we find an increase of programs in hospitals, nursing homes, recreational centers, and the like, providing new opportunities for trained educational drama and theatre leaders.

In her article Wendy Perks found that forty colleges and universities offered undergraduate and/or graduate degrees in child drama. Five others offered coursework in the field, with an additional thirteen anticipating creative dramatics related programs.[2]

In 1981 Lin Wright, professor of child drama at Arizona State University, published "a partial listing of college programs that have coursework in child drama."[3] Although not as complete as Perks's survey, Wright found that sixty colleges and universities throughout the country offer degrees or coursework in child drama.

One would hope that with so many course offerings and training programs that there would be jobs available. In a recent interview Lowell Swortzell, director of the Program in Educational Theatre at New York

University, and Vera Mowry Roberts, former chairperson of the Department of Theatre and Cinema at Hunter College in New York City and past president of the American Theatre Association, discussed the vocational opportunities in the field of educational drama and theatre:[4]

Interviewer: Are there jobs?

Lowell Swortzell: There are jobs. I brought proof of the fact. This is a folder of letters announcing jobs all across the country in our field, on the college level. But there are jobs at all levels. It's very much a growing, expanding, developing field.

Interviewer: Do you get requests for community positions as well?

Swortzell: Yes. There are jobs in community theatre and children's theatre, summer recreational programs, camp programs, community centers, all looking for drama directors. Churches, hospitals, and museums also have drama directors.

Interviewer: Dr. Roberts, do you have such a folder?

Vera Mowry Roberts: Yes and it keeps growing all the time. Twenty-five years ago, it was pretty ridiculous for young people to think of making a life in theatre, and we told them that. But today, it's perfectly possible, because the opportunities are so various.

Interviewer: Let's start from the beginning. Would you agree that it's important for a student interested in a profession in educational theatre to ask himself: "Am I qualified to work in educational theatre?"

Roberts: I think the most necessary thing if one is thinking about a life in the theatre is to make a self-assessment. If, for instance, one thinks: "I'm going to be a big star," then you say that's the wrong reason for pursuing a career in theatre. I like to think about Stanislavski saying to love not yourself in the art, but the art in yourself.

Swortzell: It's difficult to know how or why we're motivated, but certainly a love of the theatre is not enough. I think you need to know what contribution you can make to the theatre, as well as knowing the field. The only way you will know your contributions is to explore where your particular talents and strengths may be. They're not always creative. Aside from creative artists we also need administrators and people who can guide and shape the theatre in other ways.

Roberts: The whole area of design is also important. Someone who has those skills can put them to good use in educational drama. People who have an interest in community work are also needed. Educational drama requires, above everything else, a sensitivity to where other people are coming from and the ability to work in a community endeavor together. So that sometimes the person of very high creative ability, who becomes impatient with the shortcomings of the people around him or her, is likely not to be the best person.

Swortzell: And sometimes the person from the professional theatre is not the best teacher in the classroom.

Interviewer: Would you say that in educational theatre we are looking for the combination of artist-teacher or teacher-artist?

Swortzell: Absolutely.

Interviewer: Does it matter which way we start? Which comes first?

Swortzell: I don't think you can isolate the two.

Interviewer: I think we are seeing more of the theatre professional who decides to come back to school for an M.A. or B.A. in educational theatre.

Roberts: As long as he doesn't see teaching as a fall-back position for a career which has not gone where he wanted it to go.

Interviewer: That sounds like another wrong reason to go into educational theatre. Let's explore the wrong reasons further.

Swortzell: The one I was getting at is: "I want to help people to change their lives." Drama can certainly do this. But you can't just be a do-gooder. There has to be more than that. There has to be quality drama that's brought into people's lives, well used, and followed through. I firmly believe that a bad play seen by a child can do serious damage. I'd rather children see no theatre until a certain period in their lives then something whipped up because someone thinks they need a play.

Interviewer: What are some of the right reasons why students choose educational drama as a career?

Roberts: I think theatre in all of its many forms is one of the most humanizing pursuits in which anybody can engage, because it requires an investigation into a great many bodies of knowledge; it requires a sympathy and concern for a group process; and it requires a creative imagination. Put all that together and you have a pretty wonderful package of humanistic studies.

Swortzell: It is the one art that utilizes all the other arts. I include education in art. That's why I say you can't really separate the two.

Roberts: Let's not forget artist-teachers, teacher-artists.

Interviewer: When you look over the graduate students that come into your departments, what kinds of patterns do you find? Is there a standard background of students studying educational theatre or a diversity of backgrounds?

Roberts: We get a pretty diverse group at Hunter. Some come from school settings, some from community settings, some from professional theatre settings.

Swortzell: So do we. We run an enormous gamut. They may be established teachers who have somehow just discovered the potential of drama and theatre. They try it out by doing a short play or a drama lesson, and they become tremendously excited. They have no theatre background, but suddenly they want it. They come from all professions. We have people from the professional theatre who want to teach. We have parents, community leaders, recreational leaders.

Interviewer: Could we talk about the specific jobs available in some of these areas. What kind of training is most appropriate for these jobs? Let's begin with jobs in schools.

Swortzell: There are jobs for drama specialists in various states. I would hope that the day would come when every elementary schoolteacher would be trained in how to use drama, thereby eliminating the specialist.

Roberts: This is also one of my concerns. If we're ever going to make effective use of drama in education, particularly at the elementary school level, the teachers already there have to have the knowledge and training to be able to use it.

Swortzell: And now we have the mainstreaming law, requiring full educational opportunity for all in the public classroom, bringing new populations of students on the scene. Drama is the most marvelous means of getting them to work together and interrelate.

Interviewer: So we're talking about two levels of jobs in schools: the drama specialist who might teach drama classes or in-service workshops for teachers on a part-time basis and the regular classroom teacher who has some training in educational drama and theatre. What about the opportunities for educational drama and theatre in the community?

Swortzell: In recent years money has been made available in urban areas. But very often when money is made available, there is not a trained drama person to take advantage of the job.

Interviewer: At one time you had mentioned the notion of the adventure playgrounds in England. Could you talk about that concept?

Swortzell: An empty lot or piece of an abandoned urban landscape is turned into a playground that houses a whole arts program. One that I was particularly fascinated with in London used space underneath a super-highway. Painting, drama, and theatre were going on in that space all summer long. Think of how many spaces like that we have throughout the country. Youngsters and adults gravitated to the adventure playground. They made marvelous posters and had art exhibitions. It cost no one any rent. Most of the adventure playgrounds in England are staffed by maybe one person. . . .

Roberts: . . . and volunteers.

Swortzell: The community creates the program.

Interviewer: This is, then, an example of avocational work or play in educational drama. Could we talk now about drama/theatre work for the elderly. Is this a growing field?

Roberts: Since the numbers of senior citizens are increasing in our society, a good deal of attention is being paid to them now. All kinds of services are being projected to help that population. I became concerned about the fact that our society tended to put older people in file drawers and to forget about them. I raised some money to do a project with a group of older adults whose average age was seventy-five. Over a period of weeks we went to see plays—new plays, plays of the moment, avant-garde plays, so that the group would be involved in the present day.

Then we did readings of the same kind of plays. And then we did drama exercises. After that we improvised plays, then went on to work with scripts. We put together a troupe who then toured senior citizen centers.

Interviewer: If I want to work with senior citizens through drama, I'm not going to find an advertisement in the newspaper for a job working on a project such as yours. What do I do?

Roberts: You can go out and create a job. You get an idea that a certain kind of thing needs to be done; then you visit the YMCA or YWCA, and they tell you of local settlement houses or senior citizen centers in their neighborhood. One of our graduate students found the roster of a senior citizen's center and wrote the people a letter inviting them to a drama group. She got about fifteen people. Since that time she's become a staff member of that center.

Swortzell: We also have a number of instances. A student did puppetry work for ten sessions with a group of emotionally disturbed children. The staff was so impressed they asked the student to stay on as a staff member and a new position was created.

Interviewer: What about the area of theatre for young audiences. Are there jobs?

Swortzell: Yes, there are, especially in regional theatre, because many cities now have their own companies, attached to an adult company, in which there are directing, designing, and administrative jobs. Sometimes there are acting jobs.

Interviewer: The American Theatre Association publishes a monthly bulletin of jobs, does it not?

Roberts: Yes. It's a bulletin of the placement service. Because the American Theatre Association comprises college and university theatre, secondary theatre, children's theatre, community and army theatre, it has connections and listings of jobs in all of these areas.

Interviewer: Could we talk now about the programs at Hunter College and New York University in training drama and theatre educators.

Roberts: Our department at Hunter is in a liberal arts college. Students can, however, major in creative drama/children's theatre. In order to do that they must take some work in the division of education. They can also take an M.A. degree in this field.

Swortzell: Our program at New York University is situated in a school of education. It was called the department of dramatic arts many years ago. In the late sixties we shifted the focus to train teachers to use drama in all levels of education, from pre-school through work with the elderly. We offer an undergraduate degree, a master's, Ph.D., and Ed.D. We specialize in children's theatre and every other kind of educational drama and theatre as well. We're developing in the area of drama therapy. We also have a successful program in the summer in musical theatre, in collaboration with the music education department. For the past nine years we have had the study abroad program at Bretton,

England. The reason for this program is that a number of the new ideas come from England. We wanted not only to bring them here and adapt them, but to take our students there to study with the leaders in British educational drama. We're now beginning to see theatre-in-education teams established in the United States.

Interviewer: The picture, then, is fairly rosy, in that there are advertised jobs. It is also, though, incumbent upon an individual who is trained and has made a self-evaluation to go out and, in fact, create a job.

Roberts: Absolutely true. This is a field where one can create a job for oneself.

Swortzell: In the professional theatre we hear actors talking about making the rounds. In the educational area it's the same thing. You're looking for opportunities in any walk of life where educational theatre can be used. When you find that, and if it's something you can relate to, you build your job there.

Training programs in educational drama and theatre are not only limited to colleges and universities. Theatres for young audiences, such as The Children's Theatre Company of Minneapolis, now offer extensive internships in various aspects of performance, design, and administration. Hospitals and community centers sometimes train volunteers to work through drama and related arts within therapeutic and recreational settings. As volunteer or intern positions can potentially lead to jobs, it is recommended that the student of educational drama and theatre seek out relevant community resources.

Scores of articles have been written in recent years about the increasing population of M.A.s and Ph.D.s who have studied the arts and humanities and are unable to find work in their fields. But, as mentioned above, the quality and quantity of vocations and avocations in educational drama and theatre are limited only by one's imagination. The essential requirements are an expertise and commitment to the field and to a chosen population, a clear sense of one's own needs and abilities, and a willingness to create new jobs or revitalize old ones. With the expansive understanding of educational drama and theatre as presented in this book, the territory stretches beyond the auditorium and beyond the classroom.

NOTES

1. Wendy Perks, "Children's Drama 1976," pp. 6-12.

2. Ibid., p. 11.

3. Lin Wright, *Children's Theatre Association Newsletter*, Spring/Summer 1981, pp. 16-24.

4. WCBS-TV, *Sunrise Semester*, "Drama in Education: Career Opportunities in Educational Drama" (December 31, 1979).

13

FUTURE DIRECTIONS IN EDUCATIONAL DRAMA AND THEATRE

In a recent article Geraldine Brain Siks looked ahead to the year 1990 and imagined five changes occurring in the field of educational drama and theatre.

1. Every state in the nation requires drama to be included in the education of all children, K-12.
2. All children in kindergarten through grade six experience drama weekly in all the public schools of our nation.
3. The creative drama field is clarified.
4. At pre-service and in-service levels, classroom teachers and drama specialists are prepared to teach drama as an art; to use it as a teaching process; and to involve children in creative drama to foster their personal development.
5. Lively, artistic theatre performances for children and by children are integrated into the structure of drama education in every elementary school in the nation.[1]

Siks's predictions are based upon several present realities, including the development of arts councils in each state, the influence of the federal Alliance for Arts Education in instituting programs throughout the country, an increase in research in drama/theatre education, further attempts by the American Theatre Association and the Children's Theatre Association to support new scholars and research and to refine terminology, and the implementation of new state policies in Texas and North Carolina requiring the inclusion of drama and theatre in the curriculum of elementary and secondary schools.

In looking further into the future of the field, Professors Nellie McCaslin of New York University, and Ann Shaw, of Queens College, discussed their views:[2]

Interviewer: Before we discuss your thoughts about the future, would you comment on recent developments in educational theatre.

Nellie McCaslin: During the late 1950s and 1960s, we suddenly saw a tremendous spread of activity, particularly in professional children's theatre. Until that time theatre for young people was largely in the hands of educators, social workers, and community centers. Suddenly, the professionals entered the field. We had seen the traditional play traditionally performed up to that point. Then, in the early sixties a new format and some changes in content became visible. A group that had a great influence on these changes was the Paper Bag Players. This was a movement away from the traditional material toward the revue type of show or number of short sketches based upon a theme. This seemed to lead into improvisational techniques and mime. At that same time we were also aware of the growth of the musical. This I think was less original, because the musical comedy was already popular in America with adult audiences. Many of the young professionals thought that since it was a popular form for adults, it should be performed for children also. Everything seemed to be set to music. A few were good; many were not. Suddenly, many of us were aware we could scarcely find a traditional play traditionally done. Then toward the end of the sixties and early seventies the drama in education and theatre-in-education programs were reported in this country. These programs, as we know, began in England. American educators traveling abroad were enthusiastic about what they saw. We had a great deal of trivial content, and we felt we would like to see more substance. In the TIE programs we began to see content that could be used in American education. So in the seventies the change was in the direction of content-oriented programs.

Interviewer: Dr. Shaw, could you speak of theatre for young audiences from an international point of view, as you have been the chairperson of the American Center of ASSITEJ, the International Association of Theatre for Children and Young People.

Ann Shaw: One of the things we see happening in this country and around the world is a new concept in what is children's theatre. Children are more sophisticated then they used to be. So more and more theatres are addressing themselves to theatre for children and young audiences or theatre for young people, as it is often called.

Interviewer: How would you define a young person in terms of age?

Shaw: I think it depends upon the theatre and the material. Many of the theatres, for example, the Theatre for Young Spectators in Leningrad, consider its audience to be from about age eight or nine up through young adults, into the twenties. And, of course, some parents come in with children. The Empire State Youth Theatre Institute in Albany has a range of plays that would appeal to young children, junior high, high school students, young adults, and adults. The reason for this is that they began to realize that if they expand the purview of the theatre, they could then attract more professional directors, designers, producers, because they had more demanding material and a greater range of material to work with. ASSITEJ began in 1964, and the first international congress was in 1966. In a way, it's very young. There were about eight countries present at the original founding. There are now thirty-three member countries. This is an association made up largely of professionals who do theatre for young audiences, that is, they make their living at it. It's not theatre by children, but theatre for children and young people. There is also an amateur category in ASSITEJ of people who are not making their living fully in theatre for young audiences. Member countries include representatives from Eastern and Western Europe, South America, Australia, Japan, etcetera.

Interviewer: Could you now talk a bit about recent developments in the area of drama and theatre by/with/for the handicapped. You have been chairperson of the program by that name, which is a subcommittee of the American Theatre Association.

Shaw: A lot of this has come about because of federal funding for work with individuals with handicapping conditions. In the last five years I've seen an enormous shift in the attitudes of people interested in this area. I think the attitude has always been: "Well, yes, the handicapped individual ought to have the opportunity to see theatre." And we know that plays have trouped to nursing homes, children's hospitals, and veteran's hospitals. If the handicapped could manage to get to the theatre and into a seat without disturbing anyone, they were welcome at the theatre and often given reduced tickets. But that was always theatre for the handicapped, as if we were doing something nice for unfortunate folks. Now, I think that attitude has shifted enormously, because we have begun to see the potential of what a talented individual, who is disabled, can bring to the theatre. So the American Theatre Association program started by being called a special committee on drama, theatre, and the handicapped. Now the program has the long title of Drama and Theatre By, With and For the Handicapped. We get the "by" and "with" in first. And that started with the National Theatre of the Deaf, the whole notion that people with disabilities could really create excellent theatre. Notice that when many people refer to that organization, they still say the National Theatre *for* the Deaf.

Interviewer: Let us now speculate as to the future. What do you both see as important future directions in the area of educational drama, or what is presently called creative drama?

McCaslin: I believe that this area is expanding. We're a big country, and I suspect there are many fine teachers throughout the country whose work we haven't seen yet. My hope would be that drama would take its place among the other arts in the curriculum. It has taken a long time for the arts to be included in curricula. Music came first, then the visual arts. Dance took longer and had to come in through the gym door, as part of physical education. Drama is now incorporated in some school systems, but I would certainly like to see creative drama made available for all children in all schools in the United States.

Interviewer: Dr. Shaw, do you think that there is a possibility in the 1980s of incorporating more creative drama within school curricula?

Shaw: I doubt it. I think there's always a possibility, but I think when we see budget cutbacks and a more conservative approach to education that it won't happen unless more people who are trained and interested in the field will do creative drama and no one will stop them. In a sense that's always the greatest source of creative drama in a curriculum—the teacher who's interested in it and finds that it inspires children. But I don't think you are going to find many school systems that will decide to include creative drama in the curriculum.

Interviewer: You're saying that it's up to the individual teacher to say: "I know something about drama and I will do it in my classroom."

Shaw: I think more teachers are going to say that, because more teachers will know about creative drama. At Queens College, for example, I frequently get calls not only from colleagues in the education department, but psychology and the English department to inquire what's going on in our creative drama classes. I think we are going to find more people who may have had majors in areas outside of drama and theatre, but who have had some courses in drama and are going to use it when they become classroom teachers. Creative drama is more generally known now than ever before. When I started teaching in the 1950s and said I was teaching creative drama, everyone said: "What is that?"

Interviewer: Let's now shift to theatre for young audiences. What do you see as future directions in that area?

Shaw: I would like to see more of a spread in terms of what audience it addresses itself to. It will help us to develop a more and more professional theatre. I would like to see more good regional theatres, like the Children's Theatre Company and School of Minneapolis, the Empire State Youth Theatre Institute, the National Theatre and Academy— quality theatre that is well-produced and well-staged. I'm getting tired of the unisex jumpsuits and stepladders.

McCaslin: I'd like to see the same thing. I, too, am getting tired of the uniform costume. I think it had its place, but I think we have a tendency as a nation to do what everybody else is doing. A good idea comes along and suddenly everybody is doing it, like participatory theatre or the review type of theatre. There is a place for all kinds of theatre in this country. Since the sixties we have had a steady growth in funding for the arts. By the end of the sixties every state had an arts council giving money to the arts, including theatre, and many of them including children's theatre. Also we've had support from the National Endowment for the Arts, the Artists-in-Schools Program, and the Alliance for Arts Education. Suddenly, we are doing something we said we weren't going to do—let the government get into the arts. We found that it hasn't disturbed a thing. In the Rockefeller report *Coming to Our Senses*, it was discovered, after a very thorough survey, that this country is unanimously in favor of the arts in education, but that we were doing very little, indeed, to implement this. On the one hand, we believe it and give money; on the other hand, we haven't begun to go far enough.

Interviewer: Will this money still be available in the 1980s?

McCaslin: I hope that it will. As Ann said, there is this movement of back to basics. We are supporting the basics, but many people don't realize that aesthetic education is basic to human learning.

Interviewer: What about the area of drama therapy or, as you call it, drama/theatre by/with/for the handicapped? What future directions do you see for that area?

Shaw: I want to mention that we will see more drama work not only in terms of children and young people, but spreading across all age groups, and being useful in work with individuals with any kind of handicapping condition. I think, of course, that all drama is therapeutic in nature. If it's art it has to give you a better sense of well-being. On the other hand, I don't see it all as being therapy, because I don't think all of us are prepared or equipped to bring about behavioral changes in people, which I think is the job of the therapist. I think we are going to see a lot more theatre that involves people with and without disabilities working together. I think we are going to see more people with disabilities who are drama innovators and leaders. I hope we are going to see some really rigorous academic programs in the area of drama therapy, so that people can be trained as drama therapists, rather than hanging out a shingle.

Interviewer: That's what we are presently developing at New York University.

Shaw: I think there is going to be money available in this area. The National Committee, Arts for the Handicapped, funds some of the programs. The American Theatre Association has just funded workshops in drama/theatre by/with/for the handicapped at our national convention in San Diego. The Office of Education and a number of government agencies are funding in this area.

Interviewer: What part can the public at large play in assuring a healthy future for educational drama and theatre?

McCaslin: I think people should know their communities and support the best in their communities. I'd like to see school and community working together. I'd like to see people trusting themselves enough not to imitate somebody else's act.

Shaw: I'd like to see far more support from the media: newspapers, magazines, television, etcetera. I think we can all make a concerted effort in that direction so people can know more about what is going on.

Interviewer: There are some organizations that I think people should be familiar with. First is the American Theatre Association, with its various branches, including the Children's Theatre Association, the Secondary School Theatre Association, the University and College Theatre Association, the American Community Theatre Association, and the Army Theatre Arts Association. There is also the fairly recent organization, the National Association for Drama Therapy, as well as ASSITEJ, the international organization mentioned previously.

The 1980s are upon us. Several of the predictions made by Siks, McCaslin, and Shaw involve organizational support at the national and state levels, in terms of funding and program development. Yet the conservative governments of Ronald Reagan and Margaret Thatcher, among others, are not inclined to support the arts and education.

Given these political and economic realities of government, as well as the ingrained bureaucratic lethargy of some large arts organizations, the future of our field remains in the hands of individuals who discover for themselves, through formal study and experience, the natural relationship between drama/theatre and human learning and then apply this discovery to their work and play with family, friends, students, clients, and patients.

Also, to ensure a bright future these individuals must, as Siks suggested, work toward clarifying the field through relevant research and experimentation and through constructive dialogue with colleagues within educational drama and theatre and related disciplines such as psychology, special education, and the language arts.

What constitutes relevant research is a debatable point. Quantitative behavioral research has been minimal in the field and for good reason. Graham Scott, an Australian drama/theatre educator, has written:

Creative Dramatics is more concerned with personality development than with achieving limited behaviours and it does this by taking a total view of the child, one that accepts that we can view his behavior as acts, but that these are part of an ongoing matrix of activity.[3]

Scott and others suggested research representing a philosophical position that accounts for *imagination* and *identification, intuition* and *feeling*, all terms that seem to defy behavioral quantification. Even Ann Shaw in her seminal behavioral research, applying Bloom and his co-authors' *Taxonomy of Education Objectives* to creative drama, discovered:

there is a kind of response intended in creative dramatics which is not classifiable in either the *Taxonomy* or the model construct. Characteristic of aesthetic experiences, this response might be described as a sense of being one with what is being imagined or perceived.[4]

Relevant research, then, must take account of the notion that educational drama and theatre is an aesthetic experience, involving a confluence of human cognitive, affective and psychomotor learning, and based in non-behavioral processes such as imagination and identification. Researchers must not limit their work to behavioral methods of inquiry, but must also look toward aesthetic, existential modes such as those represented in the work of Richard Courtney and Gavin Bolton, which we have already touched upon, and Susanne Langer and Robert Witkin, who have written lucid philosophical accounts of the artistic process.[5]

More interdisciplinary research is needed, since an exploration of identification and imagination, for example, impinges upon psychology, education, philosophy, and sociology, as well as drama and theatre.

Nellie McCaslin's point that professionals in the field need to imitate less and discover their own directions is very well taken. For the field to retain its vitality, experimentation and variety of performance and improvisational styles must be maintained. The very nature of drama/theatre as an art form implies a diversity of styles. Theatre for young audiences must make room for reviews, musicals, puppet theatre, traditional stories traditionally told, participatory theatre, political theatre, and any number of possible new experiments in form or content.

Likewise, educational drama leaders must avoid the tendency to elevate the latest popular method or popular personality to an exalted position. Although new methods must be explored and developed, no one method is necessarily appropriate for all environments and all participants. The genius of Dorothy Heathcote does not lie in the many articles and books written about her, nor in her teaching of teachers, nor in the attempts of others to imitate her style, but rather in the challenges she provokes in students and colleagues and, more so, in the extraordinary personality of Dorothy Heathcote, of whom there is only one. There will never be another Dorothy Heathcote, but there are and will be other inspired leaders with inspiring methods to share with others.

Finally, to ensure a healthy future, leaders in the field must learn to engage in constructive dialogue. This means cutting through our tendencies to separate knowledge into impregnable compartments in our minds and departments on our campuses. It means risking that the sharing and debating of our ideas will not leave us open to exploitation, but rather to the building of a field much in need of clarification and cooperation. At a time in our field's development when leaders use so many different terms to mean so many different things (or, at times, the same thing), we must work to find at least a common rhetoric if we are to communicate more fully in the future. This rhetoric must be inclusive rather than exclusive of current work in the field, including work with various age groups, work in hospitals, prisons, museums, churches. There is great room for discussion and argument. But if the drama therapy people refuse to talk to the drama by/with/for the handicapped people, and if the political theatre people refuse to talk to the traditional theatre people, and if the followers of Viola Spolin refuse to talk to the followers of Dorothy Heathcote, all of us in what is, in fact, a common field, are compromised.

Given a field that promotes relevant research, a willingness to experiment and to allow diversity, and a commitment to constructive dialogue, individuals exposed to these conditions may well discover the natural relationship between drama/theatre and human learning. Hopefully, they will apply these discoveries to the many work, play, and home environments they move in. If they do so, the future of educational drama and theatre indeed looks bright, despite inevitable cutbacks in funds from the government.

NOTES

1. Geraldine B. Siks, "Drama in Education: Imagining Challenges of the Eighties," *Children's Theatre Review* 29, no. 3 (1980): 3.

2. WCBS-TV, *Sunrise Semester*, "Drama in Education: Future Directions, A Preview of Things to Come" (January 2, 1980).

3. Graham Scott, "Structures for Creative Drama: Some Comments on Shaw, Langer, and Kelly," *Discussions in Developmental Drama 1* (Calgary, Alberta, Can.: Department of Drama, University of Calgary, April 1972), p. 11.

4. Ann M. Shaw, "A Taxonomical Study of the Nature and Behavioral Objectives of Creative Dramatics," *Educational Theatre Journal* 22 (December 1970): 371.

5. See, for example, Susanne Langer, *Philosophy in a New Key* (Cambridge, Mass.: Harvard University Press, 1967); and idem, *Feeling and Form* (New York: Scribner's, 1953). See Graham Scott's discussion of Langer and George Kelly in the article cited in note 3. See also Robert W. Witkin, *The Intelligence of Feeling* (London: Heinemann, 1974).

14
SUMMARY AND
CONCLUSIONS

Approaching the conclusion of the *Sunrise Semester* "Drama in Education" series, forty-seven programs had been aired. Most of them have been documented to some degree within this book. In wrestling with the form of the final program, I considered two possibilities: one was to deliver a prepared lecture, trying to make a summary statement and articulate a definitive conception of the field; the other was to discover a more dramatic means of concluding, trying to show as well as tell in a way that left the field open to further thought and refinement. I chose the latter, deciding to retain the interview structure and conduct a dialogue with myself.

This choice was apt for several reasons. It remains within the boundaries of dramatic teaching. A process of thinking through an issue was demonstrated, as opposed to a fixed body of knowledge being spoken about. The self-interview had the spontaneity and playfulness of an improvisation as the interviewer/guest expert moved from role to role, much like a ventriloquist and his dummy. Simple theatrical properties, such as a pair of eyeglasses and an empty chair, were used to designate role changes. Also, the notion that acting in everyday life implies the taking-on or playing-out of several roles was graphically illustrated.

Furthermore, the self-interview provides a dramatic model of thinking, in that diverse aspects of the self are engaging in a dialogue that is open-ended, expansive, improvisational, and dialectical. As the self-interview represents externalized thought, it conforms to Moffett's notion of inner speech as essentially dramatic and interrelated to all other forms of discourse. The self-interview represents the interpersonal interview, as inner dialogue represents interpersonal dialogue.

In many ways the self-interview, although specifically focused on the television series, could just as well relate to this book, which is, in fact, a reflection, revision, and expansion of that series. An adaptation of that self-interview, substituting book references for television references, follows:[1]

Interviewer: As you look back over your work on this book in attempting to specify the boundaries of educational drama and theatre, what do you think is missing?

Robert Landy: There are very many resources throughout the United States, Britain, Canada, and Australia that I didn't mention out of ignorance or oversight. Also, there are many excellent leaders in the field whom I neglected to mention. I think these are our greatest resources. I would have liked to deal more with philosophy and theory. I didn't deal much with research. This is partly because I don't think there is a wealth of it available in our field. But maybe that's because we are still young; or because we are interdisciplinary and have to borrow research models from other fields, as Richard Courtney implied in *Play, Drama and Thought.* This can be problematic if we are not sure what to borrow and from where. We probably need to develop our own research methodologies that are appropriate to our peculiar mix of education, drama/theatre, and the social sciences. This will take time, especially as many do not agree that we are or should be thought of as interdisciplinary. But I think it's a mistake to fall back upon behavioral research simply because it's so readily available and used so often in educational and social science research in this country. Drama/theatre in education, therapy, or the arts has to do with a lot more than observable behaviors.

Interviewer: Do you think that you have presented a general conception of the field of educational drama and theatre in these pages?

Landy: I hope so. I think it's closest to Brian Way's conception that drama is truly for the development of all human beings. The development of the drama is secondary to the development of people through drama. By all human beings I mean just that: children, adults, the elderly, the severely disabled or gifted. Certainly, we meet our limits with profoundly disturbed or retarded individuals, but you must remember Richard Courtney's story about the student who reached an autistic child through establishing physical contact and imitating her movements. The power of drama and theatre in reaching people is still unexplored. Drama and education complement each other, as experience complements knowledge. I think that with an authentic dramatic education one learns through experience. Experience, in John Dewey's terms, implies not only that I do something, but that I undergo something in return; my understanding changes or I see things a bit differently as a result of my experience.[2] Experience is not only physical action; it's mental and psychological and social. To complicate matters further we add the term *therapy* into our understanding of the field. Like drama and education, therapy has to do with experiencing and undergoing a certain change of understanding or behavior. I think the ultimate aim of all three is the same—growth and development. We have seen how drama therapy developed out of some very basic ritual dramatic practices.

Interviewer: Is drama therapy educational?

Landy: Of course. The protagonist-client should learn more about himself if the therapy is successful. I don't even mean this necessarily must occur on a conscious level. If the clients have had an enjoyable experience through drama therapy, they learn that they are able to enjoy themselves. For some people, that is quite a revelation.

Interviewer: Is educational drama therapeutic?

Landy: I think so. Most people feel good when they do it. It releases tensions and can lead to insights. I'm sensitive to those who are fearful of the mix of drama and therapy. But I think as training becomes more available and more sophisticated, we'll find a competent group of trained drama therapists. *Drama*, *education*, and *therapy* are not, of course, synonymous terms. There are differences in method, training, specific purpose, etcetera. But they do all exist relative to one another within this general conception of educational drama and theatre I am trying to acticulate. Drama is a natural process of role-taking and role-playing. It is inborn and one of the properties that defines one's humanness. Those who have shut off feelings and/or find themselves locked into a limited repertory of roles, that is, those who have severely limited their ability to engage in drama, are those who generally are anti-social, alienated, or, in the extreme, sociopathic. The drama educator or therapist consciously decides how best to use the natural dramatic process in the education or therapy of his or her students or clients. Theatre, like drama, is also about putting oneself in somebody else's shoes, taking on the role of another. But the art of creating theatre isn't necessarily for everyone. It's for those who are ready, who are talented, who have made a commitment to their art. Drama is for everybody at every moment, everywhere. Theatre occurs at a special time and in a special place. And it's often performed for the wrong reasons—showing off, pleasing the expectations of a teacher.

Interviewer: What are the right reasons?

Landy: That the play comes from a need within the group; that the actors are developmentally ready to perform; that everybody sees a reason for working with particular material.

Interviewer: What about the audience?

Landy: Educational theatre is for all audiences of all ages, provided they have the ability to attend to the play.

Interviewer: Where does educational drama and theatre take place?

Landy: Everywhere. People play roles all the time—at work, at play, in the streets. Politicians use dramatic metaphors often; they speak of the political arena, for example.

Interviewer: But how is street drama educational?

Landy: In the same way that play is educational. In the same way that any role-taking or role-playing is educational. In presenting ourselves in role we have the potential to learn more about who we are and how we relate to others. This also happens in the mind, which is another common arena for drama. We are all Walter Mittys, taking on many imaginary roles in our fantasy, wishing at times that we were someone other than ourselves. We also transform time in our minds, as a playwright does on stage. We can flash back and relive moments, or we can pre-experience something that hasn't occurred yet.

Interviewer: What about other environments?

Landy: The most visible ones are the school, the community, and the theatre. Educational drama and theatre, as we have seen throughout this book, is active on every level of school in its many forms of exercise, improvisation, school play, and TIE. It's used as a method to teach other subjects or is taught as a subject in itself. It has been used as a way of integrating subject matter so that you don't perpetuate the compartmentalization of learning into forty-five minutes of English, forty-five minutes of history, and so on. A good example of an integrated approach is John Hodgson's use of anthology. In the community we have seen educational drama and theatre as an indigenous cultural activity and as a learning or therapeutic process applied to religion, museum education, family life, inner city life, and therapy in hospitals, nursing homes, and other community organizations. And, of course, we have seen the very rich resource of the theatre artist who creates for young and multigenerational audiences in a noncommercial, educational theatre. Here I am using the term *education* to mean aesthetic education, an education of the senses, of the intuition, not necessarily a cognitive or explicitly didactic education.

Interviewer: What are the reasons why we should use drama and theatre in these environments?

Landy: You must realize, again, that drama is alive in these environments whether you consciously choose to use it or not. I'd like to remind you of a distinction I made earlier between indigenous and applied drama. *Indigenous drama* is that part of our personality involving identification, role-playing, and so forth, and that part of our cultural experience involving our rituals and social behaviors, areas which are biologically or culturally determined. We consciously apply drama to a specific population for specific reasons. The reasons vary. As I just mentioned, the theatre artist generally doesn't see his work as didactic education, although some TIE people would admit to having didactic aims. The Creative Arts Team wants to provoke its audiences to talk about moral and philosophical issues. This whole business of the aims of educational drama and theatre is extremely difficult to speak of abstractly. All questions of objectives depend so much upon specific needs of specific people in specific environments. And let me add that a lot also depends upon the needs of the drama educator. You may remember that the *Uncle Vanya* project began when Phillip Lopate asserted his need to deal with literature that excited him. Also, I think we should avoid only talking of behavioral objectives. The aims of educational drama and theatre are often very difficult, if not impossible, to quantify, especially when we speak in terms of aesthetic aims, affective aims, therapeutic aims. So there are many reasons why we apply drama and theatre to education—aesthetic reasons, developmental reasons, therapeutic and academic reasons. But they must be spoken of in the context of specific people and specific places. Thom Turner spoke about learning how to learn as an aim. This is crucial. Through educational drama and theatre, one can learn many skills basic to all further learning —concentration, imagination, dialogue, and so forth. Maybe this is ultimately the reason why educational drama and theatre should be applied to human learning.

Interviewer: What about vocational and avocational opportunities in the field?

Landy: As Professors Roberts and Swortzell said, stake out your own territory and start your own program there. If you do that you liberate yourself from considerations of federal funding and conservative policies over which you have minimal control. And, of course, seek out a solid educational and training program based upon a self-assessment of your skills and career goals. There are more than sixty colleges and universities in this country alone with courses and programs in educational drama and theatre. There are also training programs, special summer programs, and internships in theatres and community organizations. Write letters to people in the field. Find out what they have to offer. Attend conferences of such organizations as the American Theatre Association, ASSITEJ, and the National Association for Drama Therapy and find out what kinds of opportunities are available. There are job availabilities that are advertised, but some of the most exciting opportunities are those not advertised and in some cases not even thought of yet by a personnel director or administrator. I think the field of drama therapy will grow substantially in the next several years. Also, I think there will be more regional theatres producing plays for young audiences and offering paying jobs to theatre artists, actor-educators,

and administrators. Another growing area of special interest is in working with the elderly and with multigenerational groups through drama
and theatre.

Interviewer: Are there any final remarks you would like to make?

Landy: Just a story. About ten years ago I was substituting for a junior
high school drama/theatre teacher. I had never met her, was unaware of
her curriculum, and knew nothing about her students. She left me a
lesson plan which was to allow the students to rehearse scenes that they
were required to perform the following week in class, for a grade. I
introduced myself, explained the teacher's wishes, and sat back in the
auditorium and watched. Several groups were working on scenes that they
clearly didn't understand—classical, stylized scenes, mostly. One group,
working onstage, seemed especially stuck. Their line readings and movements were mechanical, and they seemed bored. As their rehearsal
progressed or regressed a student appeared with a toy gun and shot at the
actors. They ignored him. Undaunted, he leaped from the stage and shot
another student who had withdrawn from his tedious rehearsal. The
second immediately fell to the ground, silent and cold, then suddenly
arose from the dead, grabbed the gun from the other boy, and shot his
murderer. Both boys played excellent death scenes. And their drama was
just warming up. They joined with four others and decided to stage a
wedding. The boy with the gun cast himself as the groom. Others
assumed the roles of bride, bridesmaid, priest, best man, etcetera. About
the same time the rehearsal onstage ended, and the wedding party made
their way to the stage. The priest conducted the ceremony, and the
wedding party wished the newlyweds well, sending them off with a
shower of imaginary rice. The bride and groom leaped from the stage
and began chasing each other through the rows of seats in the auditorium. By this time the full class was in on the drama. One girl cried out:
"Let's have a trial!" Another exclaimed that it should be a divorce trial.
The reason, said a third, should be bigamy. All agreed, and the players
quite naturally transformed themselves into courtroom characters—
judge, jury, witnesses, lawyers. The trial was chaotic. The groom was
pronounced guilty in less than a minute, but escaped imprisonment by
leaping from the stage and skillfully maneuvering himself through the
rows of seats, avoiding the gang of officers at his heels. Soon, he became
tired of playing. The officers captured him, roughed him up a bit, then
lost interest themselves. The improvisation ended as abruptly as it began.
The bell rang and class was over. The point is, of course, that drama will
occur, quite naturally, when there is no one around to stop it. Ironically,
this was a theatre class, but there was little evidence of drama until the
students rejected their curriculum. The reasons are unknown. Maybe
they played because their regular teacher was absent; or maybe because
the scenes were not relevant to their present needs. This is not to say that

the rehearsal and performance of scenes has no place in junior high school drama/theatre education. But sometimes in the name of theatre we cut off drama; and sometimes in the name of education we cut off play and learning. Excellence in educational drama and theatre means letting go of the names and rigid notions of what should happen and entering into the kinds of relationships with colleagues, students, and clients that are truly dramatic.

The self-interview is liberating. I can now leave behind the voice I have used throughout this book, that of the impersonal narrator-interviewer. Of course, in doing so, I violate the conventions of writing this type of book.

But for the ideas, techniques, and resources presented to be useful, you must also transform them into resources suitable to your own temperament and environment. I trust you will not violate the content presented but rather, like the young student with the toy gun, use it as ammunition to scare off any attempt to inhibit the search for the values of drama and theatre in human learning.

NOTES

1. WCBS-TV, *Sunrise Semester*, "Drama in Education: Summary and Conclusions" (January 4, 1980).

2. See John Dewey, *Democracy and Education* (New York: Free Press, 1966).

DIRECTORY OF SPECIALISTS IN EDUCATIONAL DRAMA AND THEATRE

Gavin Bolton is lecturer in drama in education at Durham University in England. He is the author of *Towards a Theory of Drama in Education* and numerous articles. He has traveled extensively throughout the United Kingdom, Europe, and the United States, leading workshops and lecturing on educational drama and theatre.

Isabel Burger is an American educational drama and theatre expert who founded the Boston Experimental Theatre in 1943. Her recent books include *Creative Drama and Religious Education* and *Creative Drama for Senior Adults.*

Marvin Felix Camillo is executive artistic director of The Family in New York City. As a director of prison workshops he developed and directed the script *Short Eyes*, based upon the prison visions of playwright Miguel Piñero.

Frank Canavan is the artistic director of Performing Arts for Crisis Training (PACT) in New York City and former associate director of the Criminal Justice Repertory Group at John Jay College of Criminal Justice, also in New York.

Richard Courtney is professor of arts in education at the Ontario Institute for Studies in Education in Toronto, Canada, and the Graduate Centre of Drama at the University of Toronto. He is the author of over one hundred articles and books, including *Play, Drama, and Thought*, *The Dramatic Curriculum*, and *Re-Play: Studies of Human Drama in Education.*

Albert Cullum is a drama educator and author whose books include *Push Back the Desks, Shake Hands with Shakespeare*, and *Aesop in the Afternoon.*

Rick Curry is the founder and director of the National Theatre Workshop of the Handicapped in New York City.

John Clark Donahue is artistic director of the Children's Theatre Company and School of Minneapolis. A recipient of the Margo Jones Award for outstanding contributions to the theatre, he is a director, designer, and playwright whose plays are collected in the volumes *The Cookie Jar and Other Plays* and

Five Plays from the Children's Theatre Company of Minneapolis.

Moses Goldberg is artistic director of the Louisville Children's Theatre in Kentucky. He is a playwright and author whose works include *Children's Theatre, A Philosophy and a Method.*

Paula Gray is director of activities at the Jewish Home and Hospital for Aged in New York City. An expert in drama and theatre with the elderly, she has written the book *Dramatics for the Elderly: A Guide for Residential Care Settings and Senior Centers.*

Aurand Harris is America's most widely produced playwright for young audiences. Among his twenty-five published plays are *Androcles and the Lion*, *Rags to Riches*, and *The Arkansaw Bear.*

Dorothy Heathcote is professor of drama at the University of Newcastle upon Tyne in England. She is a lecturer and workshop leader who has traveled extensively throughout the United Kingdom, Europe, and the United States, presenting her unique approach to educational drama. She has been the subject of many video-tapes, films, articles, and books, including the BBC documentary film *Three Looms Waiting* and Betty Jane Wagner's book *Dorothy Heathcote: Drama as a Learning Medium.*

John Hodgson is chairman of the School of Drama and Theatre Studies at Bretton Hall College and tutor in acting at the University of Leeds, England. He has written and edited several books, including *Improvisation*, *The Uses of Drama*, and the three volume series *Drama in Education: The Annual Survey.*

Eleanor Irwin is assistant professor of child psychiatry at the University of Pittsburgh. She is a drama therapist and researcher in the field of drama and play therapy and the author of numerous articles.

Coleman Jennings is the chairman of the drama department of the University of Texas, Austin. He is a creative drama leader, director, and author who has contributed to the book, *Six Plays for Children by Aurand Harris, Biography and Play Analysis by Coleman A. Jennings.*

Sue Jennings is a British drama therapist and author who has lectured and taught throughout the United Kingdom and the United States. Among her books are *Remedial Drama* and *Handbook of Dramatherapy.*

Carol Korty is a drama educator, director, and playwright who has published two collections of plays, *Silly Soup: Ten Zany Plays* and *Plays from African Folktales, with Ideas for Acting, Dance, Costumes, and Music.*

Judith Martin is the co-founder, artistic director, and performer with the Paper Bag Players in New York City. She is the author of the book *Everybody, Everybody.*

Nellie McCaslin is professor of educational theatre and associate director of the Gallatin Division of New York University. She is the author of numerous articles, reviews, and books, including the standard text *Creative Drama in the Classroom* and the anthologies *Children and Drama* and *Theatre for Young Audiences.*

Dorothy Miles is a deaf actress, writer, and educator who lives in England and has worked in America with the National Theatre of the Deaf and several educational institutions. She is the author of scripts for deaf actors as well as the books *Poems for Sign Language* and *Sign-Language Theatre and Deaf Theatre: New Definitions and Directions.*

Tom Miller is a puppeteer, director, and designer who co-founded the Mermaid Theatre in Nova Scotia. He has adapted for puppet theatre many tales of the Micmac Indians as well as other tales, stories, and plays from world literature.

James Moffett is a language arts educator, writer, and lecturer who has written extensively about the relationship between drama and the language arts. His books include *Student-Centered Language Arts and Reading, K-13: A Handbook for Teachers* and *Teaching the Universe of Discourse.*

David Pammenter is a pioneer in British theatre-in-education who developed the Coventry TIE Team in 1965 and trained many of the prominent TIE leaders in England.

Vera Mowry Roberts is former chairperson of the Department of Theatre and Cinema at Hunter College in New York City and former president of the American Theatre Association. Among her many publications are the books *On Stage: A History of Theatre* and *The Nature of Theatre.*

James Sacks is the director of the New York Center for Psychodrama Training and a psychotherapist in private practice. He is an educator, trainer, and author of numerous articles concerning psychodrama and drama therapy.

Gertrud Schattner is supervisor and trainer of student drama therapists at Bellevue Psychiatric Hospital in New York City and adjunct professor of educational theatre at New York University. An actress and drama therapist, she was the first president of the National Association for Drama Therapy and is the co-editor of the two-volume anthology *Drama in Therapy.*

Graham Scott is director of the Drama Resource Center in Victoria, Australia. He is an author, lecturer, and researcher in educational drama and theatre.

Ann M. Shaw is associate professor of communication arts and sciences at Queens College in New York. She has been instrumental in developing the American Theatre Association Program on Drama and Theatre By, With and For Handicapped Individuals and has co-edited two books, *Drama, Theatre, and the Handicapped* and *Perspectives: A Handbook in Drama and Theatre by, with, and for Handicapped Individuals.*

Geraldine Brain Siks is professor emeritus at the University of Washington in Seattle. A student of Winifred Ward and a pioneer in creative drama, she has taught and written extensively on educational drama and theatre. Among her books are *Drama with Children* and the seminal text *Creative Dramatics, an Art for Children.*

Peter Slade is an educator, lecturer, and author who has greatly influenced the development of British educational drama. His text *Child Drama* has become a classic in the field. Among his other books are the *Experience of Spontaneity* and *Natural Dance.*

Shirlee Sloyer is assistant professor of speech arts and sciences at Hofstra University in Hempstead, New York. She is a specialist in reader's theatre and has published the book *Reader's Theatre: A Guide to Story Dramatization in the Classroom.*

Viola Spolin is a director and educator who created and developed theatre games, improvisational techniques that are used throughout the world for actor training and education. Her text *Improvisation for the Theatre* is applied to many educational drama and theatre workshops, classrooms, and training programs.

Maurice Stewart is co-founder of the Puppet Centre in London. He is an educator, lecturer, and theatre and television director.

Joyce St. George is the executive director of the Performing Arts for Crisis Training (PACT) in New York City. She is the former associate director of the Criminal Justice Repertory Group at John Jay College of Criminal Justice in New York.

Lowell Swortzell is professor and director of the Program in Educational Theatre at New York University. He is the author of many plays for young audiences, including *The Arabian Nights* and *The Little Hump-Backed Horse*, and the editor of the anthologies *All the World's a Stage* and *Playhouse: Uncommon Plays for, by, and about Young People*.

Nancy Swortzell is associate professor of educational theatre at New York University. She is director of the New York University Study Abroad Program in Bretton, England, and has been instrumental in transporting principles and practices of theatre-in-education from England to America.

Lea Wallace is a puppeteer whose puppet characters and scripts have appeared on stages throughout the world. She is an instructor of educational theatre at New York University and has worked extensively with special populations through puppetry.

Brian Way is a playwright, author, and educator who for many years directed the Theatre Centre Limited in London. His text *Development through Drama* is used widely in the United Kingdom, the United States, and Canada. An expert in participatory theatre, he has written many scripts as well as the book *Children's Theatre and Audience Participation*.

Edward Welch is the co-founder and director of the Family Life Theatre in New York City. He has lectured and led workshops in theatre and health education throughout the world.

DIRECTORY OF SELECTED PROGRAMS IN EDUCATIONAL DRAMA AND THEATRE

THE UNITED STATES

School or Program	Contact Person	Description
Adelphi University, Garden City, New York	Julie Thompson	M.A. in Education or Speech Arts/ Educational Theatre. Interrelated arts program in Aesthetic Education.
Arizona State University, Tempee	Lin Wright	B.F.A. and M.F.A. in Child Drama.
Brigham Young University, Provo, Utah	Harold Oaks	Limited program in Educational Drama and Theatre.
California State University, Hayward	Jeanne Hall	Comprehensive undergraduate program in Child Drama.
California State University, Los Angeles	Pam Woody	Undergraduate and master's program in Educational Drama and Theatre. Special program in Recreational Drama.
	Roger Altenberg	Developing undergraduate and master's program in Drama Therapy.
California State University, Northridge	Mary Jane Evans	Comprehensive undergraduate program in Child Drama.
Children's Theatre Company and School of Minneapolis, Minnesota	John Clark Donahue	Internships in many aspects of theatre for young audiences.

School or Program	Contact Person	Description
Eastern Michigan University, Ypsilanti	Virginia Koste	Undergraduate and master's program in Educational Drama and Theatre. Coursework in T.I.E., puppetry, and developmental drama for the handicapped.
Emerson College, Boston, Massachusetts	John Barbetta	Limited undergraduate and master's program in Educational Drama and Theatre. Specialized course in drama for the handicapped.
Florida State University, Tallahassee	Richard Fallon	Limited undergraduate and graduate coursework in Educational Drama and Theatre.
Howard University, Washington, D.C.	Kelsey E. Collie	Limited undergraduate program in Educational Drama. Strong emphasis upon theatre for young audiences.
Hunter College, New York City	Pat Sternberg	B.A. and M.A. concentration in Developmental Drama. Coursework in Sociodrama.
Illinois State University, Normal	Pam Ritch	Comprehensive undergraduate and M.F.A. program in Educational Drama and Theatre.
Lesley College, Cambridge, Massachusetts	Shaun McNiff	Expressive Therapies Program, including coursework in Drama Therapy and Psychodrama.
Loyola University, New Orleans, Louisiana	Bob Fleshman	Undergraduate Drama Therapy program.
Moreno Institute, Beacon, New York	Zerka Moreno	Psychodrama training.
National Technical Institute for the Deaf, Rochester, New York	Bruce Halverson	Special theatre program for deaf and hearing students.
National Theatre Workshop of the Handicapped, New York City	Rick Curry	Training program for disabled and nondisabled student actors.
New York Center for Psychodrama Training, New York City	James Sacks	Psychodrama training.

School or Program	Contact Person	Description
New York University, New York City	Lowell Swortzell	Comprehensive undergraduate, master's, and doctoral programs in Educational Drama and Theatre. Coursework in T.I.E. Specializations in Drama Therapy and Musical Theatre.
Northwestern University, Evanston, Illinois	Anne Thurman	Comprehensive undergraduate and master's program in Educational Drama and Theatre.
Queens College, New York City	Ann Shaw	Undergraduate coursework in Creative Drama within Communication Arts and Sciences Department.
San Diego State University, San Diego, California	Margaret McKerrow	Limited undergraduate and master's program in Educational Drama and Theatre.
San Francisco State University, San Francisco, California	Bo Westerfield	Comprehensive undergraduate and master's program in Educational Drama and Theatre.
State University of New York, Brockport	Joanna Kraus	Comprehensive undergraduate and master's program in Educational Drama and Theatre.
University of Connecticut, Avery Point	Kay E. Janney	Limited coursework in Educational Drama and Theatre.
University of Connecticut, Storrs	Linda and Michael Gregoric	Media and Arts for Social Services—interdisciplinary program in drama, media, and social work.
University of Denver, Denver, Colorado	Annabel Clark	Undergraduate and graduate coursework in Educational Drama and Theatre.
University of Hawaii, Honolulu	Tamara Hunt	Comprehensive program in Educational Drama and Theatre.
University of Kansas, Lawrence	Jed Davis	M.A. and Ph.D. with emphasis on Children's Theatre.
University of Maryland, College Park	David Leong	Limited graduate coursework in Educational Drama and Theatre.
University of Minnesota, Minneapolis	Kenneth Graham	Limited undergraduate and graduate coursework in Educational Drama and Theatre.
University of North Carolina, Greensboro	Tom Behm	Limited master's program in Educational Drama and Theatre.
University of Northern Iowa, Cedar Falls	Scott Regan	Undergraduate and master's coursework in Educational Drama and Theatre.

School or Program	Contact Person	Description
University of Texas, Austin	Coleman Jennings	Graduate coursework in Educational Drama and Theatre. Strong emphasis on theatre for young audiences.
University of Washington, Seattle	Suzan Zeder	Comprehensive M.F.A. program in Child Drama.
University of Wisconsin, Madison	John Tolch	M.F.A. in directing with emphasis in Children's Theatre.
Western Michigan University, Kalamazoo	Ruth Heinig	Coursework in Educational Drama and Theatre.

CANADA

Brock University, St. Catharines, Ontario	Nora Morgan	Undergraduate coursework in Drama in Education.
Concordia University, Montreal	Barbara MacKay	One-year certificate program for teachers of Creative Drama and Theatre Arts.
McGill University, Montreal	John Ripley	B.A. and M.A. in English, with coursework in Developmental Drama and Children's Theatre.
Ontario Institute for Studies in Education and the University of Toronto, Toronto	Richard Courtney	M.A., M.Ed., Ed.D., and Ph.D. in Education with a concentration in Educational Drama and Theatre.
Queens University, Kingston, Ontario	David Kemp	B.Ed. in Education, with a concentration in Educational Drama and Theatre.
University of Alberta, Edmonton	David Barnet	B.A. and M.A. in Drama.
University of British Columbia, Vancouver	Lisa Manches	Coursework in Developmental Drama.
University of Calgary, Alberta	Craig Elliott	B.A., B.Ed., B.F.A., and M.A. in Drama. Extensive coursework in Developmental Drama.
University of Lethbridge, Alberta	Ches Skinner	Undergraduate coursework in Developmental Drama and Children's Theatre.
University of Victoria, British Columbia	Barbara McIntyre	B.F.A. and M.F.A. in Theatre.

School or Program	Contact Person	Description
University of Windsor, Windsor, Ontario	Susan Martin	B.A. honors program in Drama-in-Education.

ENGLAND

School or Program	Contact Person	Description
Aberdeen College of Education, Aberdeen	Charles A. Barron	B.Ed. in Drama; Diploma in Speech and Drama.
Avery Hill College, London	Mrs. K. E. Jones	B.Ed. in Drama in Education.
Bedford College of Higher Education, Bedford	Miss B. J. Congdon	B.Ed. in Drama.
Bishop Grosseteste College, Lincoln	Leonard Marsh	B.Ed. in Drama.
Bretton Hall College, West Yorkshire	John Hodgson	B.A. in Drama or Creative Arts.
Bulmershe College of Higher Education, Reading	Trevor Vibert	Postgraduate Certificate in Drama in the Secondary School.
Chester College of Higher Education, Chester	M. Carys Williams	B.A. and B.Ed. in Drama.
City of Liverpool College of Higher Education	R. B. Sutton	B.A. in Drama and Postgraduate Certificate in Education.
City of Manchester College of Higher Education	David Isenberg	B.A. and B.Ed. in Drama; Diploma in Higher Education.
College of Ripon and St. John, York	David Powley	B.A. in Drama; Diploma in Primary Education (Drama in Education).
	Sue Jennings	Two-year training program in Dramatherapy.
Crewe and Alsager College of Higher Education, Cheshire	Barry Edwards	B.A. in Drama in Creative Arts.
De La Salle College of Higher Education, Manchester	Clive Hadfield	B.Ed. in Drama and Education.

School or Program	Contact Person	Description
Edge Hill College of Higher Education, Lancaster	Miss M. W. Stanton	B.Ed. in Education and Drama for secondary level teaching.
Hamilton College of Education, Hamilton	Arthur P. Brittin	Diploma in Education (drama).
Hertfordshire College of Higher Education, Watford	Robin Rook	B.Ed. in Drama. Two-year training course in Dramatherapy within Department of Art Therapy.
Ilkley College, Bingley	Robin Butler	B.Ed. in Educational Drama.
Kingsway Princeton College, London	Graham Suter	SESAME full time course in drama and movement in therapy.
Liverpool Institute of Higher Education	J. Burke	B.A. and B.Ed. in Drama.
Queen Margaret College, Edinburgh	. . .	College diploma in Drama. Third-year option in Dramatherapy.
St. Mary's College, Twickingham	A. J. Rushforth	B.Ed. in Drama.
Salford College of Technology	Gordon Wiseman	Two-year post-professional program in Dramatherapy.
SESAME, London	Marion Lindquist	Training program in drama and movement in therapy.
Trinity and All Saints' College, Leeds	G. C. Andrews	B.Ed. in Drama and Education.
University of Durham	Gavin Bolton	Master's and doctoral study of Drama in Education.
University of Newcastle upon Tyne	Dorothy Heathcote	Master's and doctoral study of Drama in Education.
West Midlands College of Higher Education, Walsall	J. P. Hanratty	B.Ed. in Drama. Drama as part of Creative Arts integrated subject.

INDEX

51-56; drama and the language arts in, 41-51; drama and math in, 30-31; drama and reading in, 15, 49-51; drama and writing in, 15, 47-48; Dorothy Heathcote's views of, 27, 38; and school plays, 81, 83-84
Curry, Rick, 159-60, 162-65
Curtain Theatre, 64, 66

Dartmouth seminar, 46, 58 n.39
Darwin, 67
Davis, Bill C., 115
Dead Birds, 4
Deaf: drama/theatre with, 158, 166-73; puppetry with, 157
Deaf theatre, 167, 173
Dennison, George, 110
Designer in theatre for young audiences, 200-209, 215
Developmental drama, 6, 38. *See also* Creative drama
Developmentally disabled, drama/theatre with, 135, 154-58. *See also* Mentally retarded
Dewey, John, 258
Dewhurst, Colleen, 182
Director in theatre for young audiences, 200-209, 215
Dr. Faustus Lights the Lights, 114
Dr. Seuss, 217
Donahue, John Clark, 202-9, 217-18, 220
Double, in psychodrama, 141, 143, 225
Drama in education, 6., *See also* Creative drama
Drama therapy, 32, 134-48, 154, 174, 253, 256, 259; at Bellevue Psychiatric Hospital, 144
Dramatic education, 6. *See also* Creative drama
Dramatic play, 13
Drama and theatre by/with/for the handicapped, 251, 253, 256

Educational drama and theatre: in the church, 6, 109-16; in the community, 95-190; future directions in, 249-56; in the hospital, 6, 134, 144-48; in the inner city community, 6, 181-89; in the museum, 104-8; research in, 254-55, 258; in schools, 11-93; training and vocational opportunities in, 243-48
Educational objectives, 17-18, 20, 23, 24,

32; in drama/theatre with the physically disabled, 162; of The Family, 182; in puppetry and mask work, 237. *See also* Learning objectives; Behavioral objectives
Educational Puppetry Association, 231
Egypt, 105-6
Elderly, drama/theatre with, 4, 127, 135, 174-78, 246-47
The Elephant Man, 99, 207-8
Elizabethan period, 52-54, 81
"E-Man," 65
Emancipatory children's theatre, 219
Emotionally disturbed: drama/theatre with, 135, 144-45, 147-48; puppetry with, 157
Empire State Youth Theatre Institute, 251-52
"The Enchanted Calabash," 107
Endgame, 188
Epps, Ben, 68
Equus, 99
Everyman Theatre Company, 105

The Faggot, 111
The Family, 181-88
Family Life Theatre, 127-32
Fantasy, 4-6, 13, 28-29, 198, 260
Federal Theatre Project, 34
Finney, Doug, 82
First All Children's Theatre Company, 195
The 500 Hats of Bartholomew Cubbins, 217
Foreman, Richard, 202
Fornes, Maria Irene, 110
Forster, E. M., 50
Freud, Sigmund, 136, 139

Garbary, Evelyn, 232
Georgian period, 52-54
Geriadrama Taining Workshops, 174
Gestalt therapy, 139
Giant Anna (Anna Swan), 236
Glooscap, 232, 236
Goffman, Ervin, 97
Goldberg, Moses, 200-201
Gouran, Patrick, 81
Graczyk, Ed, 81
Gray, Paula, 174-78
Greek Tears and Roman Laughter, 80
Grips, 210, 219
Group for Art and Theatre Education (GATE), 106
Guess Who's Coming to Dinner, 167

About the Author

Robert J. Landy is an Assistant Professor of Educational Theatre at New York University. He is currently developing the first graduate drama therapy program in the United States. He is the author of several articles on educational drama and drama therapy and is himself an actor, playwright, and director active in community, academic, and professional theatre.